*f*P

END OF THE LINE

THE RISE AND FALL
OF AT&T

LESLIE CAULEY

FREE PRESS

New York London Toronto Sydney

FREE PRESS
A Division of Simon & Schuster, Inc.
1230 Avenue of the Americas
New York, NY 10020

The following photographs are the property of AT&T Archives.
Reprinted with permission of AT&T:
First phone, Alexander Graham Bell, opening of the 1956 transatlantic line,
Golden Boy, Charles Brown, Robert Allen, John Walter, John Zeglis,
Dan Somers, Charles Noski, Dave Dorman, C. Michael Armstrong.

FREE PRESS and colophon are trademarks
of Simon & Schuster, Inc.

For information regarding special discounts for bulk purchases,
please contact Simon & Schuster Special Sales
at 1-800-456-6798 or business@simonandschuster.com

Manufactured in the United States of America

1   3   5   7   9   10   8   6   4   2

Library of Congress Cataloging-in-Publication Data
Cauley, Leslie.
End of the line : the rise and fall of AT&T / Leslie Cauley.
        p.   cm.
Includes bibliographical references and index.
1. AT&T—History.   2. Telecommunication—United States—
History—20th century.   I. Title.
HE8846.A55C38   2005
384'.0973—dc22   2005046937

ISBN 13: 978-1-4391-2309-6
ISBN 10: 1-4391-2309-8

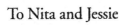

To Nita and Jessie

ACKNOWLEDGMENTS

THIS BOOK would not have been possible without the help of a lot of very thoughtful, informed people. To these people—and you know who you are—I extend a heartfelt thank you.

Books don't come together by themselves, of course. You need a community to make it happen. I'd like to thank my agent, Christy Fletcher, who believed in this project and found a great home for it. My editor at Simon & Schuster, Dominick Anfuso, gave me the time to do it right, which, for a book like this, is no small blessing. And thank you Wylie O'Sullivan, who is Dominick's ace assistant. Your sharp eye and helpful suggestions were invaluable.

A big thanks to Charlie Gasparino, who is *Newsweek*'s bulldog on the Wall Street beat. Charlie was writing his book *(Blood on the Street)* at the same time I was writing mine. Charlie, who is one of the best investigative journalists I will ever know, is a good friend and former colleague. Showing his reporter's nose, perhaps, Charlie had a way of saying exactly the right thing at exactly the right time to help get me over whatever speed bump I was trying to negotiate that day. So thanks, my friend, for being there.

I'd also like to extend a warm thanks to Howard Stringer, the newly appointed chairman of Sony. Howard, who became a legend during his 30-year run at CBS, is also a legendary friend, which is one reason he's so universally beloved. Thank you, Howard, for being so unfailingly supportive—of my journalism, as well as my ever-evolving journey in life. You are simply the best.

Thanks to John (j.) Strong for coming up with the title on the first pass. And to Rock Positano for all those late-night coffee runs. And so much more. A special thanks to my sister, Craige, for being such a rock-steady presence in my life. When I count my blessings, dear sister, you are at the top of the list.

Last, but certainly not least, I'd like to thank all the wonderfully dedicated employees of AT&T, current and former. One of my motivations in writing this book was to simply acknowledge your many contributions—to AT&T, to America, and, indeed, to the world at large. This one's for you.

CONTENTS

Genius is the ability to hold one's vision steady until it becomes reality.

—BENJAMIN FRANKLIN

Lead, follow, or get the hell out of the way.

—GEORGE STEINBRENNER

INTRODUCTION

I DECIDED TO write this book, first and foremost, out of respect. AT&T is uniquely American. It is also uniquely important in terms of its historical significance to the United States and, I would submit, the world at large.

AT&T is far more than just a grand company, however. It's family. And because of that familial tie, people have an emotional connection with AT&T that they just don't have with other companies. Look at Enron. When it blew up in spectacular fashion the business press went wild. But unless you were an investor or an employee, chances are you didn't care very much. The same can be said of WorldCom. When the company filed for bankruptcy in 2002, it was a sad day, especially for all the thousands of investors and employees who were affected. But unless you had some direct tie to the carrier now known as MCI, the blip on the emotional radar of the United States that day was barely noticeable.

But AT&T? When the company announced in July 2004 that it was backing away from the residential market, people went bananas. AT&T wasn't even bailing, mind you. It had merely decided to stop marketing its long-distance services to consumers because revenues, which had been getting shredded for years thanks to price wars, were crashing. As soon as the news hit the wires, a few people came running up to me in the newsroom: *Is AT&T really going out of business?* Their reaction wasn't unique. By the afternoon, the nation's news wires, as well as the cable TV and broadcast networks, were awash with stories decrying the end of an icon.

Keep in mind, AT&T wasn't going anywhere. It still had more than 20 million long-distance customers, and it planned to keep servicing them for as long as people wanted to stay. But no matter. People were genuinely shocked and saddened by the mere suggestion that AT&T, which had been a part of America's landscape for more than a century, was about to walk out the door for good. *USA TODAY* played the story on the front page that day, and rightly so. So did every other major newspaper in America.

To me, at least, that raw emotion has always been the thing that has set AT&T apart from the rest of the telecom pack. Verizon and SBC Communications may be bigger and better financed. But AT&T is the name, and the brand, that Americans know. And trust. And believe in. And it's been that way for more than 130 years. That's the main reason SBC Communications, which recently announced plans to buy AT&T for $16 billion, will probably wind up adopting the fabled AT&T moniker. Talking to reporters the day after the deal was announced, SBC Chairman Ed Whitacre acknowledged the historical importance of the moment. "We are preserving an American icon," he said.

Which brings me back to where I started: why I wrote this book. It's my way of giving homage to a great company and a uniquely American institution. It's also my way of showing respect to all the generations of men and women who, through their own grit and dedication, were able to turn the little Bell telephone into the ultimate corporate success story. Because of their sweat and faith, AT&T grew up to become a global icon for the ages. And nothing will ever change that.

End of the Line has another purpose: to explain what happened to AT&T, and why. Not the whitewashed version of events that was put out by AT&T's public relations department. Nor the decidedly hit-and-miss accounts that appeared in the press. But the real story-behind-the-story that explains why AT&T wound up being pushed to the verge of financial ruin. Along the way, I've also singled out the individuals who, at least in my view, were mostly to blame for the black comedy of errors that ultimately brought down the house. I had the benefit of hindsight in making my calls, of course. And I've made liberal use of it, as you will see.

I've deliberately wrapped this book around a handful of key players, starting with the then-CEO, Mike Armstrong. But it would be too easy, and also not very instructive, to simply point fingers. In telling this story, I've tried to explain what it was about the personalities or management styles of these individuals that caused them to make such flawed decisions. I'm not offering redemption to anybody—only history can do that. But I do think it's important to at least try to understand why people behaved as they did, if only so we can glean a few lessons that might be applicable to our own lives.

On a positive note, there were no bad actors à la WorldCom in the AT&T saga. Nobody cooked the books, or engaged in wholesale graft. Even the worst offenders were brimming with good intentions. Nonetheless, plenty of bad decisions were made.

In researching this book I talked to more than 100 people, some of them multiple times. That said, the conclusions contained herein are solely my own. Nobody has been spared. That includes my former co-author, Leo Hindery, who hired me a few years ago to write his memoir (*The Biggest Game of All*, also published by Free Press). To be sure, *End of the Line* is a strong book in terms of its point of view. Some might even call it a tough book. But I hope—and believe—it is ultimately a fair book, and I rest easy knowing that I've arrived at all of my conclusions in an intellectually honest fashion.

This is the story that I have sought to tell—openly, honestly, and well. Hopefully I've told it in a manner that conveys a certain amount of understanding, insight, and certainly respect for the great American institution known as AT&T, as well as the thousands of dedicated people who still work there. I hope you find the journey, and the tale, as enlightening as I did.

Leslie Cauley
February 1, 2005

1

END OF THE LINE

J OHN MALONE had a bad feeling.

The cable titan sat on the board of AT&T, and he didn't like the looks of things. In just two short years the telecom giant had committed $110 billion to buy a slew of cable TV assets. Almost half of that, $48 billion, had been used to buy Malone's former company, Tele-Communications Inc., also known as TCI. The other $62 billion went to cover the cost of acquiring MediaOne Group. The two deals grabbed headlines around the world. They also catapulted AT&T to the top of the cable heap. With TCI and MediaOne under its belt, AT&T had bragging rights to being the biggest cable TV operator in America.

It was an expensive way to get there, no doubt. But it was also fast—just 24 months from start to finish. That was by design. AT&T's chairman and chief executive officer, C. Michael Armstrong, was racing the clock. The company's core long-distance business was dying. Per-minute prices had dropped 75 percent in just two years, and they were still trying to find a bottom. The problem, for AT&T, was that long distance still accounted for 100 percent of its profits. Unless Armstrong could find a steady revenue stream to offset his jaw-dropping declines in long distance, AT&T was history.

By June of 2000, Malone's indigestion was kicking in strong. His back-of-the-envelope calculations kept leading him to the same troubling conclusion: AT&T was drowning in a sea of short-term debt. The culprit was MediaOne. As soon as the deal closed, AT&T's debt had shot up to $65 billion. Almost half of that was tied up in short-term commercial paper that would have to be paid back in less than a year. Cash was also tight. The reason, once again, was MediaOne. To close the deal, AT&T wound up having to fork over $24 billion in one lump sum. That was a big nut, even for a company of AT&T's size.

Malone was furious. As far as he was concerned, the MediaOne deal structure was just plain stupid. AT&T had no downside protection. So long as its stock price stayed aloft, everything would be fine. But if the financial markets turned, the short-term debt could eat AT&T alive. The point, for Malone, wasn't purely academic. Most of his net worth, more than $3 billion at the time, was tied up in AT&T stock. If the company took a tumble, he was going to get dragged along for the whole woolly ride.

Malone was no Chicken Little. Quite the contrary, he had a reputation for being one cool cat, and for good reason: He was. Malone never broke a sweat. Not over deals, anyway. Over the course of his 25 years in the cable business, Malone had been involved in hundreds of transactions of every size and type imaginable. His calling card was financial complexity. Malone deals were notorious for having so many moving parts that you could get cross-eyed just trying to keep up.

Malone learned his art, so to speak, at TCI. When he saddled up there as president in 1973, TCI's shares were selling for just 75 cents apiece. The banks wouldn't even think about lending money to TCI. Wall Street also looked the other way. A lot of guys would have folded their cards and walked. Not Malone. He just rolled up his sleeves and got to work.

His solution? Deals, my friend, deals. Over the next two decades, Malone bought hundreds of companies, and parts of companies, to transform TCI into the cable industry's undisputed leader with more than 11 million customers, 14 million if you included "affiliated" cable partners. (The latter was Malone-speak for companies in which TCI had an investment.) TCI had no collateral—the company was running on fumes and its stock was basically worthless. So Malone had to use his smarts to come up with unconventional deal structures to keep things moving along.

It worked. By the time Malone announced plans to sell TCI to

AT&T in 1997, that same 75-cent share was worth almost $4,200. And Malone? Owing to the financial magic he had worked for TCI, he was a fabled and feared dealmaker. So, no, John Malone was no Chicken Little, especially when it came to complicated, long-shot deals.

But the MediaOne deal—*that* one bothered him. The short-term debt, in particular. In board meetings, Malone did what he could to sound the alarm: *"How much do we owe?"* If he'd asked the question once, he'd asked it a dozen times. It was Malone's way of trying to draw a bead on the crushing debt load. It didn't do much good. AT&T was pinning its hopes to the future of Armstrong's $110 billion cable strategy. About the last thing anybody wanted to talk about was the dark side of AT&T's fast push into cable—the gut-busting debt load. Except Malone, that is. It was all he could think about.

Armstrong, known as Mike to just about everybody, wasn't too concerned. To be sure, the MediaOne deal got pushed through quickly. But he really had no choice. By the time AT&T decided to make a run for it, MediaOne had already announced plans to merge with Comcast, so he had to hustle. Sure, the $62 billion sticker price was rich—real rich. But Armstrong was in a footrace with time, and seconds counted. Revenues in AT&T's core long-distance business were falling by 10 percent a year, and the rate of erosion was accelerating by the quarter. The way Armstrong saw it, cable TV was AT&T's best, and possibly only, hope for the future.

His plan was simple but potentially effective: By using upgraded cable TV lines, AT&T could sidestep the Bells and go directly to the home with a branded package of voice, data, and video services. To make the plan fly, however, AT&T needed a long reach. That's where MediaOne came in. TCI and its affiliates had 14 million customers; MediaOne had another 5 million. Together, however, they had access to more than 41 million homes. It wasn't blanket coverage, for sure. But it was enough to at least give AT&T a firm foothold in major markets across the country.

Armstrong wasn't worried about MediaOne's financing. Dan Somers, the chief financial officer, was a seasoned professional. He also knew a lot about the cable TV business. The two of them had worked shoulder-to-shoulder to reel in TCI. Then they turned on a dime and snatched MediaOne away from Comcast. Malone had a point about the debt—

$65 billion was a big nut. But so what? It was still better than seeing AT&T go out of business, which was exactly what AT&T was looking at if his rescue plan didn't work out.

Malone could tell that his outspokenness was starting to grate. The cable titan even joked about it on occasion, referring to himself as "the turd in the punch bowl" on the AT&T board. Malone didn't really care. AT&T's crushing debt load was a financial disaster just waiting to happen. And the fact that nobody else on the board seemed bothered by that chilling possibility was driving him crazy.

AT THE VERY NEXT board meeting, opportunity knocked.

Malone found himself sitting next to Sanford "Sandy" Weill, the chairman and co-CEO of Citigroup. Within the rarefied fishbowl of the AT&T board, Weill was a singularly powerful figure. In addition to sitting on the finance committee, he was also tight with Armstrong, who sat on the Citigroup board. Malone decided to make his move.

About a quarter of the way into the meeting, Malone leaned over to Weill and calmly whispered into his ear. "Sandy, I think we could be in for a commercial paper rollover default." Malone used the gilded language of high finance to couch his concerns.

Weill's head snapped around like a slingshot.

The Citigroup chief immediately understood the gravity of what Malone was saying: AT&T was in danger of defaulting on its commercial paper. AT&T had a staggering amount of short-term paper on its books—$28 billion in all.

The implications of Malone's dire warning were enormous. One of the biggest commercial paper defaults in history—by Penn Central in 1970—had tipped the scale at just $82 million. And even that default, puny as it was by comparison, had roiled the markets for weeks. What Malone was talking about was a commercial paper default that was so big, so injurious, that it would surely cause widespread pandemonium among AT&T's investors. The stock price would probably get gutted. So would the stock prices of every other publicly traded company within spitting distance of telecom. The ripple effect could be devastating.

"You really think so?" Weill shot back, his eyes wide with dismay. Bull's-eye.

Malone settled back into his seat. "You need to look at it yourself," the cable titan coolly answered, lowering his voice just a notch so nobody else would hear. "But, yeah, Sandy, I really think so."

BY THE TIME Malone lobbed in his verbal hand grenade, AT&T's new chief financial officer, Chuck Noski, was arriving at some hard conclusions on his own.

The debt load was ugly—$65 billion. As Malone had rightly surmised, AT&T's short-term obligations were the real problem. AT&T had $33 billion in short-term loans. The majority of that, $28 billion, was tied up in short-term commercial paper. Some of the repayment deadlines were exceedingly short, 90 days or less. The problem—and it was a big one—was that AT&T only had about $20 billion in annual cash flow. And most of that was already committed to other projects. About $3 billion was earmarked to cover the annual dividend. Another $15 billion or so was budgeted for capital construction projects. That left AT&T with a grand total of just $2 billion to cover all of its other obligations, including the $28 billion in outstanding commercial paper.

In banking terms, AT&T was looking at a full-blown liquidity crisis. Put another way, AT&T, as of the summer of 2000, was just about broke.

Nobody used that term, of course. Working Joes like you and me go broke. Blue-chip stalwarts of industry like AT&T generally don't. And one big reason they don't is because they keep revolving lines of credit in place for just these sorts of emergencies. So even though AT&T was looking at a $25 billion shortfall and didn't technically have the funds on hand to make up the difference, the telecom giant had solid backup lines in place that it could tap into on a moment's notice.

Or at least that's what Noski was hoping.

Combing through the books, Noski made a stomach-churning discovery: The backup lines had been rolled back by two-thirds, leaving AT&T with a sole backup facility of just $10 billion. That was going to leave AT&T short by $15 billion, at least. The upshot: AT&T was looking at the very real possibility of a major commercial paper default, just as Malone had suspected.

Now Noski was worried.

If word got out that AT&T was about to default, investors would go wild. Retribution would be swift and brutal. AT&T as a $2 stock? It wasn't that far-fetched.

AT&T's credit rating was Noski's biggest concern. By then the Internet bubble had begun to lose steam. The red-hot telecom market was also cooling off. The shift was problematic, and here's why: By then a lot of carriers, including AT&T, had taken on enormous amounts of debt to help finance their long-term business plans. That worked fine so long as the markets were humming and the cost of debt was affordable. But if investors turned and the debt markets dried up, interest rates would soar. That, in turn, could cause the financial markets to tank. A lot of the smaller carriers that had financed their dreams using debt probably wouldn't make it.

The ripple effect on AT&T was bound to be devastating. AT&T was already paying more than $2 billion a year in interest payments, and that was with a strong "A-2" rating. If AT&T's ratings got reduced, those fees could skyrocket. Worst of all, AT&T could lose its commercial paper rating. If that happened, the carrier wouldn't be allowed to roll over, or "term out," its paper into a conventional bank loan. With only insufficient backup lines in place, AT&T would quickly find itself at the mercy of the major banks. That, of course, was about the last place you ever wanted to be in the middle of a financial emergency—over a barrel, dealing with a bunch of excited bankers.

Noski swallowed hard. At best, AT&T was looking at a major financial restructuring. At worst, if nothing went its way and the banks were unwilling or unable to extend additional facility for its backup lines, AT&T was looking at a possibility that was almost too awful, too outrageous, to even contemplate.

Bankruptcy.

The word seemed incongruous in connection with the grande dame of telecommunications. AT&T was a sturdy survivor of history. Over the course of its long, magnificent life—125 years in all—AT&T had helped birth the Industrial Age, and survived two world wars and the

Great Depression. It had also survived natural disasters, management disasters, and too many political upheavals to count. That the company could have come so far, and survived so much, only to be done in by a single cable transaction that never should have been attempted in the first place was simply unfathomable. The whole thing was so over-the-top you almost had to laugh.

Noski didn't, of course. He was too steamed. You really couldn't blame him. When he was being recruited, nobody had bothered to tell him about AT&T's shaky finances. Not Dan Somers, his predecessor as CFO. Not John Petrillo, AT&T's executive vice president of corporate strategy. Not John Zeglis, AT&T's president. Not Mike Armstrong. Just to be safe, Noski had even buttonholed a few directors. Their story was the same: AT&T was on the verge of one of the great comebacks in U.S. corporate history. They'd all waxed on for hours about the noble challenge of trying to use cable TV to turn one of the world's most beloved companies into a New Age media giant. But nobody said a goddamned word about there being a truckload of plastic explosives parked in the basement. And the fuse had just been lit.

Noski hit the roof when he found out. He later tracked Somers down and asked him point-blank why he hadn't bothered to come clean about AT&T's finances. Somers didn't miss a beat: "Because I wanted you to take the job," he joked, a big smile washing across his face. Noski got a similar shuck-and-jive response from John Petrillo. "I didn't want to oversell the opportunity," Petrillo quipped, trying vainly to coax a smile out of his inquisitor.

Noski was speechless. *You wanted me to take the job?* AT&T was within spitting distance of a major financial meltdown. Billions upon billions of dollars in shareholder value were at risk. So was the company's hard-won reputation—with customers, employees, regulators, Wall Street, and millions of small investors. Indeed, thanks to their ham-fisted handling of the MediaOne deal, AT&T's future was suddenly, and inexplicably, up for grabs. And the best they could offer up was a couple of lame one-liners? But Noski couldn't worry about any of that right then. The clock was ticking.

HOW COULD AT&T, one of America's greatest and most enduring corporate success stories have lost its way so fast?

Unlike other high-profile corporate flameouts, including Enron and Tyco, AT&T's undoing didn't stem from spectacular off-balance sheet transactions. Nor was it the victim of creative accounting of the sort that did in WorldCom, America's No. 2 long-distance company. So what felled mighty AT&T? One root problem, sad to say, was nearly as old as the company itself: good, old-fashioned mismanagement. Overconfidence and incompetence, which do seem to go hand-in-hand in the executive suite these days, played a major role. So did bad timing and the suffocating corporate culture at AT&T. WorldCom's insidious game of now-you-see it, now-you-don't revenues and profits also didn't help.

In the end, the AT&T board swooped in and saved the day. Sort of. After approving $110 billion worth of cable purchases so that AT&T could transform itself into a modern-day media Goliath, the board reversed course and decided, instead, to break up the company into four businesses: AT&T Broadband, representing the cable TV assets; AT&T Wireless, representing the old McCaw cell phone systems that had been acquired in 1994; and AT&T, representing the core long-distance business. Trying to put a positive face on things, AT&T even gave its massive restructuring a rather hopeful-sounding name: "Grand Slam."

AT&T's investors, who'd been through a lot by then, responded by driving down AT&T's shares by more than $3 that day. Investors were rightly tired of AT&T's excuses, and even more tired of its thinly veiled attempts to use financial engineering to cover up its miserable performance. The plunge, together with the previous downward ticks in the stock price, succeeded in wiping out more than $100 billion in shareholder value for the year. It wasn't quite the grand slam that AT&T had been hoping for, but it was breathtaking commentary, nonetheless.

The dividend also took its final bow. As part of the restructuring, AT&T said that it was rolling back the vaunted dividend by 83 percent. The company tried to play it cool, noting that the restructuring, including the dividend cut, would create greater long-term value for shareholders. But as symbols go, it was a primal scream heard around the world. AT&T's dividend had never been cut, not by even a penny. During the Great Depression, AT&T had slashed costs and reduced head count to scrape by. But the dividend? Untouched. Now, just 36 months into the Armstrong Era, the board was being forced to break every rule in AT&T's century-old playbook just to last until the next quarter.

To avoid the indignity of seeing AT&T's stock wind up as a $2 issue, the board also approved a 5-for-1 reverse stock split. The move was clever in that it helped sustain the stock price. But it was also cynical, backward looking, and bursting with greater meaning. In approving such a robust reverse split, AT&T was tacitly acknowledging that it was unable to keep the stock price aloft without using sleight-of-hand to get there. If only there had been an accounting trick handy that could have wiped out the 36 prior months entirely.

Armstrong tried his best to sound upbeat. "This is a pivotal event in the transformation of AT&T we began three years ago," he asserted in a prepared statement. Grand Slam, he continued, "creates a family of four national service providers that will be even better equipped" to serve customers. The AT&T chief pointed out that the four companies would continue to function as one owing to a series of inter-company agreements. In other words, the cable strategy wasn't really dead. It was just taking on a new life form.

Nobody bought it.

"It's hard to escape the feeling that a corporate funeral took place today," Ken McGee, an analyst with Gartner Group, told *The Wall Street Journal.* And McGee was being kind compared to some of the commentary that was floating around on Wall Street that day. Armstrong didn't see it that way. Talking to investors, the AT&T chief openly bristled at the suggestion that the breakup was a reversal of his famed strategy. When one analyst dared to ask him to talk about AT&T's strategic "reversal," Armstrong roared that he found such characterizations to be "not only wrong, but offensive." The quote would become an instant classic.

In hindsight, Armstrong's passionate defiance wasn't so surprising. Truth be told, nobody was more upset about the breakup than Armstrong. He'd come to AT&T to save it, not to tear it apart. But to admit that he was being forced to abandon his beloved cable strategy less than three years after its inception was to admit failure. And Armstrong wasn't willing or wired to do that—not for AT&T, not for the board, not for anybody. Imbued since childhood with a sense of raw optimism—about life, about himself, about his special place in the world—the prospect of ending his 40-year career on such a sour note was impossible for him to even contemplate. So he talked himself into a new reality, and then dared the world to challenge it.

AS THIS IS being written in March 2005, AT&T's future is once again secure. Sadly, this security owes to an outright sale of the company, not to any magic strategic fix. The buyer is SBC Communications, which agreed on January 31 to pay $16 billion for the iconic company. It's quite a bargain, especially considering that AT&T's market value, at its peak during the Armstrong Era, was more than $100 billion. Once the deal closes, AT&T will become the sole property of SBC, thus ending, for all time, its existence as an independent company.

The deal virtually guarantees AT&T a future. That, as Martha Stewart might say, is a good thing. But it's also a sober reminder of how far AT&T has fallen. When Armstrong's cable strategy was unveiled in the late 1990s, AT&T was red-hot. It was also untouchable. Its stock price soared to $95 amid high hopes that Armstrong would execute on his grand vision. Lately, AT&T's stock has been trading near $20, reflecting renewed optimism about its prospects in the arms of SBC. Before SBC showed up, however, the stock had struggled to stay in the mid-teens. AT&T's core long-distance revenues, meantime, are continuing to melt away at an astonishing rate of 20 percent a year. That is double what it was in the fall of 1997 when Armstrong first walked in the door. The acceleration is owed to the rapid decline of the long-distance business, which is being overtaken by advances in technology and the rise of wireless as an alternative to traditional phones.

It remains to be seen if SBC's chief, Ed Whitacre, can plug AT&T's holes. But if anybody can pull it off, he can. Whitacre, who hails from Ennis, Texas, is a 40-year veteran of the Bell System. He's also a singular force in telecom. Over the course of his remarkable 15-year run as CEO, Whitacre has unfailingly followed his gut instincts. And he's done so without giving in to the latest fads on Wall Street, and without compromising, even a little, his grander strategic vision. He took a lot of slings and arrows in the process. But the end result speaks for itself. Thanks to Whitacre, the smallest of the regional Bells—Southwestern Bell—is now the biggest. One can't help but wonder how AT&T might have fared if it had a bulldog like Ed Whitacre leading the way back in 1997.

You have to give Dave Dorman, AT&T's current chairman and CEO, a lot of credit for being willing to make the tough call to sell the company. Dorman ascended to the top spot in late 2002. To say that he inherited a water-weak hand would be putting it mildly. AT&T had just been broken up like Humpty Dumpty, and its future was highly uncertain. Determined to keep the ship afloat, Dorman slashed costs, reduced headcount, and pared debt. He also overhauled AT&T's business strategy to focus almost exclusively on big business customers. Dorman wasn't able to save AT&T—nobody could have, at that point. But his bold actions and level thinking did manage to put the fabled company on a fast sled to its destiny.

AT&T WATCHERS will probably spend years, if not decades, debating the finer points of what went wrong and who, exactly, was to blame for the company's spectacular collapse. To be sure, plenty of people contributed. Over the course of its long, illustrious life, AT&T churned through a dozen CEOs and scores of top managers. Some of these executives were brilliant; others not. But one name, without question, sits right at the top of the list: C. Michael "Mike" Armstrong. When he arrived at AT&T in the fall of 1997, he had a halo around his head and the future of the company in the palm of his hand. By the time he stepped down on November 18, 2002, the halo was long gone—and so was the American icon known as AT&T.

"Assume nothing" was one of Armstrong's longtime managerial mantras. He even kept a brass plaque emblazoned with those very words on his desk at AT&T. It was Armstrong's way of reminding himself, every single day, to do his homework. Be smart. Don't get caught short. It was a good instinct. It's too bad he didn't take his own advice.

Armstrong made all sorts of assumptions. He assumed that Wall Street, which had hailed him as a turnaround artist, would continue to support him. He assumed that his chief financial officer, Dan Somers, would exercise care in crafting AT&T's deals. He assumed that his cable guru, Leo Hindery, would deliver. He assumed, along with the rest of the telecom world, that WorldCom wasn't lying. He assumed that the financial markets, which had soared to breathtaking highs, wouldn't crash and burn. He assumed that AT&T's senior managers, even those who coveted his job, wanted him to be successful. He assumed that the powerful AT&T board, which had lured him in with promises of grandeur, would always see things his way. He assumed that the dense AT&T culture, even if it didn't love him, would at least give him a chance. He assumed that he would leave just as he had come in—as a hero.

Armstrong was wrong about all of it. Dead wrong, in some cases. But by the time that became apparent, his time was up. Like General George Custer at his famous last stand, the AT&T chairman, by the end, would be boxed in tight with nowhere to go but straight down to a bitter infamy. He didn't go alone. Dan Somers, the former chief financial officer-turned-cable executive, went with him.

Investors got the worst of it, by far.

Michael Balhoff, the former head of telecom equity research for Legg Mason Wood Walker in Baltimore, did an analysis of AT&T's stock performance for this book. According to Balhoff, who is now the managing partner of Balhoff & Associates, investors saw their shares erode by 53.6 percent during Armstrong's five-year run. During the same period, he notes, the S&P 500 lost just 4.6 percent of its value, and that included all the financial carnage associated with the Internet bust. The loss was even more stunning—77.9 percent—during the frenetic cable-acquisition period. *(To read Balhoff's complete stock analysis, please turn to page 288.)*

Hard to believe, but things could have turned out much worse. AT&T could have landed in the junkyard along with WorldCom and Global Crossing. Whether America's banking institutions would have permitted a company of AT&T's stature and legacy to fall into Chapter 11 is debatable—some say yes, others say no. But such academic musings miss the point. The sad fact of the matter is that AT&T should never have been pushed that far to begin with. And the fact that it was pushed that far is the real failing, and the real lesson, of the Armstrong Era. AT&T had the size and girth to weather a lot. But not even a brute like AT&T could tolerate financial recklessness, at least not for long, as her fast tumble so vividly illustrates.

No single decision felled AT&T. Rather, the company's demise came about by a thousand cuts, starting with the decision to bring in Armstrong as the CEO. That was compounded by the decision to keep Dan Somers on as the CFO. Then came the MediaOne deal, and everything unraveled from there. There were scores of other bad decisions in between, each linked to the other in a mad daisy chain of managerial incompetence. By the time it all came to a head in the summer of 2000, AT&T was teetering on the edge of financial ruin. By one measure, it was quite a feat to pull off. In just 36 short months Armstrong and his team managed to take one of the sturdiest survivors of history and reduce it to a question mark. The last time AT&T was in that much financial trouble Alexander Graham Bell, quite literally, was still on the payroll.

To be sure, Mike Armstrong didn't single-handedly drive AT&T into the ground. He had plenty of help.

His immediate predecessor, Robert E. Allen, missed the opportunity to reposition the telecom giant for a more secure future. For nine long years he debated what to do, and in the end did very little. Leo Hindery, who served as Broadband's first president, promised to deliver the entire U.S. cable TV industry to AT&T's doorstep. He didn't even come close. Dan Somers, the chief financial officer, arguably inflicted the most pain. On a positive note, Somers was energetic and creative. On the downside, he never saw a deal he didn't like. As a result, he showed none of the normal conservatism associated with the CFO's office. His optimistic style of deal making would later give rise to a new term: "Sommered." As in, "I'm not going to get Sommered [taken to the cleaners] on this deal." AT&T's suffocating corporate culture also didn't help. So dense it even has its own name—the Machine—the culture despised Armstrong and despised what he stood for: change.

AT&T's blue-chip board also deserves some blame. The board, which included such captains of industry as Sandy Weill of Citigroup, Ralph Larsen of Johnson & Johnson, George Fisher of Kodak, and Tom Wyman of CBS, sat mutely by as Dan Somers jammed through bad deal after bad deal. Then it sat by again as he rolled back AT&T's emergency backup lines—twice—to save a few million in banking fees.

The rollbacks would leave AT&T perilously exposed in the aftermath of the MediaOne deal, triggering a series of events that would culminate with the company's breakup.

Perhaps the biggest monkey on Armstrong's back, however, was the one he never saw coming: WorldCom.

Quarter after quarter, WorldCom wowed Wall Street, and bewildered AT&T, by posting impressive gains in its core long-distance business. WorldCom's stock price soared along with the reputation of its storied chairman, Bernie Ebbers. AT&T, meantime, was getting pummeled at every turn for being too slow, too dumb, too Ma Bell. Chided by Wall Street to keep up, Armstrong pushed his troops hard. When that didn't work, he started slashing budgets to reduce costs. When AT&T still couldn't seem to get clear of WorldCom's exhaust fumes, he pushed even harder. Determined to not let WorldCom waltz off with the lucrative business market, Armstrong dropped his retail prices—over and over again.

As we all know now, the AT&T chief was chasing shadows. Regulators later accused WorldCom of using accounting chicanery to achieve its stunning numbers—the whole thing was basically a farce. By the time the $11 billion ruse was revealed, however, it was too late for AT&T. By then scores of management decisions related to marketing, pricing, and more had already been made and pushed down through the organization. Careers had been made and broken. Budgets had been slashed and reworked. Customers had been won and lost. All in a valiant attempt to catch a runaway train that never existed.

IT'S HARD TO PREDICT how history will judge Mike Armstrong.

On the plus side, he had the guts to stand tall at a time when AT&T employees sorely needed someone, and something, to believe in. It's also clear that he had exactly the right strategy at exactly the right time. Armstrong's bold idea of using upgraded cable TV lines to deliver voice, data, and video services directly to the home, particularly when viewed from the rearview mirror of today, was spot-on. So was his notion of keeping everything under one roof. "One cable. One company. Countless possibilities." That was AT&T's tagline on the TCI deal. It was elegant, simple, and brilliant. Verizon, the super-sized communications company based in New York, followed a similar path, and now it's the biggest player in America with more than $70 billion in annual revenue. Verizon recently began adding video to its ever-growing bundle of services, further affirmation of Armstrong's prescient cable strategy. SBC, based in San Antonio, is following a similar path.

But when you hit the mute button on all the outside noise, including WorldCom's fraud, the dissonance of Leo Hindery, and even the dubious financial wizardry of Dan Somers, it all comes down to this: Mike Armstrong failed to execute. Period. No matter how you slice and dice the numbers—and Armstrong's supporters are quick to spin the arithmetic—he failed to save AT&T. And he didn't fail by just a little. He failed by a lot. Carving up AT&T like a retired racehorse that's been carted off to the glue factory was never the right answer. It was the easy answer in that it provided a short-term fix to AT&T's looming credit crisis. (A crisis, I would point out, that grew out of a string of bad management decisions at the top.) But it was also a hollow victory, as AT&T's current predicament so aptly illustrates.

We'll never know for sure how things would have turned out if Armstrong had managed to hang tough and soldier on. With a few lucky breaks and a sharp-eyed CFO looking over his shoulder from the start, who knows? Instead of standing on its last wobbly legs, AT&T today could have been giving the monster Bells, including SBC, an exceedingly hard time in the marketplace. Cable companies, which continue to handily dominate their local markets, also would have been well challenged. Wireless? Ditto. Though AT&T Wireless was admittedly weak in terms of its management, it had the girth and heft to become a major force in the industry. Cingular, which is a joint venture of SBC and BellSouth, certainly thought so. In 2004 it agreed to buy AT&T Wireless for $42 billion. The deal, which marked the largest all-cash transaction in U.S. corporate history, allowed Cingular to leapfrog Verizon to become the No. 1 wireless carrier in America. The man behind that transaction? SBC's Ed Whitacre. Not many people know it, but Whitacre actually tried to buy AT&T Wireless a few years earlier, but BellSouth balked. True to form, Whitacre never abandoned the idea—he just put it on ice for another day.

If only AT&T's chief had had the same sort of resolve. Sad but true, if Armstrong had made different choices at key junctures along the way, AT&T, in all probability, would still be in one piece today. Tethered to cable, wireless, and the exploding universe of IP—short for Internet Protocol, which is quickly becoming the underpinning of international commerce—AT&T would have been a global communications force to be reckoned with. Not just today, but for generations to come. Proud, iconic, formidable. It would have been the AT&T that we all grew up with, only better—just as Armstrong so boldly envisioned back in 1997. How sad, even tragic, for Mike Armstrong. And how tragic, especially, for AT&T.

2

IN THE BEGINNING

IN THE YEAR 1876, two watershed events took place. One would come to symbolize, on a grand, historical scale, abject failure; the other would spark one of the greatest success stories of our time. Both of these events took place on the same day: June 25.

Along the banks of the Little Bighorn River in Montana that afternoon, a ferocious battle was fought. On one side was General George Custer, a daring—some say cocky—young military leader, and his elite cavalry detachment of about 200 men. On the other side, sitting tall on horseback, were Chiefs Sitting Bull and Crazy Horse. They were backed by thousands of Indian warriors. By the time the battle was over, only the Indian chiefs and their men would ride out.

Back in patrician Philadelphia, another kind of history was also in the making. The city was celebrating the 100th anniversary of the signing of the Declaration of Independence. As part of the Centennial Exhibition, promising young inventors from across the country had been invited to show their wares to a panel of distinguished judges. One of the inventors was a 29-year-old Scot. He'd responded so late to his invitation that there was no room for him in the science hall. So he got stuck in a far corner of the sleepy education exhibit.

As soon as the young man unveiled his invention, *everybody* woke up. Pandemonium broke out almost immediately. Some people bolted into an adjoining space to see if the whole thing was a trick. The judges, who included such notables as Brazilian emperor Dom Pedro II and the

British physicist Lord William Thomson Kelvin, were dumbfounded. Like everybody else, they could hardly believe what they were hearing: the sound of a human voice crackling out from a small bell-shaped receiver. The emperor was so stunned that, according to some accounts, he simply blurted out, "My God! It talks!"

And, indeed, it did. By day's end, the young inventor, Alexander Graham Bell, was the star of the show, and his remarkable invention, the Bell telephone, was the talk of the town.

The world changed profoundly on that hot summer day. Custer's Last Stand, as the massacre would come to be known, paved the way for the taming of the Wild West. As for Alexander Graham Bell's invention—that little device, as rudimentary as it was, would eventually change the world. Along the way, it would also give rise to one of the greatest and most enduring corporate success stories of all time: the American Telephone & Telegraph Company.

Today, Custer's Last Stand is regarded as the Wild West's version of Waterloo—a euphemism for a bitter and decisive defeat. According to some historians, General Custer ignored the field reports of his own scouts, which had warned of large bands of Indians along the banks of the Little Bighorn River. Undaunted, the general charged ahead . . . and ran headlong into one of the largest Indian encampments on record, 10,000–15,000 in all, according to some estimates. Some historians say the entire battle only lasted 20 minutes or so. More than 128 years later, military men and women still study the tragic episode.

AT&T, sadly, has become the Waterloo of telecom—a euphemism for hubris and overreaching that reached its zenith on Armstrong's watch. AT&T's scary slide into extinction has been halted, for now, by SBC. But not even SBC can eradicate history. AT&T's collapse is now as much a part of its legacy as the invention of the storied Bell telephone, two bookend events that mark the beginning and end of one of the most fantastic business stories of our time.

HE WAS NOT an American invention himself.

Born and raised in Edinburgh, Scotland, Alexander Graham Bell, known as Aleck for years, grew up in a household that was riveted by the sound of the human voice. His father, Melville, was a professor of elocution. The elder Bell developed a technique called visible speech—it was basically a set of symbols that represented speech sounds—and used it to help teach the deaf to speak. Aleck was just 12 when his mother, a painter and musician, began to lose her hearing. Thus began his lifelong passion, even obsession, for helping the deaf to experience sound.

Aleck followed in his father's footsteps, and by the age of 20 he was using visible speech as a tool with his own deaf students in London. Bell eventually made his way to Massachusetts, where he became a professor of education at Boston University, teaching deaf students. One of those pupils was a five-year-old named George Sanders. He was the son of Thomas Sanders, a prominent leather merchant from Salem, just north of Boston. Another student was Mabel Hubbard, the teenage daughter of Gardiner Hubbard, a prominent patent attorney from Boston. On the side, Bell continued to experiment with sound using electrical currents. Sanders and Hubbard were impressed with his work, and they agreed to cover the cost of Bell's research expenses in return for a share of any inventions he might come up with.

Bell had been trying for years to figure out how to use electrical currents to carry the human voice. Conventional wisdom held that the telegraph, based on "intermittent" transmissions—an electrical current that was either present or not, producing the familiar rat-tat-tat of the old Morse code—was the way to go. Bell, however, was convinced that a continuous, "undulating" electrical current was a far better solution, reasoning that it was closer in makeup to the human voice. Working with his faithful research assistant, Thomas Watson, Bell continued to follow his hunches.

On July 1, 1875, Bell succeeded in transmitting some speech sounds using an undulating current—a scientific first. But most of the sounds were unintelligible. Bell was crushed, and immediately went back into the lab to figure out the problem. Hubbard quickly saw the promise of his breakthrough, and filed for a patent on Bell's behalf. It was a good instinct. The following year, on March 10, 1876, to be exact, Bell uttered some of the most famous words in history: "Watson, come here—I want you!" The telephone was born.

Bell, Sanders, and Hubbard quickly formed a holding company

around the new invention. Its name: Bell Telephone. The first shares were issued to just seven people: Thomas Sanders and Gardiner Hubbard each got about 1,500 shares. Gardiner's wife, Gertrude, got 100 shares, and his brother, Charles, got 10. Thomas Watson got 500 shares. Alexander Graham Bell gave all but 10 of his shares to Gardiner's daughter, Mabel, who by then was his fiancée. That left her with 1,500 shares. Bell was also named the company's "electrician" and given an annual salary of $3,000. Watson was put in charge of research and manufacturing, and he also took on some bookkeeping duties. The final documents forming Bell Telephone were signed in Boston on July 9, 1877.

Bell, who had little interest in business affairs, married Mabel two days later. The couple immediately set sail for England, leaving it up to Gardiner Hubbard to figure out a way to turn the Bell telephone into a moneymaking venture. Hubbard tried to round up some outside investors, but nobody was interested. This was, after all, 1877. Most people in America had never heard of the Bell telephone, much less used one. (For all the lather in scientific circles, only 800 devices had actually been shipped.) In a fit of frustration, Hubbard offered to sell the Bell telephone patents to Western Union for $100,000. William Orton, Western Union's president, turned him down flat. Orton told him that there was no way an "electrical toy" like the Bell telephone could ever benefit his company. The rebuff—historians peg the date as either late 1876 or late 1877—would prove to be fateful for both sides.

Determined to make a go of it, Hubbard soon hit on a novel idea: telephone franchises. With Bell's blessing, Hubbard began licensing local businessmen in cities across the country to sell telephone service using the patented Bell telephone. Owing to his own experience in leasing shoe-making equipment, Hubbard insisted that franchisees rent—not sell—customers their telephones. It would prove to be one of the savviest business decisions in U.S. corporate history.

The first telephone exchange opened on January 28, 1878, in New Haven, Connecticut. There were just 21 customers, and they could only talk to each other. Calls were handled by a telephone operator, who used a switchboard to sort and route calls by name, not number. The phone itself wasn't much to look at—a small block of wood with a magnet that acted as the receiver as well as the transmitter. There was no ringer on the phone. (Thomas Watson wouldn't invent that for another four years.) Instead, calls were announced, after a fashion, by hitting the transmitter with a hammer or whatever happened to be handy. Lag times in voice transmission made it difficult to hold a conversation. Callers had to speak slowly and succinctly, and even then they usually had to repeat themselves several times just to get out a few sentences. Despite all the aggravations, however, people loved it. The excitement of using a telephone to communicate with the outside world, even if it was just a neighbor down the street, was hard to beat.

TO BE SURE, the telephone had its share of detractors. Some people initially regarded the device with suspicion, even disdain. In Philadelphia, some bluebloods immediately decried the Bell telephone as a vulgar contraption that was sure to intrude on the city's manners and sensibility. Telephone poles, an eyesore in any era, were a frequent target of ire.

Most people, however, were fascinated by Bell's "electrical toy." The Bell telephone of the 1870s represented the latest in cutting-edge technology, and everybody wanted one. According to some historical accounts, Queen Victoria was so impressed by the device that she asked Bell to run a phone line between Osborne House, on the Isle of Wight, and Buckingham Palace. Bell agreed, and installed a telephone in the House of Commons while he was at it.

Pundits had a field day dissecting the greater meaning of phone service. Even Mark Twain, the great American writer, weighed in. "Here we have been hollering 'Shut up' to our neighbors for centuries, and now you fellows come along and seek to complicate matters," Twain chortled in one essay. Bell, for his part, felt certain that the phone would spark seismic changes in America. Writing to his father shortly after the phone's invention, Bell predicted that "the day is coming when telegraph wires will be laid on to houses just like water or gas—and friends will converse with each other without leaving home." But not even Bell, as prescient as he was, could predict the sweeping changes that his electrical experiment would help bring about.

In the 1870s, American consumers got their first glimpse of a new breed of worker: the telephone operator. The first operators were mostly teenage boys. And like teenage boys of any era, the ones manning Bell Telephone's switchboards in the 1870s were loud, impolite, and not particularly reliable. After rounds of complaints from customers, the Bell Telephone franchise in Boston hit on a novel idea: Why not staff the switchboards with young *women?* Owing to disposition and rearing, young women tended to be far more polite. Though nobody dared to say it outright, sex appeal was also a draw. Men were the most frequent users of the telephone, and the Boston franchise figured they might use the phone more often if they knew a pleasant female voice would be waiting on the other end. It was a good hunch. With female attendants in place, phone usage in Boston skyrocketed. Other franchises soon followed Boston's lead, laying the foundation of what would eventually become one of the best-known icons in the world: the female telephone operator.

BY THE LATE 1870s, Hubbard's grand experiment was teetering on bankruptcy. America was in the icy grip of an economic depression. The decline had been brought about, in part, by overzealous speculation in the railroad business. Banks were no longer lending money. Even worse, many lenders were starting to call in their loans. A lot of businesses were forced to scale back or shut down altogether. Thousands of people lost their jobs.

Hubbard, who was still trying to expand the Bell franchise business, was burning through cash quickly. By 1878 he was flat broke. Desperate to keep the business afloat, Hubbard reluctantly ceded control to a group of wealthy Boston investors. Before stepping aside, however, he made one final decision that would prove golden: He hired a U.S. Post Office worker named Theodore Vail to come on board as general manager.

The U.S. Post Office of the 1870s was widely admired for its efficiency and stellar customer care. And Theodore Vail, the superintendent of the Railway Mail Service, was its superstar. Under Vail, the train-delivery unit had become the FedEx of its day—fast, friendly, and ultra-efficient.

Hubbard, who sat on the postal committee in Washington, was an ardent admirer. With his management smarts and postal work ethic,

Hubbard figured Vail could imbue Bell Telephone with the discipline it needed to prosper as a business enterprise. Hubbard had no idea how right he was.

Vail had strong views about what a modern consumer service organization should look like—ten, twenty, or even fifty years down the road. He also had strong opinions about the telephone. Like Hubbard, Vail believed that the Bell telephone would revolutionize global communications. Anxious to move the revolution along, Vail quickly set plans to turn the company into a global leader. His high ideals were admirable, particularly considering that phone service itself was still so new that most people had never even seen a telephone, much less used one.

Vail showed up for his first day of work in June 1878. The future looked pretty bleak. For all the froth around phone service, less than 10,000 telephones had actually been shipped out. The company's manufacturing capability consisted of one shop in Boston, and the sole machinist assigned to Bell Telephone was painfully slow in turning out product.

Bell Telephone was also in the middle of a bruising legal dispute with Western Union. The telegraph giant had begun offering competing phone service using the Bell telephone, prompting Bell to claim patent infringement. Western Union pushed right back, insisting that Bell Telephone—not Western Union—was the real trespasser. Nobody expected Bell Telephone to win. Western Union, after all was rich, powerful, and monolithic. Bell Telephone was still a startup. Even worse, it was a startup that was about to get trampled by the reigning business power of the day, Western Union.

Vail refused to yield. He quickly called in a cadre of sharp-eyed patent attorneys, and before long the mud was flying in both directions. By the time it was all over, just one victor was left standing: Bell Telephone. In a stunning turn of events, Western Union dropped all its patent claims in exchange for 20 percent of Bell Telephone's rental revenues over the 17-year life of the disputed Bell patents. Western Union also agreed to sell its fledgling telephone business to Bell Telephone.

Investors went wild. Shares of Bell Telephone, which had languished at just a few dollars apiece at the height of the legal fight, shot up to an eye-popping $300—and kept heading north from there. By November,

Bell shares were trading for an astronomical $1,000 apiece. It was a dizzying level that AT&T, in all its incarnations, would never come close to seeing again.

With Bell Telephone's patent rights secure, a new era began. The company issued its first annual report to public shareholders in 1881. By then, Bell Telephone had reorganized and assumed a new name: American Bell. The number of "instruments" (phones) stood at more than 132,000, representing a 100 percent rise over the year-earlier period. All the buzz was attracting a record number of new franchisees. Even the European market, which had been slow to embrace the telephone, was perking up. "The business of the company . . . has been in every respect satisfactory," W. H. Forbes, American Bell's president, neatly summarized in his letter to shareholders that year. Though his enthusiasm was cloaked in the conservative language of the day, his message was clear: American Bell was hot.

Theodore Vail was not content. His biggest worry: Bell phone patents. Though the company's legal fight had secured the patent rights for a while, they would eventually expire. By 1885, he was spending more and more time peering into his crystal ball, and he didn't like what he saw.

Just two government-issued patents covered the main components of the Bell telephone—they had been issued in 1876 and 1877, respectively—and they were both set to expire in 1894. That was less than 10 years away. Once they expired, the Bell telephone would be up for grabs. Competition was sure to turn fierce. Price wars—always bad for profits —were bound to break out. Vail decided that he needed to figure out a way to best the competition before it even began.

Vail hit on an audacious idea: How about knitting together the Bell franchises into one, national network? The connector? Long distance. The early signs were encouraging. The nation's first long-distance line— between Boston and Providence, Rhode Island—had opened up in 1881. The route, just 45 miles in length, was strung with galvanized iron. Capacity was severely restricted—just one call at a time. As a transmission medium, galvanized iron was better than a string and two tin cups, but just barely. Interference was so bad that it was practically impossible to conduct an actual conversation.

Warts and all, people loved it. Customers loved the novelty of talking to somebody who wasn't actually in the same room with them, much less in the same town or state. The inverse proportion of quality to public enthusiasm wasn't lost on Vail. If customers were so crazy about a service that was so fundamentally flawed, how would they react once all the bugs were out? To Vail's way of thinking, the answer to that question was as good as money in the bank.

There was just one problem: Nobody had ever built a national network before. So it was going to be an engineering experiment for the ages. Vail refused to blink. Using the Bell telephone as the anchor, Vail was convinced that he could cement American Bell's leadership position in the emerging world of telecom. Even better, perhaps, it would help push along the global communications revolution that Vail and Hubbard believed in so deeply. It was a gamble, to be sure. But to Vail's way of thinking it was far less risky than if he sat pat and did nothing.

With his eye firmly on the future, Vail made his move. On February 28, 1885, American Bell set up a brand-new subsidiary in New York City and gave it a heady mission: to build and operate the nation's first long-distance network. The subsidiary's name? The American Telephone & Telegraph Company.

AT&T's first route, between New York and Philadelphia, opened up that same year. It was an instant hit. The 300-mile route was strung with copper. As a transmission medium, copper was superior to galvanized iron, but not by much. Calls still had a lot of pops and scratches. The capacity of the line was severely limited—just one call at a time. It didn't matter. People still loved it.

Two years later, Vail was gone.

By then he'd been battling with upper management for years. Most of the fights concerned money. Vail regarded expansion as the key to American Bell's success, and he constantly pushed to plow profits back into the business. The company's Boston backers, however, were far more concerned with profits, leading to some violent boardroom brawls. Tired of the constant fighting, Vail finally resigned in 1887. His stormy exit would set the stage for a remarkable second act.

The Bell telephone patents expired in 1894. Just as Vail had predicted, competition turned ugly almost overnight. Price wars broke out immediately. Within a few years, more than 6,000 independent phone companies sprang up. Phone usage skyrocketed. American Bell, which had started out with 300,000 customers at the beginning of the 1890s, was close to the one million mark by the end of the decade. The independents weren't far behind with more than 700,000 customers.

AT&T, meantime, continued working on its new long-distance network. Progress was slow, but steady. Service still wasn't all that great. AT&T's route between New York and Chicago could only handle one call at a time. The price was also steep—$9 for the first five minutes. Even so, customers loved the service.

American Bell reorganized again in 1899. The incentive was purely financial: American Bell was based in Massachusetts, which had become decidedly unfriendly to big business; AT&T was based in New York City, where the corporate laws were far more progressive. Hoping to take advantage of New York's largesse, the leadership of American Bell decided to flip all the assets to AT&T. On December 31 the plan was carried out, and by the time the clock struck midnight the deed was done. Thus, with the start of the new year and the new century, AT&T became the official parent of what was about to become the most powerful communications company on the planet.

THE YEAR 1900 was marked by a lot of political unrest in the world. The Boxer Rebellion, which would redefine territorial boundaries in China, was underway. Britain was in the midst of the Boer War. Back in America, AT&T was also at war—with itself. The company was being upended by internal power struggles among three formidable groups. Each wanted the exact same thing: control over AT&T. One group consisted of the same Boston financiers who had ousted Vail some years earlier. Clarence Mackay of Postal Telegraph, Western Union's chief rival, represented the second interest. The third group consisted of a group of merchant bankers who were headed by the most feared banker of them all, J. P. Morgan.

The three groups warred for several years, using every dirty trick imaginable to snooker one another. (In 1901, with the fight in high gear, Morgan still managed to find time to form U.S. Steel, the world's first billion-dollar company.) When the AT&T shootout finally ended in 1907, J. P. Morgan was the only Morgan who made no bones about his intentions: He wanted AT&T to become the U.S. Steel of phone service. Since Morgan controlled the banks, he figured he had a better than even shot at being successful.

Morgan already had control of AT&T's purse strings as well as the board. But he still needed an able manager who could oversee the business day-to-day. It was a crucial decision. AT&T's next president had to be somebody who could win the support of the rank-and-file. But he also needed to have the inner toughness to stay the course and bring Morgan's grandiose visions to life. It was a tall order, and Morgan had just the man in mind: Theodore Vail.

Vail, 62, had been gone from AT&T for two decades. But he was still a larger-than-life figure around the halls of AT&T. Employees revered him. Like Alexander Graham Bell himself, Theodore Vail had dared to dream the impossible. Tough, prescient, and resourceful, Vail had foreseen the explosion in long distance, and boldly created AT&T out of his own fears and imagination. Morgan admired Vail's steely resolve, probably because it mirrored his own. He also appreciated Vail's loyalty. Most important of all, perhaps, the two men shared a common vision of AT&T, and it was a vision shaped by monopolistic dreams and seemingly impossible outcomes.

Vail began his second tour of AT&T in the summer of 1907. He had his work cut out for him. His predecessors had been so consumed with political infighting that the basic needs of the business had been all but ignored. Conditions in many Bell facilities were downright dangerous and supervision was incredibly lax. On-the-job fatalities weren't uncommon. According to some historical accounts, more than 50 AT&T workers died annually falling off telephone poles.

Then there was the long-distance business itself. AT&T was still the biggest phone company in America, with more than 3 million customers. But with almost 3 million customers between them, the independents weren't far behind. Just as Vail had hoped, long distance had become a differentiator for AT&T. But its service just wasn't very good. Calls were filled with pops, pings, and other extraneous noises. The most nagging problem, by far, was attenuation—the tendency of signals to get weaker over longer distances. Until that riddle was solved, AT&T couldn't even think about offering coast-to-coast calling. For a company that aspired to become a national carrier, that was very bad news, indeed.

To shake the company out of its doldrums, Vail decided that AT&T needed a challenge, one that would energize the workforce, showcase its talents, and mesmerize the public. His solution? In a word: *quality.* It was a progressive idea for 1907, to say the least. Back then, service quality was hardly a marketing mantra. To Vail, however, it was just common sense. Given its size, AT&T couldn't compete on price, at least not for long. But competing on the basis of service *quality?* That was a game AT&T could win.

In 1910, Vail shocked the world—and some of his own researchers—by announcing that AT&T would build the nation's first transcontinental route between New York and San Francisco. Vail promised to have the route finished by the time the Panama Canal was completed. The canal was scheduled to open in 1914, less than five years away. It was an outlandish promise, especially considering that the technology did not yet exist to support a New York–San Francisco connection. But Vail, being Vail, would not be deterred. By then he had moved AT&T's scientists and researchers into one location in downtown New York, laying the foundation for what would eventually become Bell Labs. (Bell Telephone Laboratories—Bell Labs for short—wouldn't be formally established until 1925.)

Morgan, meantime, was still wheeling and dealing. He bought a controlling interest in Western Union, and named Vail as its president. With Western Union in its back pocket, AT&T was well on its way to becoming a monopoly power. Trustbusters were alarmed. The acquisition of Western Union, one of the best-known brands of its day, gave AT&T unprecedented access to American consumers. AT&T's refusal to let independent phone carriers interconnect to Bell networks concerned them even more. Morgan, perhaps not surprisingly, refused to budge. Before long, he was cranking up the pressure on AT&T's small rivals even more.

Weary of Morgan's strong-arming, the federal government sued AT&T on antitrust grounds in 1912. It would mark the beginning of a bitter and running battle over AT&T's market dominance. Morgan was enraged by the legal attack, and immediately set plans to wage a war against the government on AT&T's behalf. He never got the chance to follow through. Morgan, who was pushing 76, died the following year. His untimely death sent a shock wave through the financial community. It also gave Vail some much needed breathing room. Free at last to follow his conscience, instead of Morgan's strict marching orders, Vail quickly moved to settle the government's lawsuit.

The result was the Kingsbury Commitment. Named after Nathan Kingsbury, an AT&T vice president who had helped draft it, the document established a set of competitive principles that would guide AT&T for another 80 years. Most notably, AT&T agreed to let some independent phone companies interconnect with Bell networks. AT&T also agreed to halt its consolidation drive, and to divest its controlling interest in Western Union. The Kingsbury Commitment was later affirmed by President Woodrow Wilson and published by the Government Printing Office. It would mark the formal beginning of the government-sanctioned telephone monopoly known as AT&T. Even J. P. Morgan, no doubt, would have approved of that.

BEFORE THE transcontinental line between New York and San Francisco could be completed, a network riddle for the ages first had to be solved: attenuation. (Simply put, attenuation is the reduction of signal strength over longer distances.) Unless the mystery was unraveled, AT&T would never be able to offer high quality phone service to the masses. Even more important, perhaps, the company would never be able to provide coast-to-coast calling over its spanking-new transcontinental line. Vail, once again, would not be disappointed. In the end, a math professor at Columbia University, working in conjunction with a Bell scientist, solved the mystery: They figured out how to harness inductance, the chief cause of attenuation, and use it as a sort of force field to actually *reduce* attenuation. (Inductance is basically stored energy in the form of a magnetic field.) The happy result was the loading coil, a small device that reduced attenuation over longer distances. That breakthrough was followed by another important development, the repeater—a device that actually regenerates signals. Together with electrical amplifiers, developed by AT&T's Harold Arnold, the attenuation problem was finally solved.

Vail was ecstatic. Not only had AT&T pulled off one of the grand engineering feats of all time, it had managed to do so in record time. There was just one problem: He couldn't tell anybody about it, because the Panama Canal wasn't yet completed. Vail was determined to unveil his achievement at the World's Fair. But the fair, which was being touted as a celebration of the Panama Canal, had been pushed back by a full six months to accommodate the canal's slow construction. Vail decided to wait it out.

The big day finally arrived on January 25, 1915. Just as Vail had hoped, the World's Fair provided a magnificent stage. Reporters from all over the world jammed the area where the AT&T announcement was scheduled to take place. Nervousness hung in the air. To demonstrate AT&T's technical might, the company arranged a ceremonial four-way call between Alexander Graham Bell in New York City, Thomas Watson in San Francisco, President Wilson at the White House, and Vail, who was at his vacation home on Jekyll Island, off the coast of Georgia. Waiting around for the demonstration to start, a reporter in New York spotted Bell, and asked him to repeat the first famous words he ever uttered over a telephone. Delighted at the invitation, Bell quickly picked up the phone: "Watson, come here—I want you!" Showing great comic timing, Watson didn't miss a beat: "Well, it would take me a week now." The impromptu exchange brought down the house.

At an initial cost of $20.70 for the first three minutes, call volume on the New York–San Francisco route remained low for quite a while. But that was almost beside the point. The World's Fair demonstration, fully 40 years in the making, was proud testament to the raw power and influence of the mighty Bell telephone. America was finally, and forever, a house undivided—by geography, time zones, state lines, or coastal borders. The societal ramifications were enormous. Instead of looking at the phone as a tool of last resort, the Bell telephone suddenly became a tool of convenience, even enjoyment. For the average consumer in 1915, that was a pretty heady concept. And people couldn't get enough of it.

The device that Western Union had dismissed as a passing fad was now as much a part of the American landscape as baseball, motherhood, and apple pie. And Western Union? It was about to be eclipsed by the staggering technology developments by AT&T and the fantabulous Bell telephone. To be sure, pin-drop quality of the sort offered by fiberoptic technology wouldn't become commonplace for a few more decades. But no matter. By the time that ceremonial call at the World's Fair ended, a new era in America had already begun. Thanks to Alexander Graham Bell's imagination, Theodore Vail's perseverance, and J. P. Morgan's stubbornness, ubiquitous telephone service, with all its social, economic, and global implications, was no longer an idea ahead of its time—it was an idea whose time had finally come.

3

TROUBLE IN
(LONG-DISTANCE)
PARADISE

I N 1996, AT&T had a startling come-to-Jesus realization. The problem this time wasn't trustbusters, technology, or even political strife. It was much worse.

The problem was long distance. Thanks to years of bloody price wars, revenue growth in the company's core long-distance business was slowing to a trickle. It was only a matter of time before revenues started to decline. Once that happened, AT&T was going to have a full-blown crisis on its hands. Nobody knew what to do about it, least of all Robert Allen, AT&T's chairman and chief executive officer.

AT&T's strong balance sheet belied its dire predicament. With more than $50 billion in annual revenues, $6 billion in net profits, and 90 million customers, AT&T was one of the richest and most powerful communications companies on the planet. Long distance was the undisputed cash cow, accounting for more than 80 percent of annual revenues and 100 percent of profits. AT&T still commanded a respectable 50 percent share of the long-distance market. To be sure, it wasn't the 100 percent share that it had claimed back in its glory days before the breakup of the Bell Telephone System. But it was still more than MCI and Sprint had combined.

AT&T's growing anxiety puzzled Allen. A Bell man to his marrow, Allen still believed in the magic of the mighty AT&T name to triumph in the marketplace. His view was at least somewhat understandable. During its long, magnificent life, AT&T had overcome trustbusters, technology hurdles, economic strife, and much, much more. Bent but never broken, the company had always managed to beat the odds and soldier on. And now this proud communications warrior was going down for the count, eclipsed by a generation of AT&T knockoffs like MCI and Sprint?

I don't think so. Not on my watch.

Allen's steely resolve was easy to miss. His nickname around Basking Ridge was Mr. Rogers, and for good reason. Tall, lanky, and soft-spoken, Allen was a dead ringer for the folksy children's TV star. Like Mr. Rogers, Allen didn't come across as much of a poker player. His ruddy complexion used to turn beet red whenever he was excited or riled up. He had a habit of clearing his throat when he spoke, creating the impression that he was a little unsure of himself. True to his Midwestern roots, he was exceedingly polite. Some people mistook his reserved manner for weakness. That was a big mistake.

Indeed, Allen was no Mr. Rogers. Known universally as Bob, he was cagey, smart, and politically astute. He was a hardened survivor of the Bell System, and those who crossed him usually lived to regret it. Allen also had a lot of pull on the powerful AT&T board. That made him dangerous to anybody who was foolish enough to get in his way. As a result, not many people did.

A native of Missouri, Allen started working for Indiana Bell in 1957 right out of college. Managers were impressed by his polite manner and earnest ways. His golf game didn't hurt. Allen started playing when he was in his twenties. Trying to learn the game, he bought a second-hand set of clubs for $35 and honed his stroke on public courses. By the 1970s he was quite the duffer. Bill Cashel, the former president of Bell of Pennsylvania, was so impressed that he once wrote an essay extolling Allen's golf game. The article, which ran in *Bell Telephone News,* was ostensibly about golf being an analogy for a man's inner core. But it was mostly an excuse for Cashel, also a golfer, to rave about Allen's seamless style on the links.

Like many Bell executives, Allen worked a lot of different jobs—

more than 20 in all over the course of his career. He also moved around a lot, pulling stints at Illinois Bell, Bell of Pennsylvania and Chesapeake & Potomac Telephone Co. in Washington, D.C. By the time Allen landed at C&P Telephone in 1981, it was clear to insiders that he was headed for the top. C&P, which provided telephone service to the White House, the Federal Communications Commission, and other politically important customers, was considered a training ground for future CEOs. After a few years, as expected, Allen got called up to AT&T's New York headquarters. In baseball terms, it was alike a farm-team player getting called up to the majors. Allen had arrived.

AT&T IN THE 1980s was a beehive of activity. A lot of the activity was aimed at keeping AT&T's telephone monopoly intact. Trustbusters had long accused AT&T of using its size and clout to disadvantage rivals. Starting in 1913, the U.S. Department of Justice had filed a string of legal actions aimed at curbing its market power. AT&T, which by the 1970s was the world's largest corporation with more than a million employees, refused to bend. Determined to maintain its dominant position, AT&T spent millions of dollars defending itself in court. By the time Allen arrived at corporate headquarters in New York, the dance had been going on for decades.

In January 1982, the music stopped. Right in the middle of yet another stinging anti-trust lawsuit, AT&T chairman Charles "Charlie" Brown let loose with a jaw-dropper: He announced that AT&T would work with the government to dismantle the century-old phone monopoly. People were flabbergasted. AT&T had been fighting the government, at that point for more than 70 *years*.

A lot of Bell insiders were livid. Brown, after all, was one of the staunchest defenders of AT&T's service credo, which was inextricably tied to its status as a government-sanctioned telephone monopoly. Employees were outraged that Brown would even think about selling out like that. Brown wasn't so happy, either. A dedicated Bell man, he'd started working for the company digging ditches when he was just 18— and never left. Brown loved AT&T, and loved what it stood for. But he was also a realist. The federal judge who was hearing the case, Harold

Greene, had already made it clear that he didn't think AT&T stood a chance of winning. Neither, apparently, did Brown.

His decision had a lot of logic behind it. By then AT&T was defending itself against anti-trust charges in dozens of states. AT&T had hundreds of lawyers working around the clock just to keep up with all the motions and counter-motions. The paperwork was overwhelming. So was AT&T's legal bill: more than $360 million. Adding to AT&T's growing migraine, a telecom newcomer named Microwave Communications Inc.—the name was later shortened to MCI—was on the warpath in Washington. Regulators, who had been complicit with AT&T for decades, were suddenly gunning for AT&T. So was almost everybody else, for that matter. To be sure, AT&T had the resources to fight back. But Brown read the smoke signals, and decided to call it a day.

Brown spent the next two years negotiating with the Justice Department on behalf of the entire Bell Telephone System. During these negotiations, the Bell System's 22 operating companies got collapsed into seven "Baby Bells" of roughly equal size. AT&T was carved out in its entirety and set aside as a stand-alone company. These and other terms eventually got folded into a final breakup "decree," which was overseen by Judge Greene in Washington. The AT&T divestiture, as the breakup came to be known, officially took effect on January 1, 1984. All the state actions went away concurrent with the settlement.

Brown tried his best to be evenhanded in divvying up the booty. But in practice he wound up stacking the deck—some say wildly—in AT&T's favor. (Or so everybody thought, but read on.) AT&T, as expected, got to keep the crown jewels—long distance and the world-famous AT&T brand name. It also got Bell Laboratories, which had one of the richest collections of technology patents in the world, more than 19,000 in all. AT&T also got to hold onto its manufacturing arm, Western Electric. In addition, AT&T got a free card to enter the computer business. Brown, for his part, felt certain that the computer business was the future of AT&T.

The Bells, at least initially, felt they'd been short-sheeted. While AT&T got to sashay off with the high-glam long-distance business, they got stuck with 80 percent of the physical plant—a fuddy-duddy collection of 100-year-old copper phone networks that were incedibly expensive to maintain. They also had to tend to local phone customers, who were notoriously finicky and cheap. Their upset was understandable. Local phone service was relatively inexpensive—just $10 a month or less in most places. It was also heavily regulated. AT&T's customers, by comparison, were paying 40 cents or more a *minute* for long-distance. And since long-distance was largely unregulated, AT&T could boost its prices anytime it felt like it, which was often.

One of the Bells' biggest upsets was related to the so-called long-distance subsidy, which had been used for years to prop up profits. Prior to divestiture, long-distance was priced artificially high to offset the artificially low price of local. After the breakup, local phone service prices increased slightly to make up for some, but certainly not all, of the difference. Needless to say, the Bells weren't too happy about that. And there was more bad news. Under the new rules, the Bells were banned from manufacturing and anything that even remotely smacked of long distance. They were also stuck with a bunch of made-up corporate names that nobody had ever heard of: Nynex, Bell Atlantic, BellSouth, Ameritech, U S West, Pacific Telesis, and Southwestern Bell. Not exactly catchy.

To be sure, the Bells got a few bones thrown their way, like yellow pages and Bellcore—short for Bell Communications Research Inc.—an efficient but wholly uninteresting research consortium that had been carved out of Bell Labs. They also got AT&T's operational licenses for a brand-new service that appeared to have no future.

Most people on the AT&T side sort of snickered. In comparison to AT&T's haul, the Bells' goody bag looked downright puny. On the day the breakup terms were announced, ABC News ominously declared that AT&T was the hands-down winner. So did just about every other news organization, for that matter.

EVERYBODY WAS WRONG. The Bells weren't the ones who'd just gotten skinned alive—it was AT&T. Charlie Brown, as it turned out, had just handed the Bells the keys to telecom kingdom. And he'd even managed to wrap up his accidental present with a big red bow. That cache of operational licenses? They were *wireless* licenses. For the entire

United States, from the concrete canyons of New York City to the real canyons of California. At the time nobody expected wireless to amount to much. AT&T's own internal studies had concluded that the wireless market might attract 1 million users, at most. So when a young attorney named John Zeglis urged Brown to give the licenses to the Bells as a consolation prize, he didn't hesitate.

And AT&T? It was suddenly looking at a very uncertain future.

Why? It all went back to those 100-year-old copper networks. Even though the familial ties had been broken, the engineering ties remained. Theodore Vail, as prescient as he was, had never contemplated a world in which AT&T and the Bells would be separated. So he'd never concerned himself with trying to figure out a way to untangle their networks.

And tangled they are. AT&T had been founded strictly as a long-haul carrier—its sole purpose in life was to ferry calls from one Bell territory to another. The Bells, in sharp contrast, controlled the "last mile" of copper that runs between the central switching office, where long-distance calls are received and sorted, and the customer's premises. These "last mile" connections are deceptively simple—just a piece of copper wiring strategically placed, really. But they are ingenious from a competitive standpoint because you can't get into or out of a home or business without them. (Wireless-to-wireless and Internet calls are a different story, which is one reason VoIP—short for Voice over Internet Protocol—services are so threatening to the Bells, and so enticing to rivals.) This symbiotic relationship worked well so long as AT&T and the Bells were living under the same roof. But as soon as the court-ordered breakup took place, the fighting began.

Money was the real rub. AT&T and the Bells had always compensated each other for handling calls. When they were part of the same family, the money was just going from one pocket to another, so nobody really cared. After the breakup, however, these so-called access fees became a major bone of contention for both sides. AT&T was especially anxious, because it was looking at the prospect of seeing 40 percent of its annual revenues get sucked down the drain in the form of access fees. The Bells, on the other hand, would get to keep every nickel they collected.

AT&T tried to get the Bells to lower their fees, to no avail. Over time, AT&T did manage to eke out a few concessions here and there. But by and large the Bells had AT&T by the short hairs, and that was pretty much that. Meantime, both sides continued to search for ways to expand their borders while protecting their competitive flanks. It was an exercise that would turn into a 20-year obsession.

ADDING TO AT&T'S MISERY, the long-distance market was undergoing rapid changes. But AT&T's monolithic mindset, which had long ago become convinced of its own supremacy, wasn't changing along with it.

On the upside, call volume was exploding. AT&T was carrying an average of 37.5 million calls a day in 1984. By 1989, the number had shot up to 105.9 million. By 1999 the number had more than doubled to 270 million. The bad news was that long-distance prices were crashing. (That's why call volume was exploding.) In the gravy monopoly days, AT&T had commanded 40 cents a minute or more for long-distance. By the mid-1990s, per-minute prices had plunged to just 15 cents, and they were still dropping.

The seven Baby Bells, meantime, were pushing hard to jump the fence. That was AT&T's worst nightmare. Once the Bells got into long distance, AT&T was certain to lose even more business—the only question was how much. AT&T had already lost about 40 percent of its overall market share, and its lock on long distance was loosening by the quarter. The Bells, in sharp contrast, still controlled more than 95 percent of the local phone lines in their respective markets.

How was it possible for long distance to be a Mad Hatter's Ball of competition, while local phone service, for all practical purposes, was still stuck in a 1984 time warp? Easy: No access. So long as the Baby Bells had a lock on those "last mile" connections, nobody had a way to get calls into and out of the home. And until that changed, competition was never going to develop in America's local phone markets. Not in a decade. Not in a century. Not ever.

By 1996, Congress had seen enough. Hoping to jump-start competition in the local phone business, lawmakers passed a sweeping law aimed at deregulating the U.S. market. The landmark Telecommunications Act of 1996 was signed into law that February. The law, 10 years in the making, encouraged local and long-distance companies to invade each other's markets. It also offered some incentives to cable TV operators to jump the fence and get into phone service. Ditto for gas and electric companies. So there was a little something for everybody.

Tucked into the law was a huge carrot for the Bells: long distance. It wasn't a slam dunk, mind you. Before the Bells could start selling long-distance services they had to meet a "14-point checklist," devised largely by AT&T, showing that their local phone markets were open to competition. Approval wasn't assured—they had to get signoffs from regulators at the state and federal levels. But after 10 years of pushing and prodding, the Bells finally had a pathway for entering the $100 billion long-distance market.

AT&T also got a little something—a clear shot at the local phone business. Under the new law, the Bells were obliged to lease out their "last mile" lines to AT&T and other rivals, an arrangement known as resale. For AT&T, that was the sweetest piece of the pie. Within hours of the law's enactment, AT&T boldly announced its intention to enter the local phone business in all 50 states. To get things rolling, AT&T said it would promptly enter into resale negotiations with all seven Bells. AT&T predicted that customers would switch in droves, noting that a recent survey had indicated that 30-50 percent would cross over to AT&T in a heartbeat. Bob Allen, the AT&T chairman and CEO, was practically beaming. "We're ready to play," Allen crowed. "We're ready to win."

But the Bells weren't ready to roll over and play dead just yet. They had some ideas of their own about how to beat back competition. And unlike AT&T, they had the means to make good on their threats—100 percent control over those "last mile" connections to the home.

RIGHT AFTER THE 1996 Telecommunications Act was signed into law, the Bells made their move.

That April, Bell Atlantic, the Philadelphia-based Bell, announced plans to buy Nynex, its neighbor in New York. Southwestern Bell—the name was later changed to SBC—announced plans a few weeks later to buy Pacific Telesis, based in San Francisco. The twin announcements landed like a one-two punch to AT&T's jaw. Once the deals closed, Bell Atlantic and Southwestern Bell stood to take control of the eastern and western halves of the United States, respectively. Bell Atlantic, which already controlled the heavily populated Mid-Atlantic, including Washington, D.C., would pick up Nynex's markets in the industrial Northeast, leaving it with a commanding position from Maine to Virginia. SBC which already controlled five Sunbelt states, would also control California and parts of Nevada. The back-to-back acquisitions sparked a lot of speculation in the press about who might be acquired next.

All the blood in the water sent investment bankers into a drug-induced feeding frenzy. The drug, of course, was money. The Bells had plenty of it, and they were clearly in a buying mode. The three remaining Bells—Ameritech, U S West, and BellSouth—were immediately besieged by would-be suitors. So was GTE, the big Stamford, Connecticut, based telecom carrier, sometimes referred to as the "eighth Bell" because of its size and national reach. Microsoft, never very far away whenever big media deals are in play, made the rounds. So did a lot of other would-be investors. The press, as you might expect, ate it up. So did Wall Street, which was energized by the prospect of Ma Bell being reconstructed, one big, expensive deal at a time.

Ray Smith, Bell Atlantic's chairman and CEO, and SBC chief Whitacre played it cool. In public statements, both men dismissed critics who said they were abusing the spirit of the Telecommunications Act, which had been intended to create competition, not just extend the monopoly reach of the Bells. They also denied accusations that they were trying to re-create the glory days of Ma Bell, with its monolithic grip over America's phone markets. Taking the high road, Smith and Whitacre talked about "synergies," "cost savings," and other terms of art that get thrown around any time two like-minded giants combine. But they also left no doubt that their buying sprees, funded by money from monopoly businesses that aimed to stay that way, were far from over. With billions in their respective war chests and the $100 billion long-distance prize finally within reach, the real fight of the century—with AT&T—was just getting started.

4

CHANGING OF
THE GUARD

D EEP INSIDE the corporate offices of AT&T in Basking
Ridge, New Jersey, another drama was unfolding. This one
involved the AT&T chairman himself, Bob Allen. After eight
years in the job, pressure was mounting for Allen to name a successor.

Allen, who was 61 at the time, knew it was time to make his move.
His immediate predecessor, James Olson, died just two years after his
appointment. Olson's predecessor, Charlie Brown, had a seven-year run.
Brown's predecessor, John deButts, also left after seven years. Now Allen
was pushing into his ninth year, and there was no successor in sight.
Adding to his growing sense of personal embarrassment, Allen didn't
think any CEO should stay in the job for more than 10 years. As he'd
told the AT&T board many times, people just get worn out, tired. Not
good for the CEO or the company.

For a while, Randy Tobias, the AT&T vice chairman, looked like a
shoo-in. Allen had hired Tobias when he was working at Indiana Bell in
the 1960s. Both men hailed from the Midwest, but the similarities
stopped there. Tobias was high-strung, gregarious, and openly ambitious. Allen wasn't. Even so, the two men got along famously, and they
spent several decades climbing AT&T's long corporate ladder together.
By the 1980s they were both working at AT&T's corporate headquarters
in New York City.

In 1986, James Olson, AT&T's then-chairman, elevated Tobias to vice chairman. The move put Tobias on equal political footing with Allen, who was already AT&T's president and chief operating officer. Olson was set to retire a few years out, and some people were convinced that he wanted to get a closer look at the two contenders before making his final selection. Allen, who was older, was considered the odds-on favorite. But others insisted that Olson actually favored Tobias, who was regarded as far more dynamic and forward-looking than his plodding rival.

The world will never know whom Olson would have picked. Tragically, he was diagnosed with colon cancer in March 1988 and died less than a month later. Within 48 hours of his death, Allen was elevated to chairman and CEO. It was a logical if uninspired choice. Allen had joined AT&T in 1957; Tobias wasn't hired until 1964. So on paper, at least, Allen had a lot more seasoning. Tobias agreed to stay on as vice chairman, putting him squarely in line to succeed Allen.

For the next four years the two men continued to work side by side much as they always had. They also spent a lot of time together socially, often meeting up on the golf course for leisurely afternoons on the links. Their wives, united by the AT&T corporate bond, also became best friends.

By the early 1990s, it was finally time for Allen to give Tobias the official nod as the next chairman and CEO of AT&T. That's when the whispering began.

As it got closer to the time to name Tobias as the official heir apparent, Allen started complaining, quietly at first, about his qualifications. Tobias, he pointed out, had no operational experience. Allen, always artful at taking out a target, was also careful to heap praise on his No. 2. "One of the best strategic thinkers I've ever met," Allen would often say. But the AT&T chief took care to point out that Tobias had never actually managed a business. Most of his experience was based in government affairs, marketing, and policy. How could Tobias run one of the biggest and most complex business operations on the planet if he had never actually managed a business? Allen's insinuation was wickedly clear: Tobias wasn't qualified to sit in the CEO's chair.

There was also the matter of Tobias's personal style. Allen pointed out that Tobias wasn't very tolerant of new ideas. (Translation: As chairman, he'd hold AT&T back.) Allen also thought that Tobias managed by fear. (Translation: Tobias couldn't win the support of AT&T's rank and file.) In addition, Allen thought Tobias was way too fast to shoot messengers bearing bad news. Because of that, a lot of his direct reports were reluctant to level with him. (Translation: As chairman, Tobias wouldn't be willing to listen to others.)

Allen didn't like the fact that Tobias, who'd been openly ambitious for years, was so, well, openly ambitious. Allen also didn't like the fact that Tobias sometimes took credit for ideas that weren't necessarily his. Tobias's habit of grabbing the spotlight also grated on him. So did Tobias's preoccupation with titles and perks. The list went on and on.

When you put it all together, it added up to a whole lot of nothing. Raging egos are hardly unusual in the executive suite. As for the idea that Tobias was hard on his people—that was in the eye of the beholder. A lot of Tobias's staffers adored him, so he couldn't have been too awful. Even so, when you tallied it all up, it didn't paint a very appealing picture. All of a sudden, in fact, the chairman-in-waiting started to look like a blindly ambitious jerk.

After a while, perhaps not surprisingly, the board's support for Tobias started to slip away. By 1993, he was out of the running for good. Tobias got the bad news in classic fashion: from a press release. Allen dryly informed Tobias that he was giving him a new, international-related work assignment. The AT&T chief followed up by giving Tobias a draft of the press release announcing the news, then asked him to read it over and send it back with comments.

As he read through the press release, it became apparent that things weren't exactly as they seemed. For starters, Tobias wasn't going to have anybody reporting to him. Nor was he going to have any budgetary responsibility—Tobias had no growth targets to meet, no expense budgets to manage, nothing. Day-to-day operations? Same thing—he didn't have any. In short, Tobias's "promotion" wasn't a promotion at all. It was Allen's way of telling him that he was no longer a contender for the top job.

Tobias apparently got the hint, because he left shortly thereafter to become the CEO of pharmaceutical giant Eli Lilly. Hewing to tradition, AT&T gave him a big going-away party. Since Allen was one of Tobias's dearest friends, he naturally gave him a warm toast.

ANOTHER CEO HOPEFUL was Alex Mandl. Hired from the outside in 1991 as AT&T's chief financial officer, Mandl quickly gained kudos for his cool, commanding style. He also proved to be a quick study. In meetings, Mandl wasn't shy about offering up new ideas, or challenging old ones. Wall Street liked his global perspective, which owed, at least in part, to his run at Sea-Land, the big international shipper. (Mandl had been the chairman and CEO of Sea-Land just prior to arriving at AT&T.) His European polish—Mandl was a native of Austria and spoke four languages—probably didn't hurt. Other AT&T execs were impressed. So was Allen.

After Tobias resigned, Allen quickly elevated Mandl to president and chief operating officer. It was an appointment heavy with implication. Allen had never had a COO before. The mere fact that he was creating the position for Mandl left no doubt that he was the clear heir apparent. The one unspoken caveat, however, was that Mandl had to prove himself worthy of the job. And he had to prove himself worthy, in particular, to Bob Allen.

Mandl delivered impressively. In short order he set plans to buy Mc-Caw Cellular for $11 billion, returning AT&T to the wireless business that it had abandoned a decade earlier. Meantime, Mandl continued to slash costs and accelerate growth by squeezing new efficiencies from AT&T's century-old piece-parts. Wall Street cheered him every step of the way. So did employees, who seemed energized by Mandl's fresh eye and boundless energy.

By 1996, even Allen was sold. In January of that year, the AT&T chief took Mandl aside to deliver the good news: Assuming he continued to perform well, the CEO's job was his. Allen made it clear he still thought Mandl needed additional seasoning. And the board, of course, would still have to weigh in. But providing there were no last-minute snags, Mandl had the job.

Allen was relieved. For him, it was a watershed moment that marked the first step toward his formal retirement. Mandl was grateful for Allen's support. But he was also suspicious. As far as he could tell, Allen had no intention of stepping down anytime soon. Until he did, Mandl would never be able to put through the big strategic changes that he thought AT&T needed. That was the real rub.

By then, Allen and Mandl had been butting heads for months over AT&T's business strategy. Mandl wanted to do a complete overhaul, and even came up with a four-part plan to get the job done. The plan called for AT&T to: 1. Partner with TCI and the other big cable TV operators to offer AT&T-branded local phone service across the country; 2. Aggressively upgrade the McCaw Cellular systems that had just been purchased; 3. Do the same for WorldNet, which was AT&T's dial-up Internet access service (à la AOL), and 4. Use AT&T's credit card business, (brand name: Universal Card) to help sell consumers a bundle of voice, data, and video services.

On the plus side, the plan had the potential to create multiple revenue streams, lessening AT&T's dependence on long distance. On the downside, the plan was going to be hugely expensive, costing tens of billions of dollars. AT&T's earnings growth would probably be affected. And the AT&T dividend might also have to be reduced, or even eliminated.

Allen blinked hard. He liked the plan in theory. But he wasn't willing to do anything that might whack the stock price. As for the notion of cutting or even eliminating the dividend—get real. Allen pointed out that AT&T had never cut its dividend not by even a penny. Not during the Great Depression. Not during two world wars. Never. Allen wasn't about to become the first chairman in AT&T's history to have that sort of fame attached to his name.

Allen tried to let Mandl down easy.

"I like the strategy a lot," the AT&T chief finally told him, trying to sound a positive note. "But I really think we can do all of this without cutting the dividend or affecting earnings." After all, Allen intoned, his voice swelling with pride, "this *is* AT&T."

Mandl was dumbfounded. The mere fact that Allen believed that AT&T could use its weight to stave off the inevitable—the collapse of its core long-distance business—was shocking to him. It also convinced him that Allen was living in la-la land. The AT&T chief would never consider any strategic solution that involved short-term financial pain, no matter how necessary. That meant no fiddling around with the dividend, earnings projections, or the famous brand name. Those were immovable pieces of furniture in AT&T's century-old house of antiquity, and Allen clearly intended to keep it that way.

Not too long after that, Mandl got a call from a headhunter. A wireless startup was looking for a CEO. It represented a great growth opportunity for the right person. And, oh yes, there also might be a big signing bonus involved—no sum was specified. Was Mandl interested in talking about that?

He was.

In July 1996 Mandl left AT&T to join Teligent. As part of his package, Mandl got a staggering $20 million signing bonus. Allen was disappointed—he really believed that Mandl would have been a great CEO for AT&T. Allen's disappointment turned to anger when he learned that Mandl had started talking to Teligent just a few weeks after their confidential chat. The AT&T chief later read in the papers that Mandl had decided to leave AT&T, in part, because he didn't think Allen was serious about stepping down. That *really* frosted him.

Even if Mandl had stuck around, however, it's not clear he would have lasted. By then Allen was starting to complain about Mandl's management "style." And in Allen's hyperpolitical world that usually only meant one thing: Somebody's head was going to roll—and it wasn't going to be his.

MANDL'S HASTY EXIT created a problem for Allen, and it was a big one. All of a sudden, there were no heirs apparent left. AT&T's executive cupboard was bare.

Determined to fix the very problem that he had helped to create, Allen decided to go outside for his successor. His No. 1 pick: George Fisher, the chairman and CEO of Kodak.

Allen thought Fisher was ideal. He'd started out as an engineer at Bell Labs. Then he'd jumped to Motorola, where he spent 17 years working his way up the corporate ladder, eventually becoming its chairman and CEO. In 1993, Fisher had flirted with the idea of leaving Motorola to become IBM's CEO. But he didn't pursue it, paving the way for Lou Gerstner, who was then at RJR, to take the job.

With the blessing of the AT&T board, Allen flew up to Rochester, New York, where Kodak is based, to personally make his pitch. Allen offered Fisher no firm timetable for stepping down. But the AT&T chief also tried to make it clear that he wouldn't have to wait long—six months, tops.

Fisher punted. The Kodak chief told Allen that he was deeply honored by the vote of confidence, but the timing wasn't right. Fisher had only been at Kodak about three years, and he still had two years left on his contract. Fisher told Allen he thought it wouldn't look so good if he jumped ship right then. Kodak was starting to have a tough time in the marketplace, and Fisher didn't want to leave the company in a lurch. At least that's what Fisher told him. (Some people later speculated that Fisher demurred because he didn't want to work for Allen.) Allen was crushed. But it was also clear that Fisher wasn't going to budge, so he moved on to Plan B. The problem? There was no Plan B.

BACK IN BASKING RIDGE, the tension was mounting. With three strikes under his belt, Allen was under pressure to come up with a fix. Fast.

John Zeglis, who was AT&T's longtime general counsel, desperately wanted the job. Privately, he also thought he deserved it.

Quiet and unassuming, Zeglis was a legend unto himself at AT&T. Born and raised in Momence, Illinois, a little farming town of about 2,500, Zeglis grew up thinking he'd become a local lawyer like his dad. But life had other plans for him.

After graduating from Harvard Law School, Zeglis landed a job with the white-shoe law firm of Sidley & Austin in Chicago. He wound up working as an assistant to Howard Trienens, one of the firm's managing partners. Trienens later became AT&T's lead attorney in the divestiture of AT&T, a landmark case that still stands as one of the most important legal proceedings of our time. Zeglis stuck to him like white on rice every step of the way.

Zeglis managed to leave his mark on the case in a profound way. In the eleventh hour of the negotiations, AT&T found itself looking for a bone to toss to the Bells. Zeglis had a suggestion: Why not give them

AT&T's national wireless licenses? Zeglis was convinced that wireless would never amount to much. His dim view was shared by many at AT&T. At the time, cell phones were the size of a suitcase and reception was awful. AT&T heeded Zeglis's suggestion. It would become one of the worst business decisions in AT&T's history. (The irony, of course, is that Zeglis would later become the chairman and CEO of AT&T Wireless. But more on that later.)

Trienens retired in 1986, and Zeglis succeeded him as AT&T's general counsel. Zeglis was just 39.

Allen had an extremely high regard for Zeglis. The AT&T chairman used to tell people that Zeglis was the smartest person he'd ever met, with one possible exception—his former roommate at Wabash College in Indiana. And he was such a brainiac that he finally went off the deep end and killed himself. Zeglis wasn't about to off himself. But he was awfully good at offing other people in the political sense. It was a characteristic that Allen shared, and also admired.

All that said, Allen could never bring himself to recommend Zeglis for the CEO's job. Why? It all came down to credentials. Despite the Harvard sheepskin and his many years of faithful service, Zeglis had never actually managed a business. He'd managed AT&T's legal department. But he had no hands-on operational experience. Without that basic credential, Allen thought Zeglis wouldn't be taken seriously on Wall Street.

In hindsight, Allen would have done everybody a favor, especially Zeglis, if he'd just leveled with him. Because of his high profile, Zeglis was always going to be known as AT&T's general counsel. Just like John Wayne, he was typecast for life. But Allen didn't do that. Instead, the AT&T chief urged his old friend to aim high, and shoot for the stars. It was a kind gesture in that it gave Zeglis, who was still a small-town lawyer at heart, a much-needed boost of confidence. But as a management approach it was simply short-sighted, because it gave Zeglis a false sense of hope, even entitlement, about his future at AT&T. It was an illusion that would eventually crash-land into reality, with bitter implications for AT&T.

DESERVED OR NOT, a lot of people regarded Allen as an old-fashioned "Bell head" who wasn't very good at making the big move. Not that he didn't try.

Just two years into his reign, Allen made a valiant attempt to put AT&T on the map in the computer business. In 1990 he set his sights on NCR, a major supplier of computers to the banking and retail industries based in Dayton, Ohio. AT&T investors were befuddled as to why AT&T even wanted NCR. The long-distance giant had already lost close to $2 billion trying to make a name for itself in the computer industry, and gotten nowhere. Moreover, AT&T had a lousy track record of buying companies outside its core area.

But where others saw problems, Allen only saw opportunity. His thinking appears to have been influenced, at least to some degree, by Charlie Brown, AT&T's legendary chairman. Allen revered Brown, who had come to believe that AT&T and the computer business were a natural fit. Before the breakup, Brown had high hopes that Western Electric could become a formidable power in the computer business. That was one reason he'd made sure that AT&T, post breakup, had the right to get into the computer business—so that it could pursue his dream.

Allen shared Brown's vision. NCR, he felt sure, was the perfect entry point. NCR was a leader in networked computing, a red-hot niche that was growing three times faster than the computer industry as a whole. Allen planned to use NCR to grow AT&T's overall profitability, offsetting the carrier's dependence on long distance in the process.

That December, AT&T lobbed in an unsolicited offer of $6 billion, or $90 a share, for NCR. Wall Street gasped. The offer presented an 88 percent premium over NCR's stock price, so the offer was rich, to say the least.

NCR, which was generating almost $6 billion a year in revenue at the time, turned Allen down flat. The former cash register machine maker had a proud heritage of its own to protect, and it didn't see AT&T as a good fit. It also didn't need, or want, the money. So thanks for thinking of us, Bob. And don't let the door hit you on the way out.

Allen came back swinging. NCR refused to budge. That only made Allen even madder. Before long, the two companies were rolling around in the dirt, trading insults, threats, and counter-threats. When it was all over five months later, AT&T finally had a deal—for a jaw-dropping $110 a share, or $7.4 billion.

To help offset the cost of the acquisition, AT&T sold its 19 percent stake in Sun Microsystems for $700 million. The stake had been acquired in the late 1980s for around $520 million, so the sale represented a respectable gain on paper.

Allen was jubilant. By combining the planet's two premier networking companies—one specializing in communications, the other in computers—Allen felt confident that he finally had the long-distance problem licked. In an open letter to investors, Allen bragged that the NCR deal was one for the record books. "There has never been a merger like AT&T and NCR," he wrote, his self-satisfaction practically wafting off the page.

He got that part right.

Almost immediately AT&T and NCR started clashing—about everything. The grande dame of telecom, as it turned out, didn't speak the language of computers. NCR was just as strongheaded. It found AT&T's meddling to be intrusive—forget that the telecom giant had just shelled out $7.4 billion to buy NCR. As the months dragged on, their spats escalated.

Desperate to bring NCR into the AT&T fold, Allen churned through four CEOs in five years. Nothing worked. Exasperated, he finally recruited Lars Nyberg, a 20-year veteran of Philips Electronics, in June 1995. Three months later, AT&T announced plans to fire 20 percent of the workforce and spin off the unit, which by then had been renamed Global Information Solutions, or GIS for short.

As part of the overhaul, AT&T said the computer maker would no longer manufacture . . . computers. Investors howled. Trying to put a positive spin on things, AT&T pointed out that GIS was only bailing out of the *personal* computer business, not the networking business in general. Nobody was fooled. After years of trying to turn AT&T into a computer darling, Allen was giving up.

Some later pointed out that AT&T's ill-fated marriage with NCR had cost it a lot more than pride. By September 2000, the 19 percent stake in Sun that AT&T had sold for a mere $700 million was worth more than $35 *billion*. AT&T would have had to sell at the top of the bubble to reap the full benefit. But the paper loss is still staggering to contemplate.

To be sure, lots of CEOs do ill-advised deals and emerge unscathed. But Allen would not be so fortunate. In the face of an eroding long-distance business, a messy succession situation, and growing dissatisfaction among investors, the NCR deal only reinforced the idea that it was time for Allen to go.

Even ardent supporters couldn't help but notice that Allen seemed to be tired, frustrated, and completely drained of fresh ideas. His lifelong passion for golf probably didn't help. In 1995, when the fate of AT&T was on the line in Washington, a lot of Bell CEOs were walking the halls of Congress daily. And Allen? He preferred to let AT&T's lobbyists do his talking for him, for the most part. But he still managed to make time for his sideline passion, golf, which rankled a lot of people.

Allen made no apologies. Golf? He loved the game. He was good at it, too. With a nine handicap, Allen was better than most amateurs. But so what? His reason for getting out of bed in the morning was still AT&T. Moreover, Allen thought he was doing a damn good job.

To be sure, NCR was a disaster—even Allen thought so. But he'd also had his share of successes. The 1996 spin-off of Lucent, which had occurred simultaneously with the spin-off of NCR, was a huge success. So was the 1994 acquisition of McCaw Cellular. Mandl had put the deal together, but Allen backed him up every step of the way.

The AT&T chief was also proud of his work on the Telecommunications Act. Just because people didn't see him wandering the halls of Congress didn't mean he wasn't involved. Behind the scenes, he and Zeglis had spent hours talking through AT&T's political strategy.

Allen considered himself to be an exceptional steward for AT&T. He'd ascended to the top spot in 1988 under the toughest of circumstances. AT&T's beloved chairman and CEO, James Olson, had just died. It wasn't exactly the best way to come into the job. Employees were upset, customers were upset—everybody was upset. Hell, even *Allen* was upset. But like any good CEO in a tough spot, he bucked up and soldiered on.

And after eight long years in the job, Allen still believed—in the company, in the employees, in the magic of that world-famous brand name.

AT&T's core long-distance business had big problems, no question. But to Allen's way of thinking, the long-distance conundrum was only a jag in the road, not the road itself. With a few breaks and a solid game plan, Allen felt certain that he could turn things around. And he'd do it without goring the company's earnings or hallowed dividend. All he needed was a little more time in the job.

Time, unfortunately, was the one thing Allen didn't have right then.

Thanks to Mandl's ragged parting, the succession question was hanging in the air like the stench of a cheap cigar. The press was beating on Allen like a drum. So were big institutional investors. The AT&T board still supported Allen—100 percent, in fact. But the clock was ticking.

Since there were no internal candidates left, John Zeglis notwithstanding, the board decided that it had no choice but to look outside. It was at this point that the board made a fateful decision: It would let Allen screen potential candidates in private. That way, the AT&T chief could make his move on his own timetable. It was a generous gesture that spoke volumes about the strength of the board's confidence in Allen.

But talk about bone stupid.

By then, Allen had chewed through three candidates: Randy Tobias, Alex Mandl, and George Fisher, with John Zeglis as an outlier. Didn't that tell the board anything? Even assuming that Allen had good intentions—and on some level, surely he did—the hard fact of the matter was that Allen, for whatever reason, was clearly incapable of selecting a successor. And the fact that the AT&T board couldn't see that said as much about the board as it did about Bob Allen.

THE BOARD BROUGHT IN two top search firms: Korn/Ferry, represented by Paul McCartney, and SpencerStuart, represented by Dennis Carey. Allen told the recruiters he wanted a star, preferably a top CEO of a major corporation. But the AT&T chief also made it clear that he intended to stick around for a while—no time was specified—to give the winning candidate time to learn the business.

That was the first red flag.

The second red flag: John Zeglis. Allen wanted Zeglis to be included in the pool of candidates. But he also made it clear to the recruiters that Zeglis wasn't a serious candidate. He was a fallback option, at best. Allen probably wanted to show his respect for Zeglis, which was why he'd insisted on putting Zeglis on the short list. But in practice Allen was just setting his friend up for a very nasty fall.

Allen's instructions put the recruiters in a tough spot. Most top CEOs—think Lou Gerstner of IBM or Lew Platt of Hewlett-Packard—wouldn't even consider a No. 2 spot, much less under the watchful eye of a longtime CEO who clearly doesn't want to leave. So AT&T, almost by definition, was going to have to settle for a second-tier player.

Within a week or so, the recruiters came back to Allen with their wish list of candidates. Lew Platt, the chairman and CEO of Hewlett-Packard, and George Fisher of Kodak were both on the list. Most of the names, however, were second-tier players. They included Kenneth Lay, the chairman of Enron; Lewis Campbell, the chief financial officer of General Motors; Mike Armstrong, the chairman and CEO of Hughes Electronics, a division of GM; and John Walter, the chairman and CEO of RR Donnelley, a big publisher based in Chicago. And John Zeglis, of course.

Allen, who was working closely with Hal Burlingame, AT&T's human resources chief, ran through the names, and made his picks.

One name caught his eye immediately. Ken Lay. Allen had met the Enron chairman at a number of social functions. Allen liked Lay's Midwestern values and easygoing manner. He also thought Lay was strategically expansive in his thinking. Lay's company was in the energy business, which was a far cry from telecom. But thanks to Lay, Enron was becoming a rising star on Wall Street. (As it turned out, Enron was a shooting star that was about to implode, but that didn't happen until much later.) Lay was interested.

The two men met at AT&T's hangar at Morristown Airport in New Jersey. (AT&T kept its corporate jet there, and its hangar had private offices.) Lay came across as amiable, smart, and engaging, just as Allen had remembered him. But for a CEO, Allen thought he was remarkably uninformed about the details of his own business. To Allen's dismay, even the simplest of questions about Enron elicited rambling responses that went nowhere. Lay, in turn, asked very few questions about AT&T's operations, strategies, or challenges. Allen was troubled by his responses, and kept pressing for more. Nothing.

Needless to say, by the end of the conversation Lay was no longer on Allen's short list.

Mike Armstrong of Hughes was another familiar name. A 31-year veteran of IBM, Armstrong was highly regarded for his turnaround efforts at Hughes. He got particularly high marks for his handling of DirecTV, Hughes's satellite-TV arm. At IBM, Armstrong had earned a reputation as an ace salesman—big business customers loved him. He was also charming, polished, and politically astute. Owing to his time abroad, Armstrong had a global perspective, another plus.

There was just one problem: Allen couldn't stand him. And he had no interest in working with him. Ever.

Allen's bias owed, at least in part, to the nascent AT&T–DirecTV partnership. AT&T had just invested $137.5 million for a 2.5 percent stake, with options to purchase another 27.5 percent later. As part of the agreement, AT&T had agreed to sell DirecTV's services and equipment. AT&T soon fell short on its sales targets. Armstrong tracked Allen down to personally complain. *Loudly.* One of those calls came flying into Allen's house late one night. Allen was peeved, to say the least. The AT&T chief later told some people that Armstrong had chewed him out like a second-rate lieutenant who'd fouled up. Allen never forgave Armstrong for treating him in such a disrespectful manner. Armstrong, for his part, barely remembered the conversation.

After a lot of discussion with the recruiters, Allen agreed to meet with Armstrong and give him a second look. The AT&T chief promised to keep an open mind.

The meeting took place at the Pierre Hotel in Manhattan. To ensure privacy, Allen conducted the interview in one of the suites. Burlingame also sat in. Armstrong showed up at 6 P.M. sharp. He was by himself. After exchanging a few pleasantries, Allen got right to the point.

"Why are you interested in coming to AT&T?," the AT&T chief asked.

Armstrong seemed a bit confused by the question, and told him that he didn't have the foggiest idea. A headhunter, he explained, had called and asked if he might be interested in coming on board as AT&T's chairman and CEO.

Allen bristled at that.

"AT&T is *not* looking for a CEO," Allen shot back. "But we are looking for a No. 2" who can work into the top position.

Armstrong pushed right back. A smile affixed to his face, Armstrong made it abundantly clear that he had no interest in coming on board as anybody's No. 2. He'd consider the No. 1 job—*Allen's* job. But never the No. 2 slot.

Silence.

Since it was clear that the conversation was going nowhere, Armstrong quickly shifted gears and started talking about his early days at IBM. That made for a nice segue into talking about his first salesman's job in Indiana, which, as Armstrong was well aware, was Allen's home state. The chill in the room quickly evaporated.

The two men continued talking for the better part of an hour, polishing off a bottle of wine in the process.

By the time he rose to leave, Armstrong felt good about the meeting. Despite the rough start, Armstrong thought they had really clicked. He also thought Allen had been a pretty good sport, especially considering that he'd turned him down on the spot like that. Allen, however, was dumbfounded. He couldn't believe that the CEO of a measly $5 billion-a-year company like Hughes would even consider turning thumbs down on a global icon like AT&T. And he was staggered that Armstrong would be so brash as to think that he could just unplug at Hughes and belly flop into the top job at AT&T. As if. Suffice it to say, Armstrong was off Allen's list for good after that.

JOHN WALTER, the CEO of Donnelley, was also interested.

Allen knew Walter from his work with the American Society of Corporate Executives, a think-tank organization composed of about 25 CEOs. They both belonged to the group, and they sometimes ran into each other during social events. Allen liked Walter a lot—he was solid, smart, and well mannered too. Walter wasn't exactly a star. But he was certainly well known within telecom circles thanks to Donnelley, which published yellow pages directories. Walter also had a great track record. He had risen up the ranks at Donnelley with remarkable speed, becoming its president at just 39. The only question was whether Walter, who'd been calling the shots as CEO at Donnelley for almost nine years, would be interested in taking the No. 2 spot.

He was interested. After a quarter century with Donnelley, Walter was itching for a change. He didn't particularly relish the idea of relinquishing his CEO's title. But he was willing to give it a shot if it meant getting a crack at the top job at AT&T. The timing was also good. At 49, Walter was still considered young by CEO standards. Assuming things worked out, he had time to put in a nice, long run at AT&T. So, sure, he was game.

Walter's first meeting with Allen went spectacularly. The two men talked easily and, even better, they spoke the same language. Allen liked Walter's easygoing manner and self-deprecating style. Walter, in turn, found Allen's forthrightness to be refreshing.

That led to a second meeting, which Hal Burlingame sat in on. Same result. Allen and Burlingame were both impressed by Walter's depth of understanding of the telecom business. He also asked a lot of good questions—another big plus. Walter scored even more points by challenging Allen on the question of why he should even consider taking the No. 2 job. After all, he was already the CEO of a major company. It was a cheeky move on Walter's part, but also effective. By the end of the meeting Allen was sold. He decided to introduce Walter to the board.

The directors met with Walter at the Pierre Hotel. Each director spent about 20 minutes talking to him. In hindsight, it was a heck of a way to pick a CEO—by conducting quickie interviews in a hotel room. It was the sort of thing you might have expected from a department store trolling for Christmas help, but not from a global icon trying to pick its future leader. But no matter. The board had a lot of faith in Allen's judgment, so that's how it was done. By the end of the Pierre sessions, Walter had the job.

The news of Walter's hiring was announced on October 23, 1996. Walter was named president and chief operating officer, with the firm understanding that he would replace Allen as CEO when he retired in

1998. AT&T downplayed Walter's lack of hands-on telecom experience, focusing instead on his leadership qualities. In an interview with CNN that day, Walter seemed genuinely appreciative of the unique opportunity that had just been laid at his doorstep. But he also made it clear that he knew big challenges were ahead.

"I have very few illusions," Walter told CNN, choosing his words carefully. "I know this is not going to be a walk in the park." Walter had no idea how right he was.

WALTER ARRIVED for his first day of work on November 1, 1996. He only brought one person with him: a press representative who doubled as a speechwriter. That caused a fair amount of tittering among senior AT&T executives. Things pretty much went downhill from there.

Walter wasted no time asserting himself. He soon set off on a global meet-the-troops trip, glad-handing all the way like a politician running for re-election. Employees loved his pep talks, which were sprinkled with catchy phrases like "Let there be no light between our shoulders!"—a metaphor for teamwork. Other Walter ditties—"When the pace of change outside the business exceeds the pace of change inside the business, the end is near"—were downright dramatic.

Trying to save money, Walter shut down the executive dining room where Allen and other senior executives typically took their meals. Walter, who frequently ate in the cafeteria with employees, didn't think that much about it. He should have.

Compared to Allen, Walter came across as hip, inspiring, and slightly irreverent. He frequently chatted up employees in the halls, openly encouraging them to e-mail him with complaints and suggestions. His habit of poking fun at AT&T bureaucratic ways endeared him to employees even more. Joking around, he sometimes referred to AT&T's plush headquarters as "Carpet Land," a dig that had been used by the rank and file for years. (The name referred to the miles of thick carpet covering the halls that connected the executive offices in Basking Ridge.)

Walter's jokes fell flat with AT&T's senior executive staff, especially Allen. They had all worked for decades to get to where they were on AT&T's corporate ladder. And they didn't take the honor lightly.

Walter's comments also seemed a bit hypocritical, especially considering that his office was smack dab in the middle of Carpet Land.

Determined to make their working relationship a good one, Allen set up a series of meetings with his new No. 2. Allen hoped to use the sessions to coach Walter about AT&T's business, including its ethos and many time-honored traditions. Walter basically said thanks but no thanks. The way Walter looked at it, he'd been hired to tend to AT&T's future, not its past. He also had a lot of work to do, and he was never going to get it done by sitting around listening to Allen prattle on about AT&T's history.

On the rare occasions when the two men did sit down and talk, things didn't go so well. Walter annoyed Allen by constantly checking his cell phone for messages. A few times he even cut off the AT&T chairman altogether so that he could answer his phone. Adding to Allen's slow burn, Walter fidgeted—constantly. He also seemed to be incapable of sitting through an entire meeting. Oftentimes, Walter would duck out early, claiming he had important business elsewhere. Walter, for his part, found Allen's plodding style to be excruciating. As far as he was concerned, the less time spent with Allen the better.

One thing Walter and Allen did agree on, however, was Joe Nacchio, the pugnacious head of AT&T's Consumer Services division: they both thought he was overrated. Nacchio returned the favor. As far as he was concerned, Allen was out of touch, and Walter was in over his head.

At an executive session in early November, things came to a head. With more than 30 senior executives and support staff looking on, Nacchio delivered some sobering news: The long-distance business was failing at a precipitous rate, and the situation was only going to get worse. Once the Bells entered the market, he warned, they'd own the long-distance business. Nacchio threw out four or five possible scenarios. In each and every one, revenue and cash flow in AT&T's core long-distance business were declining for as far as the eye could see.

Nacchio's dire predictions hit the room like a ton of wet concrete. Nacchio was the Dark Prince of AT&T, a never-say-die salesman renowned for his ability to beat back the competition using brass-knuckle tactics. Now he was telling AT&T, essentially, that its core long-distance business was basically unsalvageable.

Nacchio hadn't intended to be so dramatic. But his commentary was heartfelt. Signs of trouble were everywhere. MCI had just agreed to merge with British Telecommunications, with the aim of creating a global communications Goliath with staying power. The mere fact that MCI was selling out spoke volumes about the declining fortunes of the long-distance business. Now it was AT&T's turn to acknowledge reality.

Allen and Walter were astonished. They had expected Nacchio to deliver an upbeat report, not a doomsday manifesto. With the entire room looking on, Allen and Walter tried to turn the tables. Taking direct aim at Nacchio's core assertion—that long distance was dying—the AT&T chiefs insisted that the communications market was teeming with growth opportunities. All Nacchio had to do was find them. As for Nacchio's bleak predictions about the coming war with the Bells: wrong again. AT&T was a singular power unto itself. The bottom line: With the right management, it was perfectly reasonable to assume that Consumer Services could continue its healthy growth trajectory well into the future.

The embedded message in their frontal assault was crystal-clear to everybody in the room. Consumer long-distance wasn't dying. Nacchio just wasn't managing his business very well.

Nacchio got the message. And he didn't take the insult lightly.

Planting his fists on the table in front of him, Nacchio bored in for the return volley.

"Who knows more about long distance," Nacchio shot back, hurling his words directly at Allen and his startled No. 2 "me and the management team of MCI, or you two?"

Nacchio was right, of course. AT&T's long-distance business was, indeed, about to be gutted. His prediction about the Bells was also spot-on. As for his assertion that MCI was selling out in a desperation play for survival, right again. Not that it made a difference. Thanks to his verbal slap shot, which had been delivered with deadly precision in front of the entire leadership of AT&T, Nacchio's career was over. Nacchio knew he was finished the moment those immortal words came flying out of his mouth. ("Who knows more about long distance. . . .") All you had to do was look at Allen's beet-red face to know that.

Nacchio resigned the very next month, in December 1996, to become the CEO of Qwest Communications, a long-distance upstart catering to the business community.

THE NACCHIO EPISODE did nothing to ease the strain between Allen and Walter. If anything, in fact, it only exacerbated things, particularly when Allen found out that Walter was bragging that Nacchio had only left because Walter was about to fire him. That really made Allen's blood boil. As the AT&T chief was quick to point out, only he had that kind of pull.

The dueling didn't stop with Nacchio. At cocktail parties, Walter was a little too quick to tell people that he, not Allen, was the one who was really calling the shots. He also suggested that Allen was losing political juice. It didn't take long for word to make its way back to Allen.

The AT&T chief didn't openly criticize Walter—that would have been far too obvious. But he did make his displeasure known. Longtime AT&T execs read Allen's smoke signals, and responded accordingly. Before long, executives started traipsing into Allen's office with a string of negative reports about Walter. Their complaints were all over the map. Some questioned Walter's business acumen, saying his analysis was superficial and uninformed. Others said he seemed to have a hard time focusing . . . on just about anything. A few questioned whether he understood even the basics of AT&T's business.

There was also a lot of talk about Walter's personal habits. A number of people said that Walter regularly got drunk at AT&T functions. On one occasion, so the story went, Walter got so sloshed on the company jet that he had changed into his pajamas in front of startled AT&T execs and their wives. Some said Walter, who was married, was having an affair.

It's not clear if any of these allegations were true. As a personality type, Walter was outgoing and gregarious, so it's possible that some of his actions were simply misinterpreted. But what is clear is that John Walter, in the short space of just three months, managed to alienate almost every single power player at AT&T. And that included the biggest and most important power player of them all, Bob Allen.

BY THE SPRING OF 1997, Allen and Walter were both working feverishly to put together a big merger with SBC Communications. News of
the deal soon spilled out into the papers, causing a huge sensation in
Washington. Regulators were concerned that AT&T and SBC were trying
to rebuild Ma Bell, and they didn't like the antitrust implications. Telecom
companies were also alarmed. If the deal went through, after all, they
would have to compete against this supersized communications gorilla.

AT&T wasn't talking publicly. But behind closed doors Allen and
Walter were talking up a storm. Allen claimed he was the one who had
reached out to SBC chief Ed Whitacre. Walter begged to disagree, insisting that he was actually the one who had gotten the ball rolling. Making
matters worse, each was convinced that the other was doing everything
he could to kill the transaction. Why? Because once the deal closed, Walter—or Allen, depending on which version of the story you believed—
was going to be out of a job. Whitacre, for his part, didn't remember
who called him first. And moreover, he didn't care. All he cared about
was getting his hands on AT&T.

The SBC deal never got out of first gear. Alarmed that the transaction
would deliver a serious blow to the high-minded goals of the Telecommunications Act of 1996, the FCC pulled out all stops to kill it before it
had even been announced. Allen tried to push back, but his efforts were
clumsy and mostly missed the mark. Then he started trading verbal slaps
in the papers with FCC Chairman Reed Hundt. For SBC, that was the
last straw. Sensing a political bloodbath, Whitacre wisely pulled the plug
and walked. (But he never did abandon the idea of buying AT&T, as
events would later show.)

The whole messy episode left AT&T looking a little clueless. But nobody looked more clueless, perhaps, than John Walter. Even if he was the
one who had dreamed up the idea of an SBC merger—and it's not at all
clear that he did—Walter should have had enough sense to share the credit
with Allen. Even a third-rung AT&T manager could have told him that.

The SBC episode, for Allen, was the final insult. All the months of
strained working relations, capped by the SBC debacle, had finally con-

vinced him that Walter wasn't just out of his league—he was a human square peg that would never fit into AT&T's perfectly round hole. Allen mostly blamed himself. After all, he was the one who had recruited Walter to the company. Now it was up to him to fix it.

It was right around this time that Allen came to a bizarre conclusion: Walter, he decided, surely must have attention deficit disorder, or ADD, a neurological condition that makes it difficult for sufferers to focus on virtually anything. One of Allen's grandchildren had ADD, so he recognized the symptoms—short attention span, extreme nervousness, erratic behavior. In adults, sexual promiscuity can also be a symptom.

Certain that he was on to something, Allen shared his suspicions with AT&T's medical director. The doctor agreed that it was, indeed, possible that Walter had ADD. While the condition is far more prevalent in children, the doctor explained, ADD isn't uncommon among adults, particularly among high achievers like Walter. The good news, however, was that ADD could be controlled with medication.

Allen took his suspicions, now buttressed by the weight of a certified medical professional, directly to the board. Some AT&T directors responded to his bombshell announcement by saying how sorry they were to hear of Walter's "condition." It was a curious response, especially considering that Walter hadn't yet been informed of Allen's armchair analysis, let alone diagnosed.

A few days later, Allen lowered the boom. In a closed-door meeting, Allen told his No. 2 that he felt certain he had ADD. Furthermore, Allen told Walter, he wanted him to be evaluated by a medical professional who could give the board advice as to the manageability of his "condition." The AT&T chief had more bad news: An ADD test wasn't optional. It was now a condition of Walter's continued employment.

Talk about a no-win situation. If Walter agreed to take the test and was found to have ADD, he'd be damaged goods. But if he didn't agree to be tested, there'd always be questions about his mental ability, so he'd still be damaged goods. Walter couldn't just quit, however. His employment contract didn't allow for that, not unless he wanted to walk out empty-handed, that is. Allen thought he was being quite reasonable. After all, Walter was in line to take over the CEO's job in less than a year.

AT&T couldn't afford to elevate Walter, only to find that he couldn't meet the demands of the job.

The AT&T board, which had heaped accolades on Walter less than a year earlier, refused to discuss the matter with him directly. Walter did manage to buttonhole one director, Ralph Larsen, the powerful chairman and CEO of Johnson & Johnson. It didn't do much good. "I know you're a friend of Bob's," Walter started, "but there is another side to this story." Larsen coolly cut him off. "Yes, you're right, I *am* a friend of Bob's," he said, then turned on his heel and walked away.

With his reputation on the line and his pride on his back pocket, Walter finally agreed to Allen's demand.

Dr. Kenneth Freundlich, a neuropsychologist with the Morris Psychological Group in Parsippany, New Jersey, was hired to administer the test. (Hal Burlingame found Freundlich through AT&T's employee assistance program.) In addition to having a specialty in ADD, Freundlich did a lot of work with big companies.

Walter met with Freundlich ahead of time to negotiate the details. The standard ADD evaluation consists of a battery of tests that are designed to assess intellect, memory, and attention. Walter told the doctor that he was willing to take all of the tests except one: the IQ test. Freundlich thought it was an unusual request, but he also assumed that Walter was intelligent, otherwise he wouldn't have had the No. 2 spot at AT&T. Walter's concern was political. No matter how high he scored, Walter was convinced that Allen would try to use his IQ against him. As it turned out, Allen wasn't the one he should have been worried about.

The first test was administered on May 6. The final session wrapped up about six weeks later, on June 18. Dr. Freundlich's conclusion: Walter did *not* have ADD. Quite the contrary, Walter had scored high on every test except memory. In that particular category, Walter had only tested average, not above average. The doctor noted as much in his written report, which was sent directly to Hal Burlingame. The Freundlich report was immediately handed over to Allen, who in turn shared it with the entire AT&T board.

After that, the subject of ADD and John Walter was never brought up again. But that didn't mean he was safe. Absent an affirmative diagnosis of ADD, Allen instead concluded that Walter's behavior was just odd. And certainly not in keeping with the sort of behavior that one expects from an AT&T chairman-in-waiting. In short, Walter had to go.

On the evening of July 15, Allen told the board that he didn't think Walter was ready to succeed him as CEO. Furthermore, Allen thought it would be best if his hand-picked successor resigned immediately. The board readily agreed, and together they plotted Walter's ouster.

The hit went down the very next morning.

Walter was in the middle of a meeting when a secretary strode in bearing an urgent message from Walter Elisha, a longtime AT&T board member. The message was curt and to the point: Elisha needed to see him. Now. Walter quickly excused himself and walked down the hall to the room where Elisha was waiting. An AT&T attorney was also present. Elisha didn't mince words. Walter no longer had the support of the AT&T board. As such, he would not be succeeding Allen as CEO. Walter could resign on his own volition. Or he could stay on as Allen's No. 2 with the firm understanding that he would not be promoted.

It was a clever offer. Under the terms of Walter's employment contract, he had to be elevated to the CEO's post by January 1, 1998. Otherwise, the generous terms of his contract, including his golden parachute, would become null and void. In other words, Walter could stay and keep his pride. Or he could leave and take the money.

Walter carefully considered his choice. He desperately wanted to become the CEO. He admired the company, loved the employees, and enjoyed the challenge. But it was also clear to him that Allen would stop at nothing to drive him out. Anticipating trouble, Walter had already retained a top employment lawyer, and he was locked, loaded, and ready to go.

But Walter didn't want to fight. After nine months of being chewed up by the AT&T political machine, he was bone tired—tired of the ugly insinuations, tired of the lack of support, tired of the board's refusal to hear him out, tired of the whole damn thing. Sure, he could hang around and try to prove himself. But to what end? Allen's mind was made up. So was the board's. By staying on, he'd only be delaying the inevitable.

Walter took the money.

His abrupt resignation rocked Wall Street. AT&T's public relations department was deluged with calls from reporters. Everybody wanted to know the same thing: What happened?

Elisha tried to explain, but words kept failing him. Elisha finally got so rattled that he stammered that Walter didn't have the "intellectual leadership" to become AT&T's next CEO. The phrase got picked up as a sound bite, and promptly took on a life of its own. Since nobody on the board had ever used that phrase to describe Walter, it was never clear where, exactly, the term had come from. Some people thought Elisha had simply concocted it on the spot. Others, however, insisted that it was actually a twist on a phrase in the Freundlich report that related to Walter's memory skills, not his intellect, which had never been tested.

But no matter. Elisha's stinging comment, which had been spewed at a moment when the world's microphones were pressed to his lips, would inflict more damage to Walter's reputation than any ADD report ever could. It was a breathtaking turn, to say the least. In the short space of just nine months, Walter had gone from being the heir apparent at one of the most revered companies on the planet to being a corporate reject with no hope of redemption. But that was, indeed, his fate. Thanks to Elisha's careless choice of words, no company of any import would ever hire him. Walter's career, for all practical purposes, was dead.

Walter did his best to hold on to the tatters of his dignity. "I believe I am perfectly qualified to be the CEO of AT&T right now," he said in a prepared statement. He closed by praising AT&T employees for their dedication to customers, and wished the company well. Walter never did get a farewell party. But he did get a nice sendoff all the same—a $25 million-plus severance package from AT&T.

THANKS TO WALTER walking out the door with a marching band trailing behind him, the succession issue took on crushing urgency.

This time the board took firm control of the process. The board immediately dumped Korn/Ferry, which had recommended Walter, but kept SpencerStuart. Heidrick & Struggles was brought in to replace Korn/Ferry. Gerard Roche, the legendary chairman of Heidrick, agreed to personally handle the assignment.

Almost as storied as his famous clients, Roche was renowned for his ability to convince reluctant candidates, especially longtime CEOs of top companies, to consider new opportunities. Over the years, Roche, known to just about everybody as Gerry, had handled such top CEOs as Lou Gerstner, Larry Bossidy and George Fisher. But even for a seasoned pro like Roche, the AT&T search presented a challenge. Because of Walter's public hanging, every CEO in the country was effectively on notice that AT&T was in the middle of a management crisis. Convincing a top CEO to come into a job under those hairy circumstances wouldn't be so easy. But then again, that's why companies hired Roche—to deliver miracles.

Allen, meantime, was working on a miracle of his own. In a last-ditch attempt to influence the outcome, Allen urged the board to pick John Zeglis as his successor. By then Allen had elevated Zeglis to vice chairman, putting him in charge of a big chunk of AT&T's operations. With a little more seasoning, Allen argued, Zeglis could easily step into the top job.

For the first time ever, the board turned Allen down flat. The directors really had no choice. By then there'd been too many embarrassments. Too many dead ends. Too many broken promises. Walter was the last straw.

Back at Heidrick & Struggles, Roche was twirling through his Rolodexes trying to figure out the perfect fit for AT&T. It was a tall order. Whoever stepped into the AT&T job needed to be part visionary, part mechanic, part God. The ideal candidate needed to have enough star power to blow away the Walter overhang. But he also needed to be grounded in the complexities of the communications business. And he also had to have enough clout to impress Wall Street, but enough empathy to win over the rank and file.

There was also AT&T's culture to consider. Allen's replacement needed to be comfortable with big, bureaucratic companies on the one hand, and on the other he had to have enough backbone to make bold, transforming changes. Inner toughness was key. AT&T's next CEO would be laboring under the unblinking glare of the public eye. If things went well, he'd be hailed as a hero for life. If he failed, well, that was another story entirely.

Roche's top pick, hands down, was Lew Platt, the chairman and CEO of Hewlett-Packard. Platt was a certified superstar. He was also considered untouchable. Platt had been on every headhunter's wish list for years. His story was the stuff of legends. A mechanical engineer by training, Platt had joined H-P in 1966 right out of Cornell and Wharton, and kept moving up from there. Under his watchful eye, H-P employees, inspired by his challenge to ignore the box and shoot for greatness, had succeeded in reworking the company's famous product line over, and over again. The impressive result: year-over-year revenue gains of 20 percent or more. Roche figured AT&T could use a change-agent like that. The only question was whether Platt would be interested.

Roche lobbed in a call to Platt's office that day. The call itself wasn't unusual. The two men had known each other for years. Roche made it a point to check in with Platt a few times a year just to say hello.

But this call was different.

After exchanging some pleasantries, Roche wound up his fastball and drilled in for home plate. "I have something I'd like to discuss with you," Roche began. Then he went on to describe, in broad strokes, the AT&T opportunity.

Platt, who'd been reading about the John Walter debacle along with every other CEO in the country, already knew where Roche was heading. And, yes, he was interested. After 30 years at H-P, Platt was ready to make a change, provided the right opportunity came along.

AT&T represented a tantalizing set of business challenges. To survive over the long haul, AT&T needed to transition to another, higher art form—but what? AT&T clearly had the name and resources to peel off in almost any direction. The trick was to figure out which strategy to embrace, and then convince everybody to start rowing in the same direction. Making a seismic transformation like that wouldn't be easy or cheap. And the path to success would be fraught with risk, even peril. Every decision would be scrutinized. Every stumble would be magnified. The challenge was thrilling, yet terrifying because the stakes were so high. In other words, it was just the sort of opportunity that Platt had been hoping for.

Things moved along pretty fast after that. After a few trips East to talk through the particulars, Platt was sold. His compensation and other details of his employment contract still had to be finalized. But for all practical purposes, the H-P chief was ready to sign on the dotted line.

And then, just when everybody thought the deal was done . . . a snag developed.

The snag? Walter Elisha.

With Roche and the other members of the search committee working feverishly to close the deal, Elisha almost blithely informed Platt that AT&T intended to elevate Zeglis to president. The promotion was being given to Zeglis in recognition of his many years of faithful service to AT&T. *You don't have a problem with that, do you, Lew?*

Well, yes, actually, he did.

Zeglis had been passed over for the CEO's job not just once, but three times at least. That kind of public humiliation doesn't leave a man easily, even a man as smart and as well respected as John Zeglis. Platt wisely concluded that it probably wouldn't be such a good idea to have a battle-scarred survivor, one with a sizable ax to grind, no less, serving as his No. 2. There was no upside margin for anybody in that proposition. Least of all for Platt.

Elisha didn't see it that way. He was determined to make sure that Zeglis got the recognition that he deserved and craved, even if it meant taking a pass on one of the most sought-after CEOs in America. And as the chairman of AT&T's search committee, Elisha was in a position to press the point. Platt refused to budge, and the deal quickly unraveled from there.

That left the board with Plan B: Mike Armstrong, the chairman and CEO of Hughes.

By then, the AT&T search committee had been stringing along Armstrong as it tried to reel in Platt. The deception was intentional, but also necessary. If Platt bailed, it needed to be able to switch to the alternative candidate quickly. Trying to maintain utter secrecy, the board used the AT&T jet to pick up Platt and Armstrong and fly them to New York for a series of interviews, always making sure to space them out so nobody caught on. But the board blew its own cover by dutifully sending the jet's bills, which included itineraries and other trip details, to AT&T's legal department. That, of course, was the power stronghold of John Zeglis.

Armstrong didn't know about Platt. All he knew was that he was being seriously courted by AT&T, and he was seriously interested.

Unlike Platt, the Hughes chief had no qualms about having Zeglis as his No. 2. A 31-year veteran of IBM, Armstrong was accustomed to working within the established managerial frameworks of big, bureaucratic companies. He expected it, in fact. At IBM, executives ascended up the ladder based in part on their ability to work with, and learn from, entrenched veterans. Armstrong's only requirement—and it was one that Platt had shared—was that Allen had to step down immediately. The board quickly agreed, and that was pretty much that.

Allen took the news hard. In his mind, Armstrong was just another version of John Walter. Taller and more charismatic, perhaps. But they were essentially the same person. Armstrong was a sales and marketing guy. Just like Walter. Armstrong knew very little about the nuts and bolts of the telecommunications business. Just like Walter. Both talked a good game about technology. Both claimed to have a lot of familiarity with AT&T thanks to their time in the sales trenches.

There was, however, at least one glaring difference between the two men. And that, perhaps, was the most troubling difference of all.

Unlike Walter, Mike Armstrong could never be fired. Thanks to the grievous circumstances under which he'd been brought in—on the heels of one of the worst management bungles in AT&T's history—Armstrong was Teflon. So unless he got caught red-handed doing something pretty awful—and Armstrong was a Boy Scout, so that was unlikely—he was AT&T's for keeps. That was fine so long as Armstrong delivered. But what if he didn't?

Allen aired his concerns with the board, but nobody paid much attention. After all, the Allen Era was over.

5

THE SALESMAN FROM
CENTRAL CASTING

T HE ARMSTRONG ERA began like almost everything else at
AT&T: with a well-crafted press release.

Armstrong's appointment was officially announced on October 20, 1997. In a prepared statement, Walter Elisha, the board's bag-
man on the John Walter fiasco, called Armstrong a "perfect match" for
AT&T, "a leader with exceptional technological vision, a good understanding of the forces transforming the communications services industry, and a strong record of accomplishment." In other words, he was no
John Walter.

AT&T also said that John Zeglis had been elected president. That
made Zeglis, who had just lost his dream job to Armstrong, the firmly
entrenched No. 2. Elisha was positively effusive. "Over the past few
years, but especially in the last three months, all of us on the board have
developed a deep respect and deep admiration for John Zeglis," he said.
The board, he added, "is especially pleased that Mike shares that view."
It was a not-so-subtle dig at Lew Platt of Hewlett-Packard, who had just
refused the CEO's job because of Zeglis. The inside comment was so inside, however, that few people even noticed.

Bob Allen also got some ink. Speaking on behalf of the entire board,
Elisha commended the longtime chairman for building on the "legacy

of his predecessors," noting that AT&T was the "undisputed leader in long distance, wireless, and data communication services." Elisha added rather inexplicably that to his knowledge "no other American company has been put through such a regulatory and court-ordered 'wringer' and emerged so strong." Allen, who'd been through the wringer himself by then, probably could have done without the empty accolades.

There was no mention, of course, of the fact that AT&T's long-distance business was falling off a cliff. Or that the wireless business, which had been purchased three years earlier with so much fanfare, was languishing. Or that AT&T, for all its data networking might, had no Internet strategy to speak of. Elisha also failed to point out that the only reason an outsider, a telecom novice, no less, was being dragged onto the field in the final minutes of a losing game was because there were no internal candidates left—Allen and the board had managed to run them all off. Elisha also said nothing about his own handling of Lew Platt, who was arguably the one CEO in America at the time who had the experience, backbone, and temerity to see through a culture-rattling transformation of the sort that AT&T needed. No, there was no mention of any of that. Instead, Elisha waxed on about Armstrong and Zeglis forming the nexus of a new leadership team that would be "unmatched anywhere in this industry," and just left it at that.

As for Armstrong, he was pleased as punch. After 31 years with IBM and six years at Hughes, he was officially an overnight sensation. Just 24 hours earlier, few people outside IBM and the aerospace industry had ever heard of him. Now he was headed to New York to become the CEO of one of the most storied companies in the world. Sure, AT&T had problems. But it was also iconic, powerful, and rich. The company had $50 billion in annual revenue and just $4 billion in short-term debt (total debt: just $126 billion). With that kind of financial leverage, AT&T could afford to aim high and dream big. Real big. It was a heady position for anybody to be in, much less a working stiff from Detroit who'd spent his whole career trying to prove to everybody, especially himself, that he could hang with the best of them.

CHARLES MICHAEL ARMSTRONG was born in Detroit on October 18, 1938. The eldest of three boys, Armstrong was named after his father, Charles, an engineer, who had been named after his father. Mrs. Armstrong didn't particularly care for the family name, so young Charles quickly became known as Mike. The name stuck.

Armstrong's biggest influence, bar none, was his mother, Zora Jean. A strong woman with a big heart and a ready smile, Mrs. Armstrong imbued her son with a keen sense of purpose early in life. She was also a rock-steady source of support and encouragement. Mrs. Armstrong's cheery advice was as constant as the sunrise: "If you work hard and give it your all, there's nothing you can't accomplish." As for new opportunities, those were meant to be explored—never ignored. "Go for it!" was her personal motto. Her buoyant outlook was infectious, to say the least, and all three Armstrong boys grew up embracing life's crazy quilt of challenges. Especially Mike.

Under the watchful eye of his mother, Armstrong started playing the piano when he was just seven years old. He practiced an hour a day, six days a week, diligently trying to finesse the complicated keyboard arrangements of Mozart, Bach, and other classical composers. Seven years later, he had gotten good enough to win a coveted spot in the annual music recital. Armstrong played one of his mother's favorites, "Concerto," by Sergei Rachmaninoff, the great Romantic pianist and composer. The sight of his mother weeping in delight in the audience as he played would become one of his most cherished memories.

Armstrong broke his wrist in a schoolyard scrap not long after that, forever ending his piano career. Mrs. Armstrong was crushed. Mike, however, was not. By then he was a freshman in high school and anxious to try his hand at another kind of fine art—football.

There was just one problem: Armstrong was a pipsqueak.

At five feet, six inches and 126 pounds, Armstrong was hardly football material. No matter. With his mother's encouragement, he worked up the nerve to ask the coach for a tryout anyway. Sizing up the half-pint before him, the coach marched Armstrong into the locker room and introduced him to a couple of players, strapping boys who tipped the scales at 230 pounds or more. "These guys can break you in two!" the coach bellowed to a chorus of rising snickers. "And that's *not* going to happen on my record, so get outta here!" Thoroughly humiliated, Armstrong turned beet red and scrambled for the door.

But he didn't give up.

After talking it over with his mother, Armstrong decided to see how far he could push the laws of nature. In short order he bought a set of weights and started working out. He also starting eating—constantly. Before long, he was wolfing down five meals a day. When he wasn't eating, he was lifting—two times a day, six days a week. The results were impressive. Within two years, he'd gained a full six inches in height and put on a whopping 54 pounds. By the time football tryouts came around his junior year, Armstrong was a football Adonis with six-pack abs and bulging biceps. His mother, as always, cheered him along.

That August, Armstrong marched his re-engineered frame back into the same coach's office and made his pitch. This time, he wasn't taking no for an answer. "Coach," Armstrong began, "only you can determine if I'm good enough to play on this team. But you are *not* going to kick me off for not being big enough."

Armstrong got his tryout. He made the cut, and eventually became the captain of the football team.

In his senior year, Armstrong landed a football scholarship to Miami University of Ohio, located in Oxford. That was the good news. The bad news was that Armstrong's longtime girlfriend was in Detroit. Her name was Sarah Anne Gossett—known to everybody as Anne—and Armstrong couldn't bear the thought of leaving her behind. The two had been together since they were 14, and they hoped to marry right after college. Armstrong finally worked up the nerve to ask her father to let Anne join him at school. Mr. Gossett turned him down flat, insinuating that his hard-earned football scholarship was a one-way ticket to nowhere. "As far as I can see," Mr. Gossett intoned, "you're going to end up selling popcorn at Tiger Stadium."

Crushed, Armstrong left town alone and enrolled at Miami University. Anne, also heartbroken, enrolled at the University of Michigan. They continued to stay in touch, but the distance soon took its toll on the relationship.

Just a year into his football career, Armstrong got sidelined with a recurring shoulder injury. The doctor said he could fix it, but the muscle tear was significant enough that if he hurt it again the damage might be permanent. Armstrong felt he had no choice but to leave the team. Once he did that, however, his scholarship money dried up. To pick up some extra cash, Armstrong decided to drop out of school for a semester and work. He got a job unloading cargo on the Detroit docks, volunteering for the night shift because it paid an extra nickel an hour. A childhood buddy, Bill Moody, worked the same shift. Between hauling bales of corn, wheat, and other cargo, they hatched a plan to visit Europe the following summer.

Armstrong re-enrolled in school the very next semester. He tried to focus on his studies, but nothing really inspired him. Like a lot of 19-year-olds, Armstrong exuded confidence. But deep inside he felt lost and lonely. Football had at least provided some structure to his life. Now that was gone. So was Anne. By the time summer rolled around, he was itching for a change.

Europe turned out to be just the ticket. Traveling like Gypsies in a beat-up VW Bug, Armstrong and Moody hit the road—and kept going. They took in the sights and sounds of Europe by day, and slept in the car at night. It was Armstrong's first trip abroad, and he loved every minute of it. Surrounded by Europe's rich history and culture, he felt oddly inspired, even moved. He also got some much-needed clarity—about his life, his heart, and his special place in the world. By the time the trip was over, he'd made himself two promises: He was going to hang up his cleats for good. And he'd do whatever it took to win back the hand of his one true love, Anne Gossett.

When he got back to school that fall, Armstrong got the best surprise of his life: Gossett was there waiting for him. Unbeknownst to him, she had switched schools and enrolled in Miami University over the summer. Armstrong found out later that Anne and her mother had finally prevailed upon Mr. Gossett to let her make the change. Never one to ignore a thump on the head from fate, Armstrong took it as a sign that he'd made the right decision about school, and about his life. With that, Armstrong quit college sports forever and got busy building a new life for himself and his cherished bride-to-be.

Armstrong still didn't know exactly what he wanted to do. But he did know what he *didn't* want to do—boring stuff. Accounting bored him to tears. So did finance. But marketing? On an abstract basis, at least, that appealed to him. A summer job between his junior and senior years convinced him that he might actually have a talent for it. Owens-Illinois, a major glassmaker, had just introduced a glass bottle for the beer industry, and it hired some students, including Armstrong, to help market the idea to retailers. By the time the summer was over, Armstrong had had his fill of beer. And he was more convinced than ever that his future lay in marketing.

Armstrong graduated from Miami University in January 1961. He had a degree in business and economics, but it didn't do him much good. The United States was in the middle of a deep economic recession, so nobody was hiring. He managed to line up interviews with a couple of companies, including IBM. But they all canceled at the last minute. The reason was always the same: no jobs. Undaunted, Armstrong kept scouring the classifieds.

A fraternity buddy who worked for IBM managed to get him an interview for a systems engineer job in Indianapolis. The job wasn't very glamorous. Back in those days, a systems engineer basically installed punch-card systems, one step above a repairman. It also wasn't very high paying—just $400 a month. But at least it would be a steady paycheck. Armstrong didn't have a car. He also didn't have enough money for bus fare. So he hitchhiked the 150 miles to and from the interview in Indianapolis.

He got the job. Armstrong found out later that he was one of just two people who got hired by the Indianapolis office that year. It would mark the beginning of what would eventually become a 31-year ride.

AFTER THREE YEARS of installing punch-card systems, a marketing job in Muncie, Indiana, opened up. Armstrong had no marketing experience per se—just a few summer jobs. But heeding his mother's advice to "Go for it!" he put his hand up. He got the job.

By then Anne Gossett was no longer his girlfriend—she was his wife. The couple moved to Muncie and bought the only house they could afford, a small Cape Cod that cost $17,200. Armstrong didn't have enough cash for the 10 percent down payment. He only had $1,400, leaving him $320 short. The real estate agent took a liking to the couple, and lent him the rest.

IBM's new Muncie office was a one-man operation. Plus Anne Gossett who gamely offered to act as her husband's answering service. Armstrong didn't have a budget for office furniture. So he got two filing cabinets, stained a door, and laid it across the tops of the cabinets to form a makeshift desk. The office, which was in the couple's attic, had one phone, a chair, and some boxes for storage. The sole office "machine" was a manual typewriter, an old Royal that Anne had been toting around since college.

The sales didn't exactly pour in. One month turned to two months turned to six months—and still, no orders. Most small businesses in Muncie couldn't have cared less about IBM's office products. And forget about data processing. As for computers—no way. This was, after all, 1963. Like most small businesses in America, the ones in Muncie kept their books by hand. Undaunted, Armstrong started knocking on doors. And he kept on knocking, for months. Day after day he pitched his IBM wares to anyone who would listen. Most Muncie businessmen were polite enough to hear him out. But it was clear from the blank looks on their faces that they had no interest. Refusing to cede the point, Armstrong kept circling back around, over and over again. Local businessmen couldn't help but be impressed by his seeming endless capacity for rejection. But the answer was always the same: Thanks, but no thanks.

After nine hard months of nonstop selling, Armstrong finally got his first order—from a local auto parts dealer, Muncie Auto, for a small punch-card system. That order paved the way for a second order, which led to a third, and so on. After that, word-of-mouth advertising started kicking in. Before the year was out, IBM's new Muncie office was humming. Armstrong's IBM bosses noticed, and eventually sent two systems engineers down to Muncie to help him out.

Armstrong got moved up to the Indianapolis sales office less than three years later. There, he continued to prove his mettle as a top salesman, tending to a number of major regional accounts, including Allison, a division of General Motors that made jet engines. The IBM gods noticed, and in 1970 he was invited to interview for a job as an executive assistant to Jack Guth, a regional vice president in Chicago. Two other IBM employees got similar invitations.

At the appointed hour, all three candidates for the job were ushered into Guth's office. Then, in an almost Socratic type of roundtable, they were each asked to respond to a series of questions. After a few softballs, Guth threw out a rather complex question that went to the candidates' views about customer care, specifically day-to-day management of sales accounts. The first two candidates, their nerves frayed, offered up short, polite responses. Not Armstrong.

Bursting with the convictions of his youth, Armstrong tore into the question, challenging Guth on myriad points about the art of the sale. Guth, who wasn't accustomed to being called out by anybody, much less a low-level salesman from Indianapolis, pushed back hard. As the other two candidates watched slack-jawed, Armstrong and Guth debated, cajoled, and jabbed at each other for several heated minutes. When they were finally done arguing, the room fell silent. Dead silent.

Oh, my God. What have I done? Mortified by his brazen outburst, Armstrong started sweating profusely. But it was too late—the interview was over. Seeing the trio to the door, Guth thanked the candidates for coming and told each of them how much he'd enjoyed chatting with them. Fixing an icy stare in Armstrong's direction, Guth pointedly added, "Even *you,* Armstrong."

Thoroughly humiliated, Armstrong raced back to his office and put in an emergency call to his branch manager. The panicky IBM salesman told his boss that he'd blown the interview. Armstrong was sure that his IBM career was over, and offered to resign on the spot. The branch manager listened patiently to Armstrong's concerns, and told him to settle down. It was good advice: Armstrong got the job.

Guth told Armstrong later that even though he disagreed with the substance of his argument—Guth thought he was hopelessly wrong, in fact—he admired Armstrong's willingness to stand up for his beliefs. Guth thought it said a lot about his character, as well as his courage. Armstrong never forgot that lesson.

———

IN 1975 ARMSTRONG was offered yet another promotion: a staff job as the director of systems management in IBM's Data Processing Division in White Plains, New York. Armstrong, who was a sales manager in St. Louis at the time, was deeply flattered by the invitation. But he turned it down, explaining that he and his wife really liked their St. Louis lifestyle. He soon got an urgent call from his mentor, Jack Guth, who quickly explained how things worked around IBM. The "invitation" wasn't actually an invitation. It was a mandatory promotion, so pack your bags and go. He did.

In White Plains, Armstrong quickly won notice for his ability to pick out technology pearls. On one occasion, he heard through the grapevine that the National Science Foundation was preparing to solicit bids for a new computer project. The government was trying to convert an old Department of Defense communications network into one that could be used by America's colleges and universities. The details were sketchy. All Armstrong knew was that the project was big, potentially prestigious, and involved a lot of computers. IBM wound up submitting a joint bid with the University of Michigan's engineering department—and won. The victory put IBM and its partner in on the ground floor of the Internet.

On another occasion, Armstrong was in Tulsa visiting Amoco's research lab when something caught his eye: an in-house office system that employees had patched together. Intrigued, Armstrong asked for a demonstration, and was shocked to see how easy it was for people to send private messages to each other. Though he didn't understand the underlying technology, his gut told him he was on to something big. When he got back to IBM, Armstrong called up Jack Kuehler, one of the company's top technical experts, and asked him to take a look. Kuehler and Armstrong went back out to Oklahoma a few weeks later. Kuehler was blown away by what he saw. Armstrong, as it turned out, had stumbled across a rudimentary version of e-mail. IBM later teamed up with Amoco to build a version of the Tulsa system for its mainframe computers. That system would pave the way for the development of a number of other groundbreaking programs, including Lotus Notes.

From there it was a short hop to the Data Processing Division, also in White Plains. In 1978, Armstrong was named president, putting him in charge of IBM's legendary U.S. sales force, a Panzer army of more than 60,000 employees in 50 states. The promotion made Armstrong IBM's No. 1 salesman. It was also strong affirmation of his personal business philosophy, which had been shaped and molded over 20 years' worth of real-life experiences. *"If you work hard and give it your all, there's nothing you can't accomplish."* For Armstrong, these weren't just the words of a doting mother—it was the secret to his phenomenal success as a salesman.

Armstrong was perfect for the job. With his Hollywood good looks, polite manner, and commanding style, Armstrong was the Salesman from Central Casting—a sales archetype right down to his firm handshake and strapping six-foot frame. Even his *voice* was ideal. Armstrong's manly baritone had no trace of an accent, so he could blend in anywhere. He also had "style," which in IBM parlance meant he knew how to get the job done. An optimist to his core, Armstrong never met a customer he couldn't satisfy, or a problem he couldn't fix. Toss the guy a lemon, and he'd kill himself trying to turn it into lemonade.

Armstrong's ability to turn on a dime was a constant source of awe and amusement at IBM. The following story is representative: Driving over to see a client, American Express, in New York City, Armstrong politely but firmly reminded Ellen Hancock, a senior systems engineer, that she was not to engage in conversation with the client. He was the account representative, Armstrong explained, so it was only appropriate that *he* should do all the talking. Hancock, who was merely tagging along as an observer, quickly agreed. She just wanted to learn more about American Express's technology plans.

A few minutes into the meeting, the Amex manager asked Armstrong to talk about IBM's global network architecture. Amex was thinking about expanding the use of its famed credit card overseas, and the manager wanted to know how IBM's global platform might help. Armstrong, who had a layman's understanding of technology, did his best to explain. But the client wasn't satisfied, and pressed for more detail. The ace salesman didn't miss a beat. "No problem," Armstrong said, then turned to Hancock with a quick, "Ellen?" The handoff happened so seamlessly that it took Hancock a moment to realize what had happened. The customer never seemed to notice.

LIKE A LOT of marketing whizzes, Armstrong had a natural aversion to hard finance. It bored him to tears, in fact. Finance executives also tended to spend a lot of their time holed up in back offices. Again, not his cup of tea. But the IBM gods regarded a tour in finance as a prerequisite for the CEO's job, and Armstrong was definitely on the short list. So it was inevitable, perhaps, that IBM's No. 1 salesman would eventually wind up with a finance title.

In 1981 that's exactly what happened: Armstrong was named vice president and assistant group executive of plans and controls in IBM's Information Systems and Technology division. All of sudden, the guy who'd spent a career studiously avoiding finance was responsible for more than half of IBM's $60 billion fortune. In addition to having a mile-long title, he was up to his eyeballs in numbers, flow charts, financial footnotes, more numbers, and enough manufacturing spec sheets to fill a warehouse.

Armstrong was petrified.

The ace salesman had no clue what he was supposed to do, or how he was supposed to do it. Armstrong only had a basic understanding of finance. His knowledge of information systems was also limited. Part of that owed to IBM's organizational structure. At IBM, salesmen weren't expected to know all the dirty details of technology—that's what the technical side of the house was for. But now Armstrong was on the technical side of the house, after a fashion, so he needed to school up fast. Since failure was not an option, Armstrong decided to rely on his tried-and-true formula for success: He'd wing it and hope for the best.

Armstrong set out on a mad tear to learn everything he could about finance, information systems, and technology. IBM's nurturing culture was only too willing to help and before long he was getting crash tutorials on everything from algorithms to zip drives. He also started wandering the floors of IBM's labs and chatting up researchers. As a young man, Armstrong had always been fascinated by technology, so his after-hours homework was hardly a chore. IBM researchers and scientists, in turn, seemed to get a kick out of the fact that the ace salesman was taking such an interest in their end of the world. IBM's finance department, accustomed to bringing new bosses up to speed, was also happy to oblige.

The organization's willingness to pull out all stops like that wasn't unusual. It was, in fact, the IBM way. Back in the 1980s when IBM was in its heyday, rising stars like Armstrong were treated like visiting dignitaries. Underlings knew that their boss's tours would be relatively short—they were there to learn before continuing up the executive ladder. Executives like Armstrong weren't *allowed* to fail, in fact. It was all part of the IBM code, which, at its heart, was really just an extraction of the old Three Musketeers mantra, "All for one, and one for all."

Armstrong never did become a financial star. But he didn't embarrass himself, either, and in 1983 he was named vice president and group executive of IBM's Information Systems and Communications Group. The division, based in White Plains, had responsibility for the full range of communications products, including IBM PCs, hardware, software, printers, and telecom gear. Mainframes, managed by another division, was still IBM's bedrock. But with the Internet coming on strong, the Communications Group was viewed as a critical part of IBM's future success. His tour there would prove fateful, in more ways than one.

IBM BEGAN WORK on a groundbreaking computer series in 1985, the IBM Personal System, or IBM PS/2. The series, which was aimed at redefining the personal computing experience, was the successor to the highly successful IBM PC, which had debuted to rave reviews in 1981. Everything about the PS/2 was state-of-the-art. It even had its own operating system, called OS/2, which was being developed in partnership with Microsoft. IBM hoped to use OS/2 to gain some ground on the IBM clones, which were built around Microsoft's original operating system, known as DOS. (Windows was kicking around at the time but hadn't yet gained dominance.) Another distinguishing feature was the hard drive, which offered greater memory capacity and superior performance. As the head of the Communications Group, it was Armstrong's job to make sure that the PS/2 delivered on IBM's promises to customers.

The development of any new computer series is an enormous challenge that involves hundreds, even thousands, of manufacturing decisions. One of those decisions, in the case of the P/S 2, concerned the hard drive. Armstrong's top managers wanted to use a single manufacturer, arguing that IBM could eke out greater volume discounts. The recommendation, on its face, was unusual. IBM discouraged single-source contracts, for one simple reason: If the maker ran into problems, IBM was stuck. Armstrong's senior executives weren't concerned. The hardware maker they had in mind was tops in its field, and everybody was confident it could easily handle the job. In addition, the maker was offering deep discounts for a sole-source contract. As the senior officer in charge, it was Armstrong's call. He approved the single-source contract.

As the shipping date approached, however, it became woefully apparent that IBM wasn't going to meet the deadline. The problem was the hard drive. It didn't meet IBM's performance standards. A lot of the drives would simply shut down as soon as the PC was turned on. That left Armstrong with a bitter choice: He could meet the deadline by shipping out product with inferior hard drives, or he could wait until all the bugs were worked out. Breaking the deadline was not a small event. By then, marketing campaigns were ready to go and customers were waiting. There were also competitive considerations. To blunt the impact of the PS/2, Compaq, Digital Equipment Corp., and other rivals were rushing out new PCs with competitive features. If Armstrong waited, IBM would run the risk of losing its first-to-market advantage. But if he shipped out product with faulty hard drives, a lot of customers would surely be dissatisfied.

He decided to wait.

Even though he knew the delay would disappoint some customers, Armstrong reasoned that the hit to IBM's reputation would be far worse if he knowingly shipped out faulty product. In the end, Armstrong had to send in an army of IBM technicians to help fix the problem, erasing any cost savings he might have reaped by opting for the single-source approach. The hard-drive problem was fixed within a few months, but by then other problems had cropped up, so Armstrong decided to go ahead and fix those as well. The IBM PS/2—there were actually four different models, some of which weren't affected—finally shipped out with perfect hard drives about six months late. A lot of customers, as expected, were disappointed by the delay. But the IBM gods were livid.

It almost didn't seem fair. Even though he'd performed flawlessly for more than two decades, Armstrong suddenly found himself in some seriously hot water. He wasn't in danger of being fired, mind you. Back in those days, IBM had a lifetime employment policy, so nobody ever got fired. But IBM had a way of expressing its displeasure, all the same. The signs were subtle, but strikingly clear. IBMers who fell short might suddenly find themselves iced out of meetings, jerked back from promotions, or moved out to a lateral job—or to a faraway continent. Known as the penalty box, it was the culture's way of reminding a person that he'd let down the team and, even worse, let down customers. No, you won't be fired. But by the time it was all over, you might wish you had been.

John Akers, IBM's chairman and CEO, delivered the bad news himself. He gave Armstrong a choice: He could stay on at Communications Group, but IBM would install a new layer of management above him, effectively busting him down to the No. 2 spot. Or he could pull up stakes and move to Paris to head up IBM's European operations. Purely from a pride standpoint, the choice wasn't so easy. If he took Paris, which was clearly a lateral career move, he'd be publicly admitting failure. If he remained where he was, however, the humiliation of being demoted to the No. 2 spot would amount to a public hazing.

What to do?

THE CLOSED-DOOR MEETING between Akers and Armstrong caused a lot of commotion around the famous orange-carpeted halls of IBM.

There were rumors that Akers had called Armstrong into his office and told him point-blank that he was off the short list for the CEO's job. Others said there'd been a big blowup, and that Armstrong was on the verge of quitting. Some said the two men were barely speaking. None of it was true. Even before the hard-drive snafu, Armstrong had already convinced himself that he was out of the running for Akers's job. His rationale, on paper, at least, made some sense. Akers and Armstrong were just three and a half years apart in age. By the time Akers reached the mandatory retirement age of 60, Armstrong would have been pushing 57. Armstrong didn't think the IBM board would ever appoint somebody who was that old. At least that's what Armstrong told Akers in that famous closed-door meeting. Akers, so they say, didn't disagree.

Armstrong and Akers liked each other personally—both of them were affable salesmen at heart. But they also had a lot of differences. Armstrong, unlike Akers, wasn't starry-eyed about IBM. Compared to fast-moving rivals like Apple and Compaq, IBM was way too slow to adapt to changes in the marketplace. IBM's costs were also way out of whack. In addition, Armstrong thought IBM's "full employment" practice—IBM-speak for lifetime employment—was about as dated as a slide rule. Armstrong told Akers flat out that he needed to slash costs and start firing people.

Akers was appalled. *Firing people?* Akers didn't want to be remembered as the first chairman in IBM's history to break its famous employment policy. He also didn't want to rock the boat by taking a machete to costs. With a little paring here and there, Akers was convinced he could use revenue gains to grow his way around the bloat. And since Akers was the chairman and Armstrong wasn't, that was pretty much the end of that.

Armstrong took the job in Paris.

Showing his utter mastery of the lemon-to-lemonade trick, Armstrong finally concluded that there were a lot worse things in life than being sent off to live in one of the most fabulous cities on the face of the planet. He remembered his college tour of Europe fondly, and he'd always wanted to go back for an extended visit. So the timing was really perfect. At least that's what Armstrong told himself, and to all appearances that's exactly what he believed on the day he boarded a plane at JFK Airport in New York to start his new life in Paris.

WITHIN A FEW SHORT YEARS, Armstrong was out of the penalty box. Way out. IBM's overseas operations had always been a big money-maker, accounting for half of its revenues and profits. But under Armstrong, expenses plummeted and profit margins soared. Wall Street loved his take-no-prisoners style of management, which was so, well, *un*-IBM like. Back in the States, Akers was struggling. IBM's costs were choking the company, and Akers's timid efforts at paring weren't yielding much. Under pressure from investors, Akers finally started beating the drum on costs. By then, unfortunately, Wall Street was beating on Akers.

Armstrong, meantime, was having a ball. The same sights and sounds that had intrigued him so much as a young man still captivated him 30 years later—the food, the music, the architecture, the spectacular surroundings. Only this time Armstrong wasn't touring on a budget in a beat-up VW—he was seeing the world in style. They flew on private jets, ate in the finest restaurants, and got ferried around in limousines. Five-star hotels became their home away from home. The Armstrongs became members of Parisian society, attending elegant dinner parties, black-tie galas, and exclusive soirees across the continent. Revived by Europe's wondrous pleasures, Armstrong's CEO aspirations began to fade. Armstrong knew that he was past his peak. But he really didn't care. After all, he was in Paris.

FATE KNOCKED AGAIN in 1989. The person doing the knocking, this time, was John Akers. The IBM chairman had an urgent message: He wanted Armstrong to move back to the States to stake a spot on the prestigious IBM Corporate Management Committee. It was the ultimate compliment. Composed of just Akers and four other senior executives, the committee was responsible for overseeing strategy and business development for the entire IBM organization. By inviting him onto the committee, Akers was saying, in effect, that Armstrong had the unflagging, enthusiastic support of the powerful IBM board as well as the personal confidence and backing of the IBM chairman himself.

Armstrong turned him down flat.

As the de facto CEO of Europe, Armstrong was master of his own magnificent universe, and he had no interest in changing that. Armstrong gamely offered to participate on the committee so long as he could stay put. But move to Armonk? No way. Armstrong loved Paris, loved his job, and loved his lifestyle. And he didn't mind being a six-hour plane ride away from corporate headquarters, either. So thanks, but no thanks.

Akers was stunned. He wasn't accustomed to hearing the word *no* from anybody, much less from a subordinate to whom he'd just offered the career opportunity of a lifetime. Akers pushed every button he could think of to get Armstrong to change his mind, appealing to loyalty, honor, even friendship. But Armstrong, an ace salesman himself, wasn't buying. The answer was no.

Akers refused to cede the point. He went to Paris a few weeks later and stopped by to see Armstrong at his apartment, a rambling abode in one of the most elegant parts of the city. They sat in the den, which had a panoramic view of the famous downtown lights. There, they opened a bottle of red wine and talked—for hours. Over the course of the evening, they compared notes about the serendipitous nature of life. They also talked about their accomplishments, their hopes, their failures, and their families. And, of course that IBM job in Armonk. It must have been quite a sight to see—two legendary salesmen, both of them masters of the art of the sell, each trying to convince the other. Two bottles of wine later, Armstrong had agreed to come back to the States and take the job. All that said, it's still not clear who exactly sold whom.

When Armstrong got back to New York, he tried to pick up where he'd left off three years earlier. But the thrill was gone.

To be sure, Armstrong still enjoyed zipping around the world representing a company that he dearly loved. And, yes, he could still puff out his chest with utter sincerity and expound on IBM's grand contributions to the world. But late at night when he was alone with just his thoughts and the quiet voice of his conscience, Armstrong knew there had to be more. He had a nice fat title—Chairman of World Trade. Within the universe of IBM, it conferred power and prestige. But within the heart and head of Mike Armstrong, it didn't mean nearly as much. His mother had always implored him to "go for it" in life. But now there was nothing to go for. At 52, he was done. The IBM management committee was the pinnacle of his career, and there was no more.

Was he really willing to accept that?

Life wasn't all that bad, mind you. Being ferried around the world in limousines and private jets wasn't exactly hardship duty. And he was financially set for life. But this wasn't about the money. Or the prestige. Or even the title. This was about something far more personal and, ultimately, something far more important. This was about not having regrets. This was about living large. This was about having the guts to walk back into the locker room and demand a spot on the team. This was about not giving up—on himself.

Then it dawned on him.

After 31 years with the world's greatest computer company, maybe, just maybe, the kid from Detroit was finally ready for a change.

That's about the time the headhunter's call came in. Hughes Aircraft Co. in Los Angeles was looking for a CEO. Was he interested in talking about that?

Hughes Aircraft provided radar systems for the F-18 fighter jet and built the Maverick missile. Compared to IBM, it wasn't very big—just $5 billion or so in annual revenues. It also had a quirky corporate structure. Hughes Aircraft was a wholly held subsidiary of Hughes Electronics, a small holding company that was owned by auto giant General Motors.

Hughes Aircraft's biggest claim to fame was its founder, Howard Hughes. The eccentric billionaire designed what is generally regarded as the Edsel of aeronautics—the *Spruce Goose*. The flying boat, which was actually built of birch, was an oversized monstrosity that could barely get off the water. It had a wingspan of 320 feet—20 feet longer than a football field—eight engines, and weighed in at a gut-busting 300,000 pounds. The *Spruce Goose* made its maiden flight in 1947. Hughes flew the plane a mile in less than a minute, and then landed it for eternity. Another Howard Hughes invention was the push-up bra. Jane Russell wore the cleavage-enhancing garment in 1943's *The Outlaw,* making men everywhere swoon. Russell became an overnight sensation. So did the bra.

Armstrong was interested.

Being a Detroit kid, Armstrong had grown up in the shadow of the company. So it had a familiar feel. He also knew a lot of people who worked there. As an IBM salesman, Armstrong had called on the company many times over the years. A jump from IBM to Hughes wouldn't be entirely risk-free, of course. As the CEO of a smallish subsidiary of

GM, Armstrong would hardly be the master of his own universe. Would he be free to call his own shots? Or would he get sucked into the political machinery of GM? There was really only one way to find out. Plus, he was bored out of his gourd with IBM, so why not? After a fairly short courtship, he took the job.

HIS RUN AT HUGHES began on a high note. Malcolm "Mal" Currie, Hughes's longtime and much-loved CEO, called everybody into the corporate office auditorium to meet his new successor. Armstrong went out of his way to heap praise on Currie, who, as everybody there knew, didn't really want to leave. Currie had reached the retirement age of 65, so he had no choice. Employees, many of them hard-core engineers from places like NASA and MIT, were a little befuddled as to why GM had brought in an IBM salesman to take over Mal's job. But they gave him a warm welcome all the same.

By then it was March 1992, and big changes were in the air. After six years as a thinly traded public subsidiary of GM, Hughes and GM were discussing the sale of additional shares to the public. The stock offering was set for the fall. The timing wasn't accidental. The Cold War was winding down and the national defense budget was shrinking like crazy. Hughes and other defense contractors were starting to think about survival in the post-Cold War economy. In anticipation of the IPO, Hughes was actively searching for ways to restructure the business.

Armstrong balked. As the new CEO, he naturally wanted to put his imprint on any big restructuring, But he couldn't very well do that until he had a better understanding of the business. He wanted to study the issues for six months or so, and then formulate a plan. Chuck Noski, Hughes's controller, shot down that idea real fast. Noski told his new boss as nicely as possible that he basically didn't have a choice. Because of the IPO, the restructuring details had to be finalized no later than June 30, which was just 90 days away. Otherwise the restructuring news might disrupt the offering. Mike Smith, Hughes's chief financial officer, delivered the same message. So did GM. Armstrong acquiesced.

Hughes met the deadline, with one day to spare. The plan, unveiled on June 29, 1992, was a jaw-dropper. Nearly a third of the workforce,

25,000 jobs, would be eliminated. In addition, more than 100 buildings would be cleared out or shuttered. A number of businesses were also earmarked for consolidation or sale. To cover the cost of the massive restructuring, which would take 18 months to complete, Hughes planned to take a $1 billion write-down, a staggering figure at the time. Employees were stunned. They'd worked faithfully for decades to help win the Cold War. Now that victory was near, they were being rewarded with truckloads of pink slips.

Armstrong insisted on delivering the news in person. Standing in the same auditorium where he'd been introduced just a few months earlier, Armstrong explained that there was no other way—the restructuring was critical for Hughes's survival. He talked for almost an hour, a lone figure on a stark stage trying his best to make sense of the awful confluence of events that was about to claim the careers and livelihoods of thousands of workers. When he was finally done speaking, a remarkable thing happened. All the people in the room, many of whom had just been put on notice that they were about to lose their jobs, rose up and gave him a standing ovation.

The following year, 1993, the Pentagon announced deep cuts in the U.S. defense budget. The reason came as no surprise: The Cold War was over. To survive going forward, the Pentagon strongly urged the defense industry to consolidate—and quickly. Armstrong stood pat. He wasn't worried. Even though the defense budget was about to plummet by 40 percent, that still meant 60 percent was left. The trick, as far as he could see, was to make sure that Hughes was one of the lucky ones that continued to get government work.

With his eye on the clock, Armstrong started making fast tracks to transform the dowdy missile maker into a post-Cold War warrior. He snapped up a few small defense contractors that had decided to get out of the business altogether. With GM's blessing, he also completed the purchase of General Dynamics' missile business. (The deal had been in the works prior to Armstrong's arrival.) The Tomahawk missile program, which was enormously popular with the Pentagon, came along with the deal. Armstrong then set his sights on far bigger prey: Westinghouse Electric. The company was shedding non-core assets as part of a major restructuring, and one of the properties on the auction block was its fabled defense business. Armstrong figured the transaction would give Hughes enough size and heft to survive the defense industry's consolidation. It would also add a marquee name to the lineup.

GM turned him down flat. By then GM had a new CEO, Jack Smith, and he was no fan of the defense business. The timing was also bad. GM's core auto business was faltering badly, and Smith was slashing costs like crazy. GM also had concerns about its public image. Tomahawk missiles weren't exactly weapons of mass destruction. But they didn't evoke warm and fuzzy feelings, either. Armstrong worked every angle he could think of to get GM to reconsider. He appealed to patriotism, common sense, even greed. But Smith wouldn't budge. Armstrong was crestfallen.

ARMSTRONG HAD BEEN hunting for ways to capitalize on commercial opportunities in space for a while. But once GM killed the Westinghouse deal, his mission took on new urgency.

The concept of a national satellite TV service had been rolling around inside Hughes since the late 1980s. The driver was "compression"— shrinking digital bits and bytes so that they take up less room in the pipeline, thus giving you more room for "content" in the form of voice, data, and video services. In a blue-sky moment, a few engineers at Hughes Communications hit on the idea of a direct-to-the-home satellite TV service. By tweaking Hughes's defense technology, the engineers were convinced that they could create a satellite system capable of delivering hundreds of video channels directly to the home via small, pizza-size dishes. It was a novel idea. At the time most satellite TV dishes were the size of a barn door, and most cable TV operators were limping along with just 25 channels or so.

With GM's blessing, Hughes cobbled together a partnership with News Corp., NBC, and Cablevision Systems Corp. In 1990 the group announced plans to build a national satellite TV network called Sky Cable, with the goal of transforming America's TV viewing habits. The press loved it, and before long Sky Cable stories were dominating the headlines. After the furor died down, however, everybody started bailing out. Before long the only partner was Hughes. The idea probably would have died right there, but a group of deeply passionate engineers, led by Steve Dorfman, refused to let it go. Moreover, they were convinced that Hughes didn't need the others to be successful. Impressed by their enthusiasm—and still hoping for a financial hit—Hughes decided to carry on alone.

Armstrong showed up on the scene about two years later. By then Hughes had gone a long way to turn its blue-sky concept into an hon-est-to-God satellite TV system. The service had a clear strategic vision— to rewrite the competitive rules of cable. It also had FCC licenses, the right satellite technology, and a new name: DirecTV. Most important of all, perhaps, it had the enthusiastic backing of the GM board, which had already approved first-round funding for constructing one state-of-the-art satellite for DirecTV.

Armstrong, to his credit, immediately saw the promise of DirecTV and lent his full backing. (So had his predecessor, Mal Currie.) He didn't know a lot about satellite technology—not an IBM product. But he had plenty of ideas about marketing, and he shared them liberally with DirecTV's creators. Among other things, Armstrong insisted that Di-recTV do a test drive before rolling out DirecTV nationally, just to en-sure that all the bugs were worked out. (It's a good thing he did, too, because DirecTV's test market turned out to be quite buggy.) He also in-sisted that Hughes build its own set-top boxes so that DirecTV wouldn't be dependent on external suppliers. Burned by his experience on the IBM PS/2, Armstrong wasn't about to get caught by the short hairs again.

With support from Armstrong, an army of Hughes engineers and the entire GM board, DirecTV was officially launched in 1994. The service took off like a Tomahawk missile: DirecTV picked up 640,000 sub-scribers its first year, and another 1 million the following year to finish up 1995 with 2.3 million subscribers overall. By 1996, DirecTV had almost doubled its customer base to 4.4 million subscribers. Traditional cable TV operators couldn't help but be alarmed, because most of those customers were coming directly out of their hides.

Satellite and compression technologies, meantime, were improving rapidly, allowing DirecTV to launch wireless Internet services, and more. That *really* got everybody's attention—especially AT&T. All of a sudden, the quirky little satellite TV service didn't look so quirky, or little. And AT&T wanted a piece of the action.

Bob Allen, AT&T's then-CEO, had never had much success at leveraging the company's gold-plated name in the Internet space. AT&T had WorldNet. But that was just an old-fashioned dial-up service like AOL, only without the creativity and content. Joe Nacchio, who was head of AT&T's Consumer Services division, thought DirecTV was ideal. By selling DirecTV and long distance as a bundled package, Nacchio hoped it might cause customers to stay with AT&T longer, stabilizing revenues in the process. Allen wasn't so sure it would work. But AT&T was pretty desperate to slow down turnover in its consumer long-distance business, so he was willing to try anything.

DirecTV was thrilled. In less than 36 months it had managed to parlay a wild-eyed engineering idea into a formidable business, and now one of the premier names in telecom was knocking on its door. In March 1996, AT&T announced plans to invest $137.5 million for a 2.5 percent equity stake in DirecTV, with options to purchase another 27.5 percent of the company later. As part of the deal, AT&T agreed to use its prodigious sales force to sell DirecTV services.

As the CEO of Hughes, Armstrong had naturally expected to attend the press conference to announce the deal along with Bob Allen. But Eddy Hartenstein, a Hughes engineer and one of DirecTV's creators, had other ideas. When the big day finally arrived, Hartenstein showed up with his press people in tow. Armstrong was nowhere in sight. Everybody just assumed that Armstrong had decided to bow out.

Not exactly.

As it turned out, Hartenstein had never bothered to tell Armstrong about the details of the news conference, including the date, time, or place. (Hartenstein had a history of being selective about the facts he disclosed to his bosses.) Armstrong got pretty upset when he found out. GM's directors wound up reading about the press conference in the papers along with everybody else, forcing Armstrong to admit that he'd been left out of the loop.

A lot of CEOs probably would have fired Hartenstein over a stunt like that. Not Armstrong. Weaned in the forgiving ways of IBM, he chalked it up to another lesson learned, and left it at that. It was a kindly side of Armstrong's managerial style that would come back to haunt him at AT&T. Over and over again.

BY THE SUMMER of 1997, Armstrong had a lot to be proud of. Thanks to a series of acquisitions, consolidations, and divestitures that had occurred on his watch, Hughes was flying high. Overall shareholder value was up more than 350 percent. DirecTV was still growing like crazy. Armstrong's idea of starting a new satellite TV set-top division had also paid off. Hughes Network Systems, his brainchild, was raking in more than $300 million a year.

He'd had a few disappointments, for sure. Armstrong never did get to transform Hughes into a sleek, post-Cold War defense giant. The DirecTV–AT&T relationship also hadn't worked out so well. AT&T, as it turned out, wasn't so good at selling video services, and by the summer of 1997 there was a lot of talk about unwinding the partnership altogether.

Armstrong's dreams of running his own company were also fading. By then he'd been trying for years to convince GM to spin off Hughes and let him run it as an independent company. But GM always nixed that idea, arguing that Hughes's technology was strategically important to the overall success of its automobile business. That was a stretch. The hard reality was that DirecTV was simply too valuable to let go. It was a tough irony: In helping to turn DirecTV into a household name, Armstrong had ensured that he'd never get to be a household name himself.

But that was okay by Armstrong. At 59, he was at peace with the idea that Hughes was his last stop. He'd even started making retirement plans. His game plan was simple: He'd retire at 62, and then sit on a beach with his wife and enjoy the rest of his life. Truth be told, Armstrong wasn't so sure he wanted to retire that early. Inside, he still felt like he had a lot to give. But he never wanted to stick around so long that somebody had to show him the door.

Armstrong and his wife had just purchased a beautiful ranch-style home in Manhattan Beach, California. The house, which sat on a bluff, had a spectacular view of the Pacific Ocean. It had windows everywhere, affording prime viewing of whales and dolphins out in the surf.

But this wasn't just a house. It was a statement. For his entire six-year run at Hughes, Armstrong and his wife had lived in a rental house. It was a nice house, but a rental nonetheless. Armstrong said he'd always intended to buy, but just never got around to it. A better bet is that he thought, and probably hoped, that a plum CEO's job was just around the corner, one that would require him to pull up stakes and leave town in a hurry. In buying that house in Manhattan Beach, which was located just around the corner from his rental, Armstrong was throwing down roots. And in doing so he was making a big statement to the world, and a big statement to himself: After 37 years of climbing the executive ladder, he was done. Hughes was his last stop, and there was no more. Within three years, the only ladder he'd be climbing was the one he dragged out of his garage on weekends.

That's not to say he didn't play the "what if" game now and again. He often wondered, for example, what might have happened if he'd stayed at IBM. Who knew that John Akers was going to be pushed out? When Armstrong walked out the door in 1992, he'd just assumed, along with the rest of the world, that Akers would finish out his term. If Armstrong had stayed on another year, would he have gotten the nod? Armstrong sometimes thought about that late at night. But not too often—conjecture wasn't his style.

To be sure, headhunters still called up him up now and again. But nothing ever came across the transom that fired his imagination. At 59 he was past his prime for a top CEO's job. He knew that. So did the headhunters. But, hey, Armstrong wasn't exactly crying in his beer, either. He'd had a fabulous run at IBM, and a tremendous experience at Hughes. He was proud of his work, proud of his accomplishments, proud of his life. And now he had this great house in Manhattan Beach to enjoy in his post-retirement years with his wife, kids, and grandkids. He also had a ski chalet in Telluride, Colorado, another beach house on the gold coast of Florida, and a real house in Darien, Connecticut. For a guy from Detroit who'd never really expected all that much, he'd done all right. At least he wasn't selling popcorn in Tiger Stadium.

That's about the time The Call came in.

Gerry Roche, one of the top headhunters in America, was on the line. AT&T was looking for a new CEO to replace Bob Allen. Would he possibly be interested in talking about that?

Armstrong didn't have to think twice.

You bet.

6

THE BIG-PICTURE GUY
(A.K.A. DAN SOMERS)

U NLIKE A LOT of hired guns, Mike Armstrong didn't bring an entourage with him to AT&T. Not even a secretary.

That raised a few eyebrows around Basking Ridge. Armstrong, after all, had just finished up a 37-year global tour of IBM and Hughes. Surely he had a few loyalists who would follow him to the ends of the earth, or at least to the suburbs of New Jersey, to ensure his continued success. Yet, there he was by himself at AT&T—alone like a gunslinger at high noon in the town square. Some people found it downright odd.

They shouldn't have.

At Big Blue, senior executives have always been like eagles—they fly alone, never in packs. It was all part of the IBM code, which encouraged senior execs to work with, and learn from, the management teams they inherited—no card shuffling allowed. Like a lot of executives weaned in the winning ways of IBM, Armstrong took pride in his ability to build teams and pick out talent.

IN PREPARATION FOR taking on the job of his life, Armstrong did his homework. Or at least he tried to.

He asked for personnel files on the top 20 AT&T executives, and started making calls. Discreetly, of course. Everybody got high marks, with one exception: Dan Somers, the chief financial officer. Armstrong couldn't find anybody who knew Somers well enough to talk about him with much specificity. Armstrong got a lot of general comments—good guy, smart, knows Wall Street—that sort of thing. He was a little puzzled by that and kept scouring his Rolodex, hunting for somebody—anybody—who might know the guy. Nobody stepped up. Armstrong mostly shrugged it off. He figured Somers must have just dropped off everybody's radar. Somers had spent the bulk of his career working outside the United States, and he'd only been at AT&T about five and a half months. Armstrong decided to give Somers a chance to prove himself, and make a final decision later. All in all, it was a very Big Blue way of looking at things.

Armstrong couldn't help but compare his new CFO to Chuck Noski of Hughes Electronics. Noski had spent 17 years working as an accountant for Deloitte & Touche, so he could tear apart a balance sheet with cold precision. Noski was also an ace deal maker. At Hughes, Noski had ridden herd over dozens of transactions, including the $9.5 billion Raytheon merger. But he was by no means star-struck. Like most CFOs, Noski viewed deals as a means to an end. Period. If something didn't smell right, Noski was the first one to throw a body block. He also had no compunction about pulling Armstrong aside if he was getting too enamored of a deal, or veering off in the wrong direction. Noski and Armstrong would sometimes go round and round trying to convince each other about the merits of a transaction. Sometimes Noski convinced Armstrong; sometimes it was the other way around.

Noski's bloodless style owed to his wiring. All his years at Deloitte had conditioned him to believe that lurking inside every successful transaction was a disaster just waiting to happen. That's why he spent so much time on the front end poring over the details—the fine print, social issues, exit clauses, financing, and all the hundreds of other line items that collectively make up "the deal." The bedrock issue, for him, was always the same: Was it a good deal for Hughes, and did it make sense in terms of the long-term business objectives? It wasn't a very glamorous style of deal making. But he never got sucker-punched, either.

Dan Somers was no Chuck Noski.

A deal maker to the bone, Somers never saw a transaction he couldn't broker, finesse, finance, or steamroll. Big ones, small ones, hostile ones, you name it. Proxy fights? No problem. Tender offers? Child's play. Tell Somers to go get a deal, and he'd kill himself, or the other guy, to make it happen. Whereas Noski spent most of his time worrying about what might go wrong, Somers was always convinced that everything would go right. In Somers's world, CFOs like Noski were a dime a dozen—suits with sharp pencils who were good at crunching numbers, but not much else. Somers, by comparison, was all about the Big Picture. He was a builder—of businesses, of dreams, of a new way of looking at the world. He had a roadmap in his head, and his foot on the pedal. To the floor, baby.

Somers's religion was cable TV. His bullishness owed, improbably, to his long run at Hardee's, the fast-food chain. On its face, cable TV and hamburgers didn't have a lot in common. But to Somers they were practically one and the same. Both were essentially cash businesses. Both emphasized cash flow over net profits. Both were inherently entrepreneurial. Both could make you rich beyond your wildest dreams.

Somers wasn't shy about sharing his opinions. He told Bob Allen flat out that he thought AT&T should consider a big cable TV play. If AT&T was smart, he said, it would buy a slew of cable TV systems, then harness the power of the pipe to sell customers a branded package of services—local, long distance, Internet hookups, and more. Armed with a load of cable, AT&T could stagger the competition and roll right over the Bells. A no-brainer, Somers crowed. And that was just during his job *interview.*

Allen was impressed by Somers's bravado. But dive deep into cable? No way. To Allen, the idea of buying up a bunch of cable TV systems and slapping the AT&T name on them was absurd. Not to mention financial suicide. Allen was well aware that coaxial cable TV lines were workhorses in comparison to the Bells' 100-year-old copper phone lines. Upgraded with new technology, one-way cable TV systems could be transformed into sleek, two-way communications conduits. At least that was the theory. In practice, cable TV operators were notoriously cheap.

As a result, a lot of them didn't make the necessary investments to keep up with technology.

Allen's bias stemmed from personal experience. In the early 1990s, AT&T secretly met with TCI, Cox, and some other cable TV operators to talk about the possibility of forging a big national partnership. The project, code-named Fast Lane, called for AT&T to work with TCI and the others to offer a branded package of services. By piggybacking onto the local cable TV networks, AT&T could sidestep the Bells and get a direct pathway to the home. Best of all, AT&T could avoid the Bells' access fees, which were draining 40 percent of AT&T's revenues annually.

Project Fast Lane quickly ran off the road. One big issue was money. The cable operators wanted AT&T to pay for most of their network upgrades. Another issue was service quality. Allen was never convinced that cable operators could ever live up to AT&T's high standards. The two sides went round and round for months trying to figure out a solution, to no avail. The Fast Lane talks broke down for good in 1996 after Alex Mandl, who had championed the idea, left AT&T to join Teligent.

All that said, Allen appreciated Somers's out-of-the-box thinking. Even if his ideas were a little blue-sky, at least Somers was willing to look beyond the four walls of Basking Ridge for strategic solutions, which was a hell of a lot more than most AT&T execs were willing to do.

Somers had been brought in to replace Rick Miller, AT&T's outgoing CFO. Miller was a solid numbers man. He was also highly regarded on Wall Street. But Allen thought he was way too conservative. Miller, a former CEO for Wang, was the one who had come up with the idea of lopping 40,000 people off AT&T's payrolls. Allen thought the company could easily reduce head count through attrition and buyout packages. Layoffs of that magnitude, Allen argued, would be far too painful for the organization, which had already been through a series of wrenching upsets. Miller refused to budge, insisting the cuts were necessary.

After a lot of hand-wringing—by Allen, not Miller—the cuts were finally announced in January 1996. Allen took a pounding in the press. He got painted as a heartless lout who didn't give a damn about his employees. Because the cuts were announced just as the presidential primaries were getting underway, Allen wound up getting dragged into a national debate about workers' rights and corporate greed. Allen, who cared deeply about AT&T employees, was mortified. He was also furious with Miller.

Allen and Miller also had words about John Walter, AT&T's ill-fated president. Miller wasn't in favor of Walter's hiring, and let Allen know as much. Allen went ahead and hired Walter anyway, with disastrous results. Not too long after that, Miller decided it might be time for him to look for career opportunities elsewhere. Allen decided to use Miller's exit as an opportunity to bring in a CFO who would be far more expansive in his thinking. He told the recruiter that he wanted somebody who wasn't afraid to shake up the status quo.

On paper, at least, Somers seemed to be perfect. Just to be safe, Allen put in a few discreet calls to Somers's former bosses in Canada. They basically told him what Allen had already been able to discern on his own: that Somers was a Big-Picture Guy who wasn't afraid to shake things up. But his aggressiveness also had to be managed—closely. So long as you keep an eye on him, Allen was told, you won't find a finer finance executive.

Somers quickly lived up to his reputation.

During his first week on the job, Allen invited Somers to sit in on his weekly management meeting. The meetings, attended by all the business heads, are used as a forum to review ongoing operations. As the meeting progressed, Somers couldn't help but notice that the verbal presentations didn't quite square with the numbers. Even more unsettling, nobody in the room, including Allen, seemed to notice, or at least acknowledge, the disparity. About a third of the way into the meeting, Somers couldn't stand it anymore. He was sitting next to Allen, so he leaned over and whispered into the chairman's ear.

"Are they all like this?"

"What do you mean?"

"The presentations," Somers countered incredulously. "They're all painting a happy picture of life, but the charts all show their businesses going to hell."

"*That's* the problem."

Sensing blood in the water, Somers leaned in even closer and asked if it was okay for him to ask a few questions. Allen was delighted at the prospect of a flamethrower being let loose on the meeting, and told him to go right ahead. With that, Somers went to work. By the time he was done whittling down the presentation in progress, the hapless division chief was beet-red, and the room was stone silent. Just as the silence was reaching the breaking point, Allen turned to John Zeglis, who was seated to his left, and drilled in for the finale: "Well, the fun's started," Allen intoned in a loud stage whisper. "Maybe *now* we'll get some answers around here!"

SOMERS' SPECIAL BRAND of scrappy didn't happen overnight. It was a lifetime in the making.

Born in Detroit, Dan was the second oldest of four children—two boys and two girls. Dan was the second-oldest boy. AT&T's future CFO was so unruly as a child that his parents enrolled him in kindergarten when he was just four, hoping the rigors of school might help to calm him down. It didn't.

Dan's father was a lawyer and a successful trucking company executive. Mr. Somers was a caring but tough taskmaster, and he tried to imbue his children with a sense of independence early in life. Compassion was another early lesson. Dan's oldest sister, Mary Alice, born in 1933, was severely retarded. She exceeded everybody's expectations, eventually learning to read and write. She also loved to sing, and had an exceptional ear for music. Mary Alice delighted in playing her own version of *Name That Tune* with family members. Dan adored his sister. He was also impressed by her strength and her courage, and he vowed to demonstrate the same in his own life.

After graduating with a B.S. degree in finance from Stone Hill College in North Easton, Massachusetts, Somers hit the career track hard. He landed a job on Wall Street with White Weld & Co. As the low man on the totem pole, Somers quickly turned into a jack-of-all-trades, acting alternatively as an analyst, investment banker, and researcher. Somers loved the adrenaline rush of Wall Street. He also like the complexities of high finance, and his expertise expanded along with White Weld's portfolio of clients.

Somers worked on a number of major financings. One of them was for Hardee's, the national fast-food chain. Somers soon struck up a friendship with Hardee's chairman, Jack Laughery. That led to a job offer to become the head of strategic planning. Somers was just 27, making him the youngest officer in Hardee's history. Two years later he was promoted to CFO. The following year, he was bumped up again, this time to executive vice president. He also got a seat on the board. By then Somers had forged a close friendship with Paul Pare, the powerful chairman and CEO of Imasco, which owned a big stake in Hardee's. In 1982 Pare invited Somers to become the CFO of Imasco. Somers was just 34.

Imasco, a big conglomerate, was the fourth largest company in Canada. Its vast holdings included Hardee's and a diverse collection of consumer products. With Pare's backing, Somers sprinted up the career ladder, eventually becoming the chief operating officer. Along the way, he helped engineer the hostile takeover of GemStar/Canada Trust for $6 billion. The deal was messy, difficult, and marked by moments of terror on both sides. Somers loved every minute of it.

In 1988 Somers decided to make a lifestyle change. By then he was traveling constantly and he missed spending time with family. A devoted family man, Somers had five young children, and they were growing up fast. That fall he pulled up stakes and moved to Nova Scotia, where his wife's family owned a small group of radio stations. To get around Canada's prohibition on expatriates running broadcast companies, he became a Canadian citizen. The deed done, Somers became the CEO of the broadcasting group; his wife, Mary Jane, became the CFO. For all his hard-charging ways, Somers discovered that he loved the slower pace of coastal living. And he especially liked calling his own shots.

Nirvana didn't last long. In 1992 the Canadian economy went into a nosedive. Interest rates skyrocketed, sending the ad market into a vicious downward spiral. His radio fortunes decimated, Somers had no choice but to put his family's business on the auction block, and start all over again.

Nobody was hiring. Canadian businesses were downsizing like mad, and there was little demand for high-priced media executives like Somers. As luck would have it, however, Somers had a friend who was a recruiter for a small headhunting firm in Canada—and it was conducting a search for BCE, a huge communications conglomerate that owned

Bell Canada. BCE needed somebody to run its pension fund business. It wasn't exactly the job of his dreams, to be sure. But with five kids and a wife to support and no other job prospects in sight, Somers was open to just about anything.

When Somers showed up for the interview, things took a sharp turn. BCE's chairman, Lynton "Red" Wilson, thought Somers might be better suited for another position that had just opened up—the CFO's job in the international group, called BCI Telecom. The division was headed by Derek Burney, a former Canadian ambassador to the United States who had no media experience. BCI owned a handful of telecom and publishing assets, and Wilson wanted to expand the portfolio. Somers was elated. He also got the job.

Somers wasted no time putting his imprint on BCI. In short order he snapped up some media properties in the United Kingdom, including a stake in a cable TV system in East London. He also bought a stake in Videotron, another cable TV operator in London, as well as Mercury, a small telephone company that competed against British Telecom. By the time the dust settled a few months later, BCI was a major force in the U.K. media market.

With Somers leading the charge, BCI decided to up the ante even more. In 1993, BCI announced plans to pay $290 million for a 30 percent stake in Jones Intercable, a Denver-based cable TV operator, with the understanding that it would kick in another $55 million later to take 100 percent control. The deal wasn't especially large by conventional standards, especially when viewed in the context of the multibillion-dollar cable deals that would become commonplace a few years later. But the strategic implications were huge. By linking arms with Jones, BCI could create a powerful platform for selling voice, data, and video services. It was a bold idea, to say the least. Until then, most phone and cable companies in the United States had steered clear of each other. Cable companies didn't try to provide phone service, and phone companies didn't mess with video. Thanks to the BCI deal, all those neat boundaries were suddenly up for grabs. Almost overnight, cable and phone companies started rethinking their game plans, because they were going to have to compete against this hydra-headed beast known as BCI.

The Jones deal would set out an aggressive pattern of deal making that would become Somers's calling card. On the plus side, the Jones deal was bold and forward-looking. Somers, to his credit, was one of the first to recognize the value of combining the powerful platforms controlled by phone and cable companies. On the downside, the deal offered no financial protection to BCE if things went south. Cable veterans were also agog at the purchase price—$26 a share. That was more than double the $12 that Jones shares were trading for at the time. The deal also assumed compounded annual growth at unprecedented levels. (BCI's buyout price down the road was $69 a share, a level that Jones had never come close to achieving in more than 25 years of operation.) Another oddity of the deal: Even though BCI paid a control premium, it didn't get any control.

Even Glenn Jones, the company's founder and namesake, was a little befuddled by BCE's generosity. A wily dealmaker, Jones had characteristically asked for the moon when he was negotiating the terms. But he had never expected the company to actually comply. Somers made no apologies. "That's what they asked for," he would later explain. His quick trigger finger and agreeable nature would become legendary within the U.S. cable TV industry.

Anxious to raise BCI's profile even more, Somers started scouring the globe for media deals. Over the Christmas break that year, Somers invited Pat Lombardi, a top deal maker at Jones Intercable, to join him for a family holiday in Florida. Somers and Lombardi spent most of the week on the golf course. By week's end, the two men had cooked up a plan to combine all of their British media properties into one company, with an eye on taking it public. (Jones Intercable owned a number of properties in the United Kingdom, including a big stake in an East London cable system in which BCI was also an investor.) They even came up with a name for the new company: Bell Cablemedia.

Somers thought it only made sense for a BCI executive to head up the entire operation. And he even had a candidate in mind for the job: himself. Somers had no actual experience running a cable TV system, much less a hybrid cable-telephone operation with a British sensibility. But with his Wall Street background and entrepreneurial spirit, Somers thought he could teach the buttoned-down Brits a thing or two about competition, American style. BCI bought the argument. Somers got the job.

SOMERS MADE QUITE a splash in London.

One of his first official acts was to demote the incumbent CEO, Alan Bates. Showing his bloodless Wall Street side, Somers called Bates and other senior staffers into his office and summarily announced that he, not Bates, would henceforth be calling the shots. With that, Somers said he had work to do and shooed everybody out. Employees were dumbfounded. Bates was speechless. In the months leading up to his arrival, Somers had left the impression that he was merely coming over to assume the title of non-executive chairman, a figurehead position that had previously been held from afar by BCI's Derek Burney. It's not clear if the misunderstanding was intentional or not. But what is clear is that the episode strained working relations between Somers and his mostly British staff. It also created the impression, deserved or not, that Somers was a cad who couldn't be trusted.

And that was just the first month.

Anxious to prove his mettle as a manager, Somers pushed his staff hard. Sometimes too hard. During meetings, he routinely yelled at people who didn't agree with him. As a result, not many people did. Trying to light the competitive fires, he often referred to his experiences at Hardee's, using hamburger sales as an analogy for cable TV sales. The problem, however, was that few people on his staff had ever heard of Hardee's, much less visited one. So his colorful in-the-trenches stories mostly missed the mark. His open disdain of the European business sensibility didn't help. On one occasion, Somers roared to a group of about 15 managers that the British were "idiots," then proceeded to pound on the table shouting, "The Americans are coming, and we're going to show you how to do it!" Nobody said a word in the meeting, but there was plenty of talk afterward. The consensus was overwhelming: Somers was a jerk. An American jerk.

Somers's insistence on being treated like a media mogul only burnished his image as the ugly American. At his request, Bell Cablemedia secured him a home in Chelsea, one of the chicest parts of London. The company also picked up his tab for Wentworth, an exclusive golf and country club, as well as his Sunday limousine rides to the tennis club. In addition, Bell Cablemedia covered the cost of his car, a top-of-the-line BMW, and even had it cleaned for him. Whereas his predecessor had always flown coach, Somers insisted on flying first class. In a move worthy of a Hollywood bigwig, Somers even commissioned an official portrait of himself, with instructions to have it hung in a prominent spot.

Within a few months of his arrival, Somers decided to relocate his office from the main headquarters in Watford, a 20-minute train ride from London, to Portland Place, an exclusive address in downtown London. Somers only took two people with him: his secretary and his CFO. Somers explained the move by saying that he wanted to be closer to investors and to regulators, who were closely monitoring Bell Cablemedia's expansion. To a lot of insiders, however, the move was just another example of Somers's grandstanding.

It didn't take long for employees' simmering resentments to boil over into the open.

A few months after he moved to Portland Place, Christine Hurst, the head of Bell Cablemedia's human resources office, went to see Somers in London. Among other things, she wanted to discuss a senior marketing manager who had been recruited by Somers. The manager, a Brit who specialized in inspirational marketing, was rather hard on her staff, and Hurst was concerned about morale. As soon as Hurst started to talk, however, Somers was on his feet, yelling.

"She's one of the finest marketers I've ever seen!" Somers shouted, leaning over his desk so that his face was within a few inches of Hurst's nose. "You'd better watch yourself!"

Hurst lost it.

Drawing herself up to her full five-foot-four-inch height, the normally buttoned-down Brit started screaming at the top of her lungs. By then she'd been dealing with a steady stream of upset employees, so she didn't hold back. Hurst told Somers that she was sick of his surliness, sick of his bullyboy tactics, and sick of his uneven treatment of the staff. Unaccustomed to being called out by anybody, much less a church mouse like Hurst, Somers pushed back hard. Hurst refused to relent, and before long, the two executives were locked in a full-tilt screaming match that could be heard on two floors. Outside in the halls, workers stopped dead in their tracks, and heads started popping out of offices. Within a few minutes, Somers gave Hurst the international sign for a cease-fire—the time-out signal. Still white with rage, Hurst turned on her heel and stormed out.

Somers and Hurst never had a cross word again. Somers even gave her the Chairman's Award for employee excellence that year, an honor that included a $5,000 cash bonus.

BACK IN AMERICA, BCI's partnership with Jones Intercable was imploding. Four years after announcing the deal, the larger strategic goals weren't even close to being realized. BCI and Jones Intercable were also locked in a bitter, escalating battle over a range of control issues. Adding to BCI's growing angst, Intercable's stock price was treading water at just $10 a share, far short of the lofty $60-plus level that Somers had envisioned. Glenn Jones of Intercable and Derek Burney of BCI were also fighting. Burney, a former aide to Canadian prime minister Brian Mulroney, was a career diplomat who knew little about media. Jones was a self-made billionaire who knew the business cold. Needless to say, they didn't see eye-to-eye on much.

Tired of all the bickering, BCE, which was BCI's parent, decided to pull the plug. By then the Canadian economy was starting to swoon. BCE figured it made more sense to focus on its core strength, telecommunications. With that, BCI's star-crossed push into media skidded to an abrupt halt.

Across the Atlantic, Somers was dealing with his own crisis. One of BCI's local cable partners, Videotron, had decided to put itself on the auction block. The sale was significant, because Videotron controlled those parts of London that Bell Cablemedia didn't. Anxious to secure Bell Cablemedia's market position, Somers tried to buy the remaining 80 percent of Videotron that it didn't already own. The purchase price was stiff: more than $800 million. Since BCE was in no mood to finance any more cable deals, Somers started trolling for a big strategic investor.

Deutsche Telecom, the German phone giant, expressed interest. But it pulled back after the CEO, Ron Sommer, balked.

While Somers was tearing around London trying to round up money, Richard Brown, the new chairman and CEO of Cable & Wireless, was hatching a plan of his own. Brown, a 27-year veteran of the U.S. telecom industry, was talking to Nynex, the New York–based Bell, about its cable TV operation in London, called Nynex Cablecomms. Brown had designs on using Nynex Cablecomms to form the foundation of a broadband partnership, with the aim of offering voice, data, and video services across the continent. Cable & Wireless was also an investor in Bell Cablemedia, so it didn't take Somers long to get wind of what Brown was up to.

Somers wasn't too wild about the idea of dismantling his U.K. empire to throw in with Brown. But the stars weren't aligning in his favor. BCE had made it clear that it had no interest in growing its global media business, and Brown was offering full value.

Somers jumped on the Cable & Wireless bandwagon. Before long, Brown and Somers had joined forces to form what would eventually become a four-way partnership between Cable & Wireless, Nynex, Videotron, Bell Cablemedia, and Mercury, a money-losing phone venture that was majority-owned by Cable & Wireless. (BCI also owned a small stake.)

Somers called up Glenn Jones, who sat on the Bell Cablemedia board, and tried to get him to approve the deal over the phone. Jones refused, telling Somers that he couldn't even think about approving a transaction of that magnitude on the basis of a verbal description. Moreover, Jones thought it was imprudent for Somers to even try. Somers pushed right back, arguing that big, fast-moving deals got done all the time over the telephone.

Jones was unmoved. "That's just not me," he told Somers. "The answer is no."

Since BCI didn't technically need Jones's approval to proceed, Somers went ahead and inked the deal without him. Jones resigned from the board that night in protest.

Somers's headaches weren't over yet. When regulators finally got a look at the terms of the deal that he had agreed to, they quickly concluded that Bell Cablemedia shareholders were getting short-changed. Somers tried to get Nynex to help him out by giving up a piece of its 18.5 percent stake. Fred Salerno, the chief financial officer, refused. Brown, anxious to move the deal along, finally gave one point of his controlling stake to Bell Cablemedia, allowing the deal to proceed.

BY THE TIME the Cable & Wireless deal was over, so was Somers's career at BCI.

Red Wilson, BCE's chairman, told Somers that he could come back and run the company's yellow pages business. Another option was the wireless division. The CEOs of both units were retiring, creating the openings. Neither opportunity grabbed him. Somers relished the adrenaline rush of the media world. For him, the prospect of taking over yellow pages or wireless was about as exciting as watching cars rust.

What Somers really wanted was a high-powered job with visibility, clout, and, of course, the chance to put his prodigious deal-making skills to work. Somers threw out a few lines here and there. Nobody bit. A few people said he put up his hand for the CFO's job at BCE, but got rebuffed. (Somers always denied it.) Somers talked to Glenn Jones about joining Jones Intercable as the CFO. Jones liked Somers personally. Thought he was a hell of a golfer, too. But Jones didn't think too much of Somers' cable smarts or deal-making skills, so that didn't work out, either.

That's about the time The Call came in.

Peter McLean, an executive recruiter for SpencerStuart in Philadelphia, was handling a search for a major client. The company, a big telecommunications carrier in the United States, was looking for a CFO. Somers was intrigued, and agreed to take the meeting. McLean flew to London a few weeks later to meet Somers for breakfast at the Hyde Park Hotel. There, over a hearty breakfast of eggs and sausage, McLean revealed that the client was, in fact, AT&T.

Somers kept his poker face on. But inside he was ecstatic. He was also deeply honored. As far as Somers was concerned, being the CFO of AT&T was like being the CEO of almost any other company out there. AT&T was rich, powerful, and iconic. AT&T was also in the middle of some big, seismic changes. Somers liked that idea a lot. As the CFO, he could have a hand in shaping the future of one of the true legends of the business world. There was also compensation to consider. American companies, on balance, tended to pay a lot more than businesses in the United Kingdom or Canada.

So, McLean pressed, are you interested?

Somers didn't have to think twice

Damn straight.

After a few rounds of calls with the headhunter, Somers was invited to meet with John Zeglis, who was AT&T's vice chairman; John Petrillo, the strategic head; and Hal Burlingame of human resources. The meeting went well. Somers was soon invited to come back and meet with Bob Allen, AT&T's chairman and CEO, as well as John Walter, AT&T's new president. Somers was headed to the States for a wedding in Detroit, so he agreed to swing by New York to see them. The meeting with Allen and Walter went well. McLean called Somers the next morning and told him the good news: Allen and Walter liked him a lot, and they wanted to push on to the next level. He asked Somers for a dozen references on the spot. About a week later, Somers got the call he'd been hoping for: He had the job.

SOMERS RESIGNED FROM BCE on May 1, 1997. He started his new job at AT&T less than two weeks later, on May 12. Within months Bob Allen and John Walter would both be gone. Armstrong would be hired to replace Allen as the chairman and CEO, marking the beginning of one of the most unfortunate executive pairings in AT&T's 125-year history.

The news of Somers's hiring was met with mixed reviews back at BCI. Glenn Jones and Derek Burney happened to be in a meeting together when Somers's name came up. Burney said he'd heard through the grapevine that Somers had been named the chief financial officer of an AT&T division.

"No, Derek," Jones corrected him. "Dan was named the CFO of *AT&T,* the parent."

Burney blinked hard, and then roared with laughter: "Well, I'm sure it wasn't because of his financial skills!"

Somers, however, was about to get the last laugh. No guts, no glory. It was a mantra Somers had been living his entire career, starting from his early days on Wall Street. Now he was about to get his chance to prove his mettle on one of the most prestigious, high-profile corporate stages in the world, AT&T.

7

RESCUE PLAN

WHAT DO YOU THINK the AT&T shareholder wants out of all this?"

Mike Armstrong had thrown out the question during his very first board interview in the summer of 1997. It was one of those round-robin questions that candidates ask when they're trying to break the ice. The pat answer, of course, was, "More shareholder value." After all, that's what every investor expects, or at least wants.

But this wasn't a typical company, or a typical situation. Ralph Larsen, the chairman and CEO of Johnson & Johnson, took the bait.

"A future," he shot back.

Larsen hit the nail right on the head.

AT&T's future, for the first time in modern history, was a real question mark. Armstrong's challenge was to figure out how to reduce the company's dependence on the very business that had defined and sustained it for more than a century. That was like trying to figure out how to make the *Queen Mary* less dependent on the Atlantic Ocean. For all its big talk about New Media and the power of broadband, good old-fashioned long distance still accounted for more than 80 percent of its annual revenues and 100 percent of its profits. Changing the math on that wouldn't be easy or cheap.

A rescue plan. That's what the board was really after. Nobody said that out loud, of course. After all, AT&T wasn't ready to keel over and die just yet. Bob Allen might not have been much of a visionary, but he'd done a hell of a job with the balance sheet. For all its problems of the moment, AT&T was still a brute with more than $50 billion in annual revenue, $8 billion in operating cash flow, and $7 billion in net income. The company's short-term debt load was just $4 billion. Total debt was less than $12 billion, insignificant for a company of AT&T's size. It also had a gold-plated brand name and 90 million customers. With that kind of financial leverage, AT&T could easily afford to buy its way out of the tight corner it was boxed into right then. All Armstrong had to do was pick an investment strategy, and execute like crazy. But he had to pick fast, because the clock was ticking.

———

A LOT OF AT&T veterans were thrilled that an executive of Armstrong's stature was joining the company. After the roller-coaster ride of the Allen years, they were ready for a CEO who could imbue the organization with a renewed sense of direction and purpose. And most important of all, perhaps, hope for a brighter future.

Frank Russo was one of those people.

A 17-year veteran of AT&T, Russo was a vice president in the strategic development office. He was so excited about Armstrong's impending arrival that he dashed off a deeply personal letter to the incoming chairman. In the letter, Russo extended a warm welcome to AT&T and described the company's problems as he saw them. Also Russo offered his personal assessment of the senior management team, including his own boss, John Petrillo, AT&T's longtime strategic head. Nothing Russo said was all that critical, mind you. But for a mid-level manager at AT&T, it was a bold move all the same.

Russo was on vacation in Florida when he got a call from one of his colleagues. What he said almost gave Russo a heart attack: Armstrong had copied his letter and circulated it to the entire senior executive staff, including his boss, John Petrillo. Russo panicked when he heard that. He was worried he might be fired. Like a lot of big companies, AT&T took a dim view of people who tried to leapfrog the chain of command. As for Russo's written critique of the senior leadership, that was unheard-of.

Russo was deeply embarrassed by the disclosure. More than anything, though, he was concerned about Armstrong. His judgment in particular.

If the incoming chairman was so guileless as to believe that circulating his letter was constructive—for him, for Russo, for *anybody*—how could he even begin to finesse the fractured, hyper-political world of AT&T? To turn AT&T into a New Age communications Goliath, he'd need patience and intellectual fortitude, not to mention sharp elbows and a keen sense of office politics. The senior management team knew the game, and played it well. Could Armstrong survive, much less triumph, in a toxic fishbowl like that? Or was he going to be completely overwhelmed—by the culture, the politics, the pure weight of the AT&T machine?

It was a core question that many AT&T insiders would struggle with as the Armstrong Era progressed. But for the moment, at least, it was just an odd situation that left Frank Russo with an uneasy feeling in the pit of his stomach. Russo never did get fired. But he didn't write any more letters, either.

FOR ALL THE HEADY expectations swirling around him, Mike Armstrong was remarkably ill equipped to lead AT&T. He knew precious little about the telecom business. He knew even less about long distance. At IBM, he'd worked closely with AT&T on its hardware and software systems. But as Bob Allen had observed, *selling* to AT&T and *running* AT&T were two different things entirely.

No matter. A can-do guy right down to his shoelaces, Armstrong resolved to fashion himself into a telecom guru as quickly as possible. It probably didn't seem like much of a stretch. After all, he'd transformed himself many times over the course of his career. During his 31-year run at IBM, he'd turned himself, alternately, into a technology expert, financial whiz, PC specialist, and international diplomat. He did the same thing at Hughes. By the time Armstrong left there, he was an expert on a circus of defense technologies, from satellites, to Tomahawk missiles. After all that, the long-distance business must have looked like a lay up.

One of Armstrong's first orders of action was to conduct a top-to-bottom review of AT&T's operations. The goal of the exercise was to come up with a strategic fix for AT&T's long-distance problem. It was a clever approach in that it enabled Armstrong to get crash tutorials on every single business that AT&T owned. It also allowed him to spend a lot of time with the various members of his management team, and take their measure. AT&T execs, in turn, got to see Armstrong in action as well.

Right off the bat, it was clear that the new CEO had his own way of doing things. To some people, it looked an awful lot like The IBM Way.

In one of his first review sessions, Armstrong asked his senior managers to round up the latest "benchmarking" data—cost ratios, profit ratios, sales costs, and other details related to AT&T's market position. Armstrong wanted to get a bead on AT&T's performance relative to the industry, and figured that was a logical place to start. At Big Blue, benchmarking was practically a way of life. AT&T execs, however, were a little flummoxed.

Benchmarking?

We don't really do that, the AT&T execs explained. Armstrong's salesman's antennae started twitching a bit at that. He wanted to see the benchmarking data. ASAP.

When the data was finally assembled, Armstrong was shocked to see that AT&T wasn't that far off the industry norm—at almost 30 percent of sales, AT&T's costs appeared to be squarely in line with those at the other top carriers, including MCI. Armstrong was incredulous, and asked to see a breakdown of the companies that had been used to compile the profile. Sure enough, AT&T, which represented 40 percent of the industry, had been included in the roundup. So compared to *itself*, AT&T didn't look so bad.

Armstrong laughed out loud at that. AT&T execs didn't get the joke. For more than 100 years, AT&T had sold its services on the basis of *quality*, not price. It was a tradition that had begun under Theodore Vail, AT&T's legendary general manager, in the early 1900s, and 100 years later it was still AT&T's religion. As a result, AT&T had never obsessed about its costs relative to MCI and the others. What it did obsess about—constantly—was customer service.

AT&T's service ethic could be traced to an exact date: March 12,

1888. On that day, the Great Blizzard of 1888 slammed the Northeast. More than two feet of snow blanketed the region. Howling winds formed snowdrifts as high as houses. Highways, trains, and telegraph lines were shut down completely. AT&T's open-wire phone lines in New York City, were also threatened. Angus MacDonald, a 23-year-old lineman, refused to yield. Turning a blind eye to the storm's fury, Mac-Donald patrolled the phone lines around the clock, making repairs by hand as he came across them. Other linemen did the same. Thanks to their valiant efforts, New York never lost phone contact with the outside world. AT&T later commissioned a painting in honor of the episode, which would become a defining moment in the company's history. The painting's title, *Spirit of Service*, pretty much said it all. MacDonald later became an AT&T folk hero. Over time, he also became an international symbol of the company's unflagging commitment to customers.

Try benchmarking *that*, Mr. Chairman.

Nobody said any of this directly to Armstrong, of course. Not The AT&T Way.

Armstrong persisted. He was convinced that AT&T's costs were way out of line, and he was determined to prove it. Let's back AT&T out of the mix and see what the data looks like, he suggested.

Bull's-eye.

Just as Armstrong had suspected, AT&T's costs were running at a fat 29.6 percent of sales—higher, by far, than any other carrier. MCI and the other big carriers were in the low 20s. The startups blew the doors off everybody with costs in the high teens. There were some long faces all around the table at that revelation. Not because Armstrong was right. But because they could see that AT&T's premium pricing strategy, a hallmark since the days of Theodore Vail, was about to go out the window. As for Armstrong, he had the self-satisfied look of a house cat that had just eaten the canary.

THE BENCHMARKING EPISODE would mark Armstrong's first brush, but certainly not his last, with the AT&T culture. Literally a century in the making, the culture was so omnipresent that it even had its own nickname: the Machine. It was an apt moniker. Almost impenetrable to outsiders, the Machine was a self-perpetuating mechanism that was loath to change. Like Hal, the megalomaniac computer in *2001: A Space Odyssey*, nothing escaped the Machine's ever-present eyes and ears. Those who dared to tread on its myopic vision of the American icon that had birthed it did so at their own peril. The Machine wasn't deadly in the literal sense. But it was deadly all the same.

Process was a big part of the Machine's artistry. At AT&T's operational headquarters in Basking Ridge, New Jersey, meetings could ramble on for weeks, or even months. It wasn't uncommon for AT&T execs to have meetings to talk about meetings. Ditto for memos about memos. John Walter, AT&T's ill-fated former president, used to openly joke about it. The rank-and-file got a kick out of his irreverence. The Machine didn't, and promptly ground him up like yesterday's hamburger. (Memo to John Walter: You're history.)

The Machine steadfastly resisted change, and embraced those who did the same. It wasn't uncommon for executive decisions to be ignored or openly flouted. The practice was so pervasive it even had its own (unfortunate) nickname: Grin Fucking. Simply known as GFing around Carpet Land, these random acts of insubordination were usually carried out in an exceedingly polite fashion. That accounted for the "grin" part of the term. ("New marketing plan? Fantastic idea. I'll get right on it.") The latter part of the term was also self-evident.

How to determine if one had been the target of an AT&T special? That was easy: Nothing happened. Executive decisions—about marketing, management, personnel, you name it—would simply fail to be implemented, or they'd be implemented in such a roundabout manner that the spirit of the original decision would be undermined completely. And good luck trying to finger the culprit. With so many layers of management to hide behind, that was easier said than done.

ARMSTRONG'S CAN-DO SPIRIT had taken him far at IBM. But within the insular world of AT&T, his buoyant optimism sometimes left him looking slick and uninformed. In hindsight, it was a classic case of miscommunication: AT&T clearly didn't understand him, and he clearly didn't understand AT&T.

Not long after he was hired, Armstrong stopped by to give a pep talk to 150 AT&T officers who were in the midst of a two-day management meeting. There had been some speculation in the press that he might start slashing head count, so there was a lot of nervousness in the air. Seizing the high ground, Armstrong went out of his way to assure everybody that there was no need to worry. "This is my team!" he boomed to effusive applause. A few minutes later, however, Armstrong let it drop that he planned to beef up the company's international presence. As part of that initiative, Armstrong said he might bring in a heavyweight to head up AT&T's overseas push.

More than 100 sets of eyeballs immediately rotated in the direction of Mark Baker, AT&T's much-lauded head of international. For all practical purposes, Baker had just been fired—and in front of an audience, no less. Armstrong, oblivious to the soap opera in progress, continued talking.

At the break, Burlingame, the human resources chief, rushed up to Armstrong and implored him to clarify his comments. As soon as the break was over Armstrong strode up to the podium—and promptly fired Baker *again*. With the overseas markets turning red-hot, Armstrong explained, it was imperative for AT&T to have a heavy-hitter in the top job. He added that Baker, "of course," would still have a job, then trailed off from there.

A few minutes later, Armstrong opened up the floor to questions. Hands shot up like emergency flares. One of the first questions concerned speculation in the press about impending staff cuts. Armstrong didn't miss a beat: Given the tough economics of the long-distance business, AT&T, indeed, might have to reduce its corporate staff by 25 percent or more. Jaws practically hit the floor upon hearing that. Less than an hour earlier, Armstrong had reassured everyone in the room that their jobs were secure. Now he was saying the polar opposite. By the time Armstrong wrapped up his pep talk, the entire room was in a deep funk. Armstrong, for his part, thought he'd done a pretty good job revving up the troops.

Then there was the famous Limo Memo.

Shortly after he arrived at AT&T, Armstrong fired off a memo saying that henceforth staffers could no longer use chauffeurs to drive them around. The company already reimbursed senior executives for the cost of their cars, and Armstrong thought it was wasteful for AT&T to also provide chauffeurs. Armstrong told staffers they could have a company car or a chauffeur, but not both. Armstrong said nothing about his own long list of perks, however, which included a company car, a driver, and liberal use of the AT&T helicopter. His habit of having a driver pick him up at the helipad and drive him halfway around the building to the front door of AT&T also grated. (There was a shorter way, but it would have required the AT&T chief to walk about 50 yards.) Senior staffers took one look at the missive . . . and completely ignored it (GF Alert). To get around the directive, they started using non-AT&T car services, and just buried the cost on their monthly expense reports.

Because of the Limo Memo, AT&T drivers suddenly had a lot less to do, and they were none too happy about that. (AT&T only had about a dozen drivers. Many of them were retired technicians and linemen who doubled as security detail.) The drivers didn't have any political clout. But some still found a way to get even. Normally a closed-mouthed group, they soon started passing along information about Armstrong's cell phone conversations, passengers, personal conversations, and more. For senior staffers, it was better than having a squawk box in the backseat of Armstrong's car. As you might imagine, the Machine got a big kick out of that.

ARMSTRONG'S REVIEW SESSIONS ground on for three long months. Day in and day out, for 12 to 14 hours a day, Armstrong and his senior executives debated, argued, and dissected the many issues confronting AT&T. When they finally came up for air, three options were on the table: (1) AT&T could stay the course set out by Bob Allen, (2) it could put itself up for sale, or (3) AT&T could put its formidable balance sheet to work.

Staying the course was risky. Per-minute prices for long distance had fallen by 75 percent, and they were still rolling downhill. AT&T's attempts to work with the Bells on "resale," industry parlance for reselling local Bell services, had also flopped.

That brought AT&T to option No. 2: putting AT&T on the auction block. Though Armstrong hadn't come to AT&T to sell it, he hadn't come to *not* sell it, either, especially if that was the best strategic solution. Just to make sure he was leaving no stone unturned, Armstrong put in a call to Ed Whitacre, at SBC, to see if there was any interest in a merger. Reed Hundt, the chairman of the Federal Communications Commission, had already made it clear that he would never approve an AT&T-SBC merger, calling the combination "unthinkable." But Armstrong wasn't so sure about that. Before he'd agreed to take the job at AT&T, Armstrong had made a discreet visit—actually two—to see Hundt in Washington.

Armstrong got right to the point: How long do I have? It was Armstrong's way of asking Hundt to predict how long he thought it would take the Bells to win FCC permission to start selling long-distance services. Hundt's answer: Two years, tops. Armstrong posed the same question to Bill Kennard, who was about to succeed Hundt as the FCC's chairman. Kennard gave him the same answer: Two years. Armstrong came away convinced that he had 24 months, at the outside, to fix AT&T.

Whitacre, as usual, was game. He'd always liked the idea of buying AT&T, and his dismal experience with Allen had done nothing to change that. Armstrong and Zeglis flew out to SBC's headquarters in San Antonio to meet with him. The two sides quickly agreed that a merger made a lot of economic sense. Married to SBC, AT&T's future would be virtually assured. SBC, in turn, would get a big jump-start into the long-distance business.

Regulators were a big concern. Even if the FCC agreed to back the deal—and that was a big "if"—the regulatory approval process could take years. And even then the U.S. government, as a condition of approval, might try to impose a raft of onerous restrictions and conditions on the combined company. Armstrong decided to pass. With just two years to make his move, Armstrong felt he couldn't afford to get tangled up in a messy merger situation that might run out the clock. Whitacre, having been taken partway down the aisle once with Allen, was disappointed. But he also understood.

That left Armstrong with his last alternative: the balance sheet.

AT&T had $50 billion in annual revenue, $8 billion in operating cash flow, and $7 billion in net income. The company's short-term debt load was light—just $4 billion. With that kind of financial leverage, AT&T could afford to peel off in a lot of directions. But which one?

Dan Somers, the CFO, had an idea: How about buying Teleport Communications Group? Founded in the 1980s by Merrill Lynch, Teleport had its own local networks in dozens of cities. Teleport, known universally as TCG, catered exclusively to business customers. But with a little tinkering, Somers thought its networks could provide a handy launching pad for attacking the Bells' $120 billion local phone market.

Somers's idea wasn't exactly new. Armstrong's predecessor, Bob Allen, had considered buying TCG for years. But Allen could never get comfortable with the idea. Teleport was a scrappy little company that was headed by Robert Annunziata, and Allen wasn't so sure he could live up to AT&T's expectations.

That bias drove Annunziata crazy. Known as Bob to just about everybody, Annunziata spent 17 years working his way up the ladder at AT&T, only to get stopped short because he didn't have a college degree. His progressive ideas about competition didn't help his career. Annunziata sent shock waves through one meeting by merely suggesting that AT&T might want to reduce its prices by 5 percent to beat back MCI. This was in the 1980s: AT&T was still the undisputed champ of long distance and MCI was just a pipsqueak. "That's an unregulated thought process," his boss snapped. "Maybe you should think about leaving."

He did.

Tired of the AT&T bureaucracy, Annunziata left in 1983 to become the CEO of TCG. The teaming was serendipitous: Merrill Lynch, TCG's backer, happened to be one of Annunziata's accounts. Merrill Lynch was so impressed by Annunziata's out-of-the-box thinking that it offered him the CEO's job.

Annunziata, a streetwise New Yorker, quickly rose to the challenge. Since he didn't have much to work with—TCG at that point was little more than a business plan—he used grit and imagination to get things going. The upstart only had one installation truck—hardly impressive to the big business customers that TCG was trying to woo. Annunziata's solution? He painted a big "No. 7" on the side of it, creating the impression that he had an entire fleet running around Manhattan. To make it look like TCG had a lot of visitors, he also put a sign-in book at the receptionist desk. That was despite the fact that most people had never heard of TCG, much less taken the time to visit its shoe-boxed sized office.

The real show stopper, however, was service. In 1983 it wasn't uncommon for big business customers to wait nine months to a year for the local Bell to install a single DS-1 line—basically a big data hookup. TCG offered installation times of three months or less. In truth, TCG was so nimble it could have easily turned around jobs in a day or less. But Annunziata, showing his salesman's savvy, quickly figured out that he could charge more for that, so he offered 24-hour installations as an extra option for a lot more money. The ruse worked. AT&T, which had to wait in line for DS-1s along with everybody else, was so impressed it signed up for 750 lines in one shot. MCI and other carriers followed AT&T's lead. The Teleport mystique was born.

By 1997 TCG had local networks in more than 90 markets, including top cities like New York, Boston, and Chicago. It also had 3,000 employees and a growing base of blue-chip business customers. Merrill Lynch had cashed out its position, and a couple of big cable TV operators, led by Cox, had stepped in. Cox, in turn, brought in Comcast and TCI. Together they owned 66 percent of the equity, but they had 95 percent voting control.

John Zeglis had his concerns. To be sure, TCG had some promise as a local phone player. But he still thought resale was AT&T's best hope over the long haul. Somers disagreed. According to his calculations, AT&T was spending $3 billion a year on resale, with little to show for it. And the situation was only going to get worse, because the Bells were doubling down on local through their own mega-mergers, and coming after long distance.

Somers and Zeglis had been going round and round for months by the time Armstrong showed up on the scene. Sensing an opportunity, Somers asked Armstrong to take a meeting with Annunziata. Just listen to his pitch, Somers urged, and make your own decision. Delighted at the chance to referee, Armstrong quickly agreed.

The two men sat down to talk in early December. It was clear to Annunziata that the AT&T chairman didn't know a lot about the dirty details of the telecom business. But he liked the fact that Armstrong, unlike Bob Allen, was willing to give TCG a fair shake. Armstrong, in turn, was impressed by Annunziata's firm grasp of AT&T's problems. He also like Annunziata's plainspoken manner. After the meeting was over, Armstrong called up Somers and uttered just three words: "Make this happen."

Zeglis, who was Mr. Resale around AT&T, was crushed. As general counsel, he had spent years trying to turn resale into a competitive weapon. When the Telecommunications Act of 1996 was being crafted, he'd labored over every sentence, word, and comma as it related to resale. After the law was passed, he continued to ride herd over AT&T's resale strategy, overseeing contract discussions with all seven Bells. Zeglis was convinced that a big breakthrough was just around the corner. By then he'd been laboring for months on a big resale project, with the goal of striking business arrangements with dozens of TCG-type carriers across the United States. By going that route, he felt sure that AT&T could finally beat the Bells at their own game. And for a relatively cheap price, too.

Zeglis never got a chance to find out if he was right. As soon as Armstrong decided to buy Teleport, he killed the resale deal. It must have been pretty galling to Zeglis. By then he'd spent half his life looking out for AT&T's interests. Armstrong was still trying to figure out the ABCs of the industry. Even worse, he was taking his strategic advice from Dan Somers, a former Hardee's executive who had less than a year under his belt at AT&T. Zeglis took the news hard—he thought buying TCG was a short-term fix, at best. But he wasn't about to challenge Armstrong publicly. Not his style. Instead, Zeglis did what he always did anytime he was handed a political defeat—he kept his head down and plotted his next move.

THE TELEPORT DEAL was festooned with red flags. But you had to be paying close attention to see them.

Early on, Somers set up a meeting with TCI, Cox, and Comcast to talk about TCG's valuation. Bruce Ravenal, who was Malone's right-hand man, showed up on behalf of TCI. Cox and Comcast were represented by Dave Woodrow and Larry Smith, respectively.

Somers wanted each company to verify, in writing, how much fiber it had in the ground, and where. AT&T's inquiry was prudent. The presence of fiber-optic lines was indicative of upgraded plant, which was far more valuable than traditional coaxial cable. The response from Cox and Comcast was immediate: No problem. Woodrow and Smith quickly flipped through their respective binders and read off their fiber numbers, by market.

When it was TCI's turn to talk, the conversation skidded to a halt. Ravenal hurriedly excused himself and made a beeline for a private telephone. About 20 minutes later he returned, but he was still dragging his feet. The problem was obvious to Cox and Comcast: TCI's upgrades had been done in such a haphazard fashion that it had no clue how much fiber it had, or where it was located. In hindsight, the mere fact that Ravenal was bobbing and weaving so hard should have been a tip-off about the condition of TCI's cable TV systems. Somers never seemed to notice.

The second red flag concerned Somers himself. Trying to gin up some conversation, Somers let it drop that he knew a lot about the cable TV business.

Silence.

The other cable executives shot side-glances at one another. They'd all known each other for years. None of them had ever met Somers, and what they did know about him wasn't too promising. Somers was the architect of the BCI-Jones Intercable deal, which was widely regarded as a great deal for Glenn Jones—but a terrible deal for BCI. Somers had represented BCI's interests. Everybody in the room knew that much.

Somers kept on talking.

He soon mentioned that he used to run a cable TV operation in the United Kingdom—Bell Cablemedia. Maybe you've heard of it?

Actually, no. But they had heard a lot about that Jones Intercable deal. Nobody said that out loud, of course. Not with an $11 billion check from AT&T just around the corner.

By now it was clear that Somers was trying to present himself as an honest-to-god cable guy. Cox and the others were happy to play along, especially if Somers was willing to write them more checks.

THE TELEPORT DEAL was finally announced on January 8, 1998. The $11.3 billion deal grabbed headlines across the country, both for its size and its strategic importance. "Joining forces with Teleport will speed AT&T's entry into the local business market, reduce our costs, and enable us to provide businesses the any-distance services they want," Armstrong crowed in a prepared statement. In short, AT&T planned to use Teleport as a battering ram to bust down the door of the Bells' $120 billion phone market. Wall Street loved the deal, and sent AT&T shares soaring by almost $3 to close at $62.63.

As part of the deal, Annunziata agreed to join AT&T as an executive vice president in Business Services, with responsibility for overseeing local phone deployment for corporate accounts. Teleport's 3,000 employees went right along with him. It was a drop in the bucket considering that AT&T had 130,000 employees worldwide. But to Armstrong's way of thinking, the Teleport workforce, as small as it was, could at least begin to infuse AT&T with a new competitive spirit. He was thrilled to have Annunziata on board. Armstrong figured longtime AT&T execs could learn a thing or two from a maverick like him. Even better, Annunziata was a former AT&T manager, so he spoke the same language.

Needless to say, the Machine just about blew a gasket upon hearing that. It had pushed Annunziata out of the AT&T litter like a runt puppy some 15 years earlier, and it was in no hurry to get him back. Ditto for his 3,000 faithful employees. Teleport as a battering ram? That was nothing compared to the iron fist of the Machine, as Bob Annunziata and his collection of telecom misfits were about to find out.

8

THE CABLE CURE

A RMSTRONG'S RUSH TO EMBRACE cable appears to have been influenced, at least to some degree, by John Malone. Shortly after he arrived at AT&T in the fall of 1997, Armstrong went out to see Malone in Denver. The cable titan, who could smell desperation a mile away, was ready for him.

The visit, for Armstrong, was mostly a courtesy call. He knew Malone from his days at Hughes Electronics, and wanted to reconnect. Malone looked forward to the visit. He remembered Armstrong well, and liked him. A couple of years earlier, Malone had spent an entire day with Armstrong and Chuck Dolan, the chairman of Cablevision, on a sailboat off the coast of Nantucket. Armstrong spent most of the afternoon trying to convince them to make a big strategic investment in DirecTV. Malone passed, but he appreciated Armstrong's enthusiasm, all the same.

This time Armstrong wasn't selling. He was just fishing. AT&T needed a new strategy otherwise it wasn't going to last very long. If you were in my position, Armstrong wondered aloud, what would you do?

Malone had anticipated the question, and he was ready with an answer. Three things, he said: One, buy Teleport to gain local transport. Two, get an Internet play going by getting involved in @Home. Three, start working with TCI to come up with a local phone service play, using TCI's cable TV networks to gain direct access to the home.

It was a clever answer that was laced with larger meaning for TCI.

TCG and @Home were both part-owned by TCI. His third suggestion—striking a phone alliance with TCI—was something he'd been pushing AT&T to do for years. Greed wasn't Malone's sole motivator—he honestly believed that the three actions would go a long way to shore up AT&T's competitive flanks. But the fact that TCI stood to financially benefit probably didn't hurt.

Armstrong was intrigued. By then, as Malone was well aware, AT&T was already looking at TCG. He also liked the idea, at least in theory, of using cable TV lines to deliver AT&T-branded local phone services to consumers. And he especially liked the idea of using cable to sidestep the Bells. After all, every dollar that AT&T didn't have to pay the Bells for handling calls was an extra dollar that it got to keep. Malone's idea about striking some sort of deal with @Home also resonated. @Home only had about 100,000 customers at the time. But it had exclusive access to 55 million cable homes in key markets across the United States, so the upside potential was terrific.

The meeting ended on an up note. Armstrong promised to think about their conversation and get back to him. The TCI chief said he'd do the same.

Malone was impressed. During his 20-year reign at TCI he'd seen a few AT&T chairmen come and go, and it was obvious to him that Armstrong was different. With his DirecTV background, Armstrong understood the cable business better than most of his predecessors. Even more important, perhaps, Armstrong understood that the iceberg AT&T was clinging to was melting away, one long-distance customer at a time. And that only meant one thing: It was opportunity-time for TCI.

SOMERS LOVED THE IDEA of using cable to stick it to the Bells.

Back in the United Kingdom, Bell Cablemedia had managed to snatch away 40 percent of British Telecom's phone customers in markets where the two competed head-on. As a result of that experience, Somers was convinced that AT&T, tethered to cable, would clean house. The big difference, of course, was that Bell Cablemedia had had the benefit of building its networks—it actually had two, one for cable TV and another for phone—from scratch, enabling it to take advantage of new technologies right out of the gate. That was a breeze compared to trying to rebuild thousands of miles of 50-year-old coaxial cable plant to accommodate two-way voice and video services. One was the equivalent of building a house from the ground up; the other was like trying to retrofit a Victorian mansion with the latest in gee-whiz technology.

Somers recognized the monumental challenge ahead. As a gut check, he called in some investment bankers and asked them to run the numbers. The bankers, who included such Wall Street notables as Gene Sykes of Goldman Sachs and Larry Grafstein of Credit Suisse First Boston, compared the feasibility of a cable TV investment versus an outright purchase of a Bell. One possibility was U S West, based in Denver. U S West had the largest footprint of any of the regional companies—14 states in the West and Northwest. But its territory, while expansive, also included a lot of wide-open spaces, as well as the Rocky Mountains. Good for sheep and wild mustangs. But not so good for a telecom icon trying to get into the local phone business.

BellSouth was another possibility. Based in Atlanta, BellSouth had an iron grip on the fast-growing markets in the South. It also had a prodigious wireless business. Even better, it was using the same wireless technology as AT&T, so melding those two businesses would be fairly painless.

The biggest obstacle to a merger with BellSouth, by far, was BellSouth. Duane Ackerman, the chairman and CEO, was a genteel Southerner. But he was also notoriously slow to pull the trigger on big deals. Ditto for his longtime chief financial officer, Ron Dykes. The pair had rebuffed potential suitors for years. Ackerman's conservatism had even earned his company a nickname in investment banking circles: Fort South. Somers was unimpressed. He told Sykes and the other bankers that he was fully prepared to make a hostile run at BellSouth if that was the best option.

As it turned out, a hostile run at BellSouth would not be necessary, or even advised. Sykes and the other bankers were universal in their advice: To get the best bang for the buck, they said, invest in cable TV.

Why cable? It all came down to the arithmetic. In the United States, just two lines run directly to the home—the local telephone line, and the local cable TV connection. Since the Bells were never going to part with their "last mile" facilities, or even rent them out, if they could avoid it, that left just one option: cable TV.

Cable TV pipes were real workhorses in comparison to copper phone lines, which still made up more than 90 percent of the Bell's networks. Upgraded with fancy new electronics, coaxial cable lines could support phone service—called cable telephony in the cable TV world—high-speed data, and video. Cable lines were also relatively free of outside interference. And fast. Using high-speed cable lines, customers could surf the Web at rates that were up to 50 times faster than traditional dial-up services like AOL. Copper phone lines, by comparison, were incredibly slow and cumbersome to use. In car terms, broadband was a Ferrari and dial-up was a Hyundai.

Forging a national partnership with America's big cable TV operators wasn't going to be cheap. AT&T would probably have to spend tens of billions of dollars to help cable operators transform their dowdy, one-way video networks into two-way broadband highways. Crews would have to be dispatched to upgrade the lines by hand. That meant rolling trucks and tearing up streets. There was also the tar factor to consider. By lending its good name to the cable TV industry, AT&T would be aligning itself with a group of companies that was widely despised—by consumers, regulators, and politicians. Some of the taint might rub off on AT&T. Since AT&T had a 100-year obsession with its famous brand name, that was no small consideration.

Armstrong wasn't worried. To his way of thinking, the risk of partnering up with the cable industry paled in comparison to what AT&T was looking at if it didn't take a gamble—complete annihilation in the marketplace. His attitude was influenced by his own experiences at DirecTV. During his Hughes days, he'd spent a lot of time studying the different transmission technologies—copper, cable, and satellite—in an effort to better gauge DirecTV's vulnerabilities. Cable, he concluded, was the biggest threat. With its superior capacity and speed, Armstrong became convinced that cable would eventually steamroll the other two—it was just a matter of time. So the idea of buying a cable TV operator, or even two, made a lot of sense to him.

But which cable company?

It was a critical question that didn't have an obvious answer. Everybody knew that TCI was the biggest. But was it the best?

Cox, the Atlanta-based cable operator, was small by comparison—just 3 million customers. But on the plus side it was known for stellar customer care. Cox also embraced the idea of cable telephony. And what about Comcast? The Philadelphia-based company only had about 4 million customers. But it was run by the father-and-son team of Ralph and Brian Roberts, who made no bones about their interest in growing the company into a major media power. Then there was Time Warner Cable, which was part of the New York–based media giant of the same name. Under its visionary chairman and CEO, Jerry Levin, Time Warner had doubled down on cable early on, winning it the No. 2 spot right behind TCI. MediaOne, based in Denver, was also tops. Even better, it had a telecom heritage. The company, which had 5 million customers, had been carved out of the old U S West, one of the original seven Baby Bells.

In early 1998, the question of which cable TV operator to pursue was given to John Petrillo, AT&T's executive vice president for corporate strategy. He, in turn, pushed the question over to Lew Chakrin, AT&T's vice president of business development, who in turn called in Jerry DeFrancisco, a 25-year network operations veteran. DeFrancisco had just returned from a stint in Alaska, where he'd spent the better part of three years integrating a local carrier into AT&T's long-distance network. DeFrancisco quickly pulled together the Cable Telephony Group, a task force of network experts that included Mark Dzuban of AT&T Labs. The team members quickly fanned out in search of answers.

Over the next few months, Dzuban and the others talked to equipment suppliers, cable operators, contractors, set-top makers, and anybody else they could find who might have a clue about cable. Then they collated their findings, ranking the various cable operators according to a set of specific benchmarks, including network quality, footprint, and geographic location. They also looked at hypothetical combinations—say, AT&T–Cox—and tried to draw conclusions about the potential success of each coupling, taking into account the various operating and network characteristics of each cable operator. The group's conclusion:

Almost any combination of the big cable TV operators would work, with one exception—TCI.

Unlike the other big operators, a lot of TCI's systems were located in smaller, rural markets that weren't very attractive. Owing to its penny-pinching ways, the quality of TCI's networks was also uncertain. Cable operators consistently decried the decrepit state of TCI's plant—the actual cable TV lines and related support systems. That was a huge red flag. After all, if AT&T's goal was to roll out local phone service quickly, it needed to have access to cable systems that were in good condition. Otherwise, AT&T ran the risk of getting pulled into extensive upgrading, which could be expensive and time consuming.

At the other end of the spectrum were Cox and MediaOne. Unlike TCI, both companies received high marks from other cable operators for the consistent quality of their upgrades.

AS DEFRANCISCO'S GROUP had rightly concluded, about the only thing TCI had going for it was size.

Based in Denver, TCI was the biggest cable TV company in America, with 11 million customers, 14 million if you counted affiliated cable partners. TCI had access to about 18 million homes, but the number ballooned up to an impressive 33 million if you included affiliates. TCI's chairman, John Malone, was the Warren Buffett of cable—closely watched, widely emulated, but never matched. Malone's legend owed to his long and storied run at TCI. An electrical engineer by training, Malone joined TCI in 1973 as president. He was 29. The company, which had been founded some 20 years earlier by Bob Magness, a former cottonseed buyer, was struggling to stay afloat. TCI, which only had about $19 million in annual revenue, was choking to death on its debt—about $132 million at the time. In hindsight, it's a wonder the company didn't sink like a stone.

Since the banks wouldn't even think about lending TCI more money, Malone started coming up with deal structures that didn't require any cash. Over the next two decades he refined his art, using his brute intellect and keen negotiating skills to snap up more than 600 cable systems.

The outcome was impressive. By the early 1990s TCI was the biggest cable TV operator in the United States. It also had a prodigious programming arm in the form of Liberty Media, which had stakes in dozens of media properties, including Discovery, QVC, and Time Warner. As for Malone, due to his dramatic, even impossible, transformation of TCI, he was the undisputed King of Cable.

In 1993 Malone set plans to merge TCI into Bell Atlantic for $33 billion. The deal electrified Wall Street. Cable and phone concerns were taken aback at the audacity of the deal, which aimed to create a media juggernaut with access to 40 percent of all U.S. homes. The deal ran off the tracks five months later, but by then the seeds of a new way of thinking had been planted. Emotionally wrung out by the experience, Malone decided to step back from the business to clear his head. He left Brendan Clouston, TCI's chief operating officer, in charge.

Malone had famously predicted that cable TV networks would one day offer 500 channels and all sorts of New Age digital services, and Clouston was determined to make sure that day arrived on his watch. Clouston set out on a mad dash to remake the TCI culture, recruiting armies of executives and consultants from the airline industry, consumer products, even a major defense contractor. He also shelled out hundreds of millions of dollars for cool but ultimately faddish enterprises, including $600 million to secure licenses for a new generation of wireless phones.

TCI's expenses and debt soared. The nation's credit rating agencies soon became concerned, and pushed TCI's senior debt to the edge of junk. To conserve cash, Clouston held off on upgrades to the networks, but kept raising cable TV rates. At the same time, he continued spending heavily to pursue the digital future. The combination—bad service, high rates, blue-sky nonsense—got a lot of attention in the press. Sensing blood in the water, DirecTV and other satellite TV operators swooped in and grabbed market share. Tens of thousands of TCI customers bolted. The exodus ate into TCI's dwindling cash flow. That, in turn, only exacerbated the vicious cycle of high prices and poor service even more.

By the fall of 1996, the elephant in the room could no longer be ignored. In less than three years TCI had lost almost half its value. Its huge customer base, which Malone had meticulously pieced together over the course of 20 years, was washing away like beach front property in a hurricane. By October, TCI shares were trading for just $11, a 52-week low, and threatening to go still lower.

Malone, watching from the sidelines, tried to exude confidence. But meantime he was being swamped with calls from worried friends and investors imploring him to intervene. Their message was universal: TCI is in trouble. Do something. *Now.*

Malone heeded the warning. That October the cable titan abruptly returned to the office and reasserted himself into day-to-day operations. Clouston kept the COO's title. But there was no question about who was running the show: Malone. Over the next several months, he slashed expenses, reworked TCI's financial structure, and jettisoned the blue-sky projects that had been so warmly embraced by Clouston. He also renegotiated a series of service and programming contracts to get TCI better terms. Convinced that digital TV would be the future of the cable industry, Malone started upgrading TCI's larger systems so they could accommodate a raft of pricier new broadband services. Before long, the pace of customer defections had slowed to a trickle. Then it stopped altogether, putting TCI back on the upswing. After that, TCI's cash flow started perking up. Within six months, it had improved by a whopping 40 percent.

Malone, meantime, was logging 12 to 14 hour days—and the grind was taking its toll. He still loved TCI, and loved what it represented. But after 23 years in the business, he was worn out.

Fatigue turned to heartbreak the very next month. On November 15, 1996, Bob Magness, TCI's beloved founder and chairman, died. Malone was devastated. Magness had been like a father to him, and he deeply mourned the loss. Malone couldn't very well abandon TCI in what was arguably its greatest hour of need. But he also recognized that he couldn't soldier on alone. He needed some help.

Since it was clear that Clouston wasn't up to the challenge, Malone decided to bring in a hired gun.

Malone's top pick for the job, hands down, was J. C. Sparkman, TCI's former, longtime cable chief. The two men had worked shoulder-to-shoulder in the 1970s and 1980s to turn TCI into an industry leader.

Sparkman was notorious for being a bull-nosed hatchet man when it came to costs. Even more important, from Malone's perspective, Sparkman delivered. During his 32-year run at TCI, he routinely under-promised and overdelivered. Sparkman was long retired. But Malone was hoping he'd agree to come back, at least for a while, so they could re-create that same magic again.

When word of Malone's plan got around, he started getting calls from concerned friends. Sparkman still had the chops to get the job done, no question. But his health was not the best. Some people worried that the stress of running TCI might be too much for him. One mutual friend told Malone flat out that Sparkman "will come back to TCI if you ask him to, but it's going to kill him." Malone dropped the idea on the spot.

Malone's No. 2 pick was Jeff Marcus, the president and CEO of Marcus Cable of Dallas. The company was America's tenth-largest cable TV operator with 1.1 million customers in 18 states. Malone had known Marcus for years. He'd managed a TCI affiliate called Marcus Communications, and done a good job. Other TCI execs objected. Smooth to the point of slick, Marcus had a spotty record as a cable TV operator. There were also some concerns that he wouldn't be a good fit with the rest of the executive team.

By then it was pushing into February. Malone was still twirling through the Rolodex in his brain when Jerry Kern, a TCI deal lawyer, lobbed in a name from left field. How about Leo Hindery?

Hindery was the CEO of InterMedia, a mid-sized cable operator in San Francisco. TCI had given InterMedia some seed money to get started in the late 1980s. Since then, InterMedia had grown into the ninth-largest cable company in the U.S. with 1.4 million customers. TCI's relationship with InterMedia wasn't unique. Over the years, TCI had made investments in dozens of cable TV operators. (These were the famous affiliates.) Still, Kern thought Hindery, who was known as a tireless worker, might be worth a look.

Malone paused. He'd met Hindery a few times, but he was hardly a confidant. The TCI chief had always marveled from afar at Hindery's willingness to overpay for cable TV properties. Hindery also seemed to have no qualms about piling on the debt. As far as Malone was concerned, that was a deadly combination.

Kern persisted, arguing that Hindery had the kind of energy and resolve that TCI needed. Besides, what was the downside? Malone would still be calling the shots as chairman. In addition, Kern said he and Donne Fisher, the CFO, would keep a close eye on him. Okay, so Hindery sometimes overpaid for his cable properties. But at least he was smart enough to structure his deals so that they minimized taxes, Kern pointed out.

That was the magic word. *Taxes.*

Malone hated paying taxes, and he would do almost anything this side of legal to avoid them. "Okay," Malone told Kern. "Let's talk to him."

Hindery was thrilled. He'd first met Malone in the late 1980s when he was thinking about striking out on his own. Hindery, who was working for a publishing company at the time, went to see Malone in Denver to talk about the cable business. Malone, who was a larger-than-life figure even back then, was gracious and encouraging. Hindery remembered their exchange fondly. Malone, for his part, barely recalled the episode. As the godfather of the cable industry, newcomers frequently sought out his advice and he was always glad to offer it.

Malone thought hard. Given Hindery's hard-driving management style, he probably wouldn't last very long. A year or two, tops. By then he'd wear himself out, or wear out everyone around him. A renowned workaholic, Hindery thought nothing of calling in people for 6 A.M. meetings. But that was okay by Malone. Hindery moved so fast he'd have TCI in shape in no time. Then it would just be a matter of time before Hindery got bored and moved on, or blew himself up. Either way TCI would be fixed. And at the end of the day, that's all Malone really cared about anyway.

MALONE'S PEP TALK about the promise of cable had only helped to convince Armstrong that cable TV, warts and all, was probably AT&T's best shot at survival. AT&T's own internal review, which had been influenced by Gene Sykes and the other bankers, buttressed that view.

Armstrong still wasn't so sure he wanted to buy a cable TV operator outright. But a broad-based industry partnership? That was definitely of interest. Malone, as always, was game. The cable titan wasn't so sure the rest of the cable industry would go along, but he thought it was certainly worth a try. Armstrong decided to make his pitch at the cable TV convention in Atlanta that May.

Everybody who was anybody showed up for the meeting—Jim Robbins of Cox, Brian Roberts of Comcast; Joe Collins of Time Warner Cable; Chuck Lillis of MediaOne; and Malone and Hindery of TCI. After exchanging a few pleasantries, Armstrong got down to business. He launched into a moving, heartfelt speech about how AT&T hoped to work with the cable industry to forge a strong partnership for the future. By teaming up, Armstrong urged, they could marry the iconic AT&T brand name with the powerful high-speed cable TV pipe, creating a broadband giant for the ages, one that could carry America into the next century and beyond. In many ways, it was Armstrong at his best: in the spotlight, selling like crazy.

The cable operators basically yawned. They weren't interested in creating a broadband giant for the ages. But what they were interested in was money. And lots of it.

Chuck Lillis, the chairman and CEO of MediaOne, took the lead in presenting the industry's view. In addition to shouldering most of the upgrade costs, the cable heads wanted AT&T to pay billions of dollars in annual access fees for handling calls. Lillis was also adamant that the cable industry—not AT&T—had to "own" the customer relationship, essentially relegating AT&T to the role of middleman. In real estate terms, the cable industry wanted AT&T to pay for the house, the furniture, and the upkeep, but AT&T itself was not allowed to step foot inside the front door.

Armstrong kept his cool. But inside he was steaming. He probably could have worked out an arrangement on the upgrade costs. To a point. But the idea of AT&T paying access fees—an artificial subsidy that had been created by the old Bell Telephone System that bore no relevancy whatsoever to cable—was simply absurd. Indeed, one of the main reasons AT&T wanted to link arms with cable was because Armstrong was trying, desperately, to find a way around access fees. As for the notion of

AT&T, one of the most trusted names on the planet, turning over its customer base to a bunch of cable TV monopolists—not happening. Not then. Not ever. (Armstrong's initial reaction to that suggestion: *Are these people insane?*)

When the meeting was over, Armstrong shook everybody's hands and thanked them for coming. Lillis promised to confer with the other cable heads and get back to him. But there was no going back. Not for Armstrong. By the time he walked out the door that day, he was done. He felt angry, dejected, and deeply disappointed. He was the chairman and CEO of one of the largest and most respected communications companies in the world. Yet he'd been treated with all the accord of a Silicon Valley startup that was begging for money.

Hindery, for his part, couldn't have been more pleased. All the weeks of listening to Armstrong yammer on about the promise of cable had only convinced him that AT&T was ready to deal. And since it was clear that the other big cable operators weren't, that left AT&T with only one option: TCI.

9

SPRINKLING
STARDUST

M IKE ARMSTRONG was pissed.
America's big cable operators weren't interested in what AT&T was offering—a chance to link arms with one of the best-known and best-loved brands on the planet. Not on terms that even approached reasonable. The only possible exception was TCI. John Malone was the only one who seemed to grasp the larger meaning, and promise, of a bigger partnership. Now, improbably, the Darth Vader of cable was Armstrong's only hope for securing AT&T's future.

As white knights go, TCI was pretty weak. Its systems, together with the TCI affiliates, only covered about 30 percent of the United States. The number was even smaller—just 18 percent—in terms of its actual demographic overlap with AT&T, which had 60 million residential customers in 50 states. But there were also some big pluses. TCI and its affiliates had direct access to 33 million homes across the United States. Not great, given AT&T's long reach. But it wasn't so awful, either, especially considering that AT&T had direct access to zero homes on its own.

Determined to not let TCI slip away, Armstrong and Somers flew out to Denver to see Malone and Hindery. They all agreed that a joint venture made sense. AT&T could carve out its Consumer Services division, which handled Internet, wireless, and residential long distance, and combine it with TCI to create a broadband giant capable of delivering

AT&T-branded voice, data, and video services directly to the home. By the time the meeting broke, Armstrong and Malone had a handshake deal. Hindery and Somers were instructed to work out the details.

The details were killer.

The problem was long distance. Per-minute prices were dropping like a stone, making it impossible to put a firm valuation on Consumer Services. For the TCI side, it was like trying to hit a moving target. Long-distance prices were down 75 percent from where they had been just 24 months earlier, and they were still dropping. AT&T tried to argue that its vaunted brand name made up for some of the uncertainty. But TCI wasn't impressed. Control was also a problem. AT&T, always obsessive about the handling of its brand name, wanted broad authority over marketing, finance, and day-to-day management. TCI, whose own fortunes were soaring thanks to Malone's turnaround efforts, insisted that it, not AT&T, had to own the customer relationship. The wrangling went on for weeks.

By early June the two sides were deadlocked. Concerned that TCI might walk, Somers finally pulled Hindery aside and asked him the question that he'd been aching to hear for months. "We ought to just merge," Somers said matter-of-factly. "This is too complicated."

The AT&T chief was ready to go. And he'd been ready to go ever since he'd gotten his head handed to him in Atlanta. Armstrong's growing anxiety was understandable. To guarantee AT&T a future, he needed to find a new revenue stream that could outrun, and eventually offset, his rapid declines in long distance. All roads seemed to lead to cable. And since it was clear none of the other operators were interested, TCI was his best, and maybe his only, hope.

When Hindery told Malone that AT&T wanted to buy TCI, he got a cool response. "That's nice," Malone shot back, not a trace of emotion in his voice. Translation: Come back to me when you have a firm offer in hand. In Malone's dog-eat-dog world, expressions of interest from potential deal partners were a dime a dozen. The only thing that mattered to him was how much the other guy was willing to throw down on the table. Period.

Hindery had a ready answer: He thought AT&T might be willing to pay a fat premium—possibly 30 percent to 40 percent—for TCI's shares.

That got Malone's attention. The cable titan wasn't especially anxious to sell. But if AT&T was willing to step up with that kind of money, he'd be crazy not to listen.

AT&T's willingness to pay up aside, the real value of TCI's stock price was an intriguing question. Wall Street had driven up the company's shares largely on the basis of Hindery's optimistic—and, some would say, unrealistic—predictions about the future performance of the business. To hear Hindery talk, TCI was a veritable incubator of hot technology that was about to sprout wings and fly into the Digital Age. In reality, however, TCI was still struggling to provide decent cable TV service. Likewise, its efforts to roll out @Home were being hobbled by the slow pace of TCI's upgrades.

The disconnect wasn't lost on Malone. The TCI chief privately marveled at Hindery's ability to spin such a colorful story to Wall Street. Malone used to tell people that Hindery wasn't necessarily lying—he was just "sprinkling a little stardust" over TCI's future. Malone, for his part, sincerely believed that TCI would eventually become a technology leader. Just not as fast as Hindery was telling everybody.

Even so, Malone was willing to consider any legitimate offer that Hindery could reel in. Would AT&T really be willing to pay that much for TCI? Malone wasn't so sure. But if anybody could prod AT&T into acting, it was Hindery. Okay, so he sometimes got a little carried away with the stardust thing. But he'd also managed, through pure moxie and willpower, to drive up TCI's stock price by more than 100 percent in just 12 months, and it was still gaining ground. If Hindery could top himself again by convincing AT&T to take all the cable systems—and all the regulatory and political baggage that went along with them—then Malone was happy to consider it. Providing the price was right, of course.

Back at AT&T, meantime, DeFrancisco and his Cable Telephony Team were still grinding out their reviews on the U.S. cable industry. John Petrillo, who was deeply involved in the TCI merger talks, sometimes sat in on the briefings. Curiously, he never asked DeFrancisco's team to dig any deeper on TCI. Neither did anybody else. In hindsight, it was the ultimate GF: The cable project had been started, ostensibly, so that Armstrong and the senior leadership could make more informed choices. But in practice it was a meaningless exercise whose key findings were blatantly ignored. All in all, it was the sort of mindless behavior that would have made the Machine mighty proud.

THE SUNDAY BEFORE the landmark merger between AT&T and TCI was announced, *The New York Times* ran a story about TCI's remarkable turnaround under Leo Hindery. The story, which appeared on the front page of the *Times* business section, heaped praise on Hindery, noting that TCI's stock price had skyrocketed by an astronomical 149 percent under his leadership.

About a quarter of the way into the story, however, it took a sharp turn and began delving into Hindery's personal history. The article basically accused the TCI president of fabricating parts of his childhood to make his early years seem more destitute, and dramatic, than they actually were. The story, written by Geraldine Fabrikant, a heavy hitter on the *Times*'s media beat, included quotes from Hindery's mother, sister, and brother. Hindery had claimed that he left home at the age of 13 to fend for himself. But his family members had far different recollections. Likewise, Hindery's plaintive contention that his parents never tried to look out for him—"They didn't care if I left . . . it was cheaper to have me out of the house"—also didn't ring true. In the article, Hindery stood by his version of events, saying, "I never exaggerate about that."

Fabrikant continued to needle. Abraham Zaleznik, a professor emeritus of leadership at the Harvard Business School, was quoted saying that "storytelling is a pattern among some American business leaders," including such notables as Henry Ford and Andrew Carnegie. And Leo Hindery, if you followed the *Times*' drift. "That an executive might exaggerate his past could send up red flags for an investor—or spur confidence that his drive to succeed could work for the benefit of his employer," Fabrikant concluded.

If some readers found the juxtaposition—Hindery's childhood versus TCI's finances—to be a bit odd, there was a reason for that. Fabrikant had decided to drop in the personality analysis at the last minute. As it turned out, a *Times* editor, Alison Leigh Cowan, happened to see an early draft of the story and questioned some of his assertions. Among others things, she had doubts about Hindery's contention that his mother had deserted him at an early age. She also thought other details didn't square. Fabrikant did some additional reporting, and reworked her story accordingly.

The timing of Fabrikant's devastating profile was serendipitous—but also spot on. Though she didn't know it right then, AT&T was 48 hours away from announcing a merger with TCI, and Hindery was leading the way.

The story hit like a bombshell.

When Hindery and his team walked into the deal room that Sunday morning, they found a neat stack of *New York Times* newspapers piled high in the center of the conference table. Just the *business* sections. Hindery, who had already read the story, was deeply embarrassed. So was Dan Somers. But like everybody else at the table, he didn't know what to do. So he wound up doing the same thing as Hindery—he tried to ignore the bellowing elephant that was camped out in the middle of the table. One of the bankers eventually got up and, without saying a word, removed the stack of papers from the room. On that rather strained note, the talks continued.

But that didn't mean the controversy was over. Quite the contrary—it was just getting started.

When George Fisher saw the story that morning, he did a major double take. Other AT&T board members had similar reactions. Their upset was understandable. By then AT&T had agreed to hire Hindery as its new cable chief, and they were concerned about another public relations disaster. Given the public drubbing AT&T had taken on the John Walter debacle, about the last thing the company needed was another high-profile recruit with credibility problems. Later in the day, with the controversy over the *Times*'s story still gaining heat, AT&T held a conference call with senior executives and a few directors. Fisher was adamant. "I think you guys better check this out," he urged.

AT&T heeded the advice. Hal Burlingame, AT&T's human resources chief, called up Dennis Carey, an executive recruiter for Spencer-Stuart, and asked him to do a background check on Hindery. Carey, in turn, called in John Keller, a former Wall Street Journal reporter whom he had just hired to help build up the firm's telecom practice. Carey also put his prodigious Rolodex to work. Within a few weeks, Carey and

Keller had managed to cobble together an exhaustive report on Hindery that delved into his personal habits, professional life, and more.

The SpencerStuart report concluded what most people in the cable TV industry already knew: that Hindery was a go-to guy who got things done. But he also tended to break a lot of glass. As for his credibility "problem," that was in the eye of the beholder. Hindery had a lot of detractors, to be sure. But he also had some loyal supporters, including John Malone. The bottom line: If you're going to hire him, you have to manage him. Closely.

Armstrong read the report, and pretty much dismissed it. No real surprises here, he thought. Guys like Hindery are like thoroughbred racehorses—great performers, but hard to handle. He'd managed his share of racehorses over the years. Take Eddy Hartenstein of DirecTV. Difficult to the point of insubordinate, Hartenstein was virtually impossible to manage. Some of Armstrong's senior managers spent years trying to get him to fire Hartenstein. Armstrong refused. He had always appreciated Hartenstein's unflagging loyalty to DirecTV. Even if Hartenstein was, at times, disruptive, secretive, and thoroughly incorrigible, he gave 110 percent to DirecTV.

As far as Armstrong was concerned, Hindery was no different. Okay, so he was a bit of a loose cannon. But he was also a tenacious executive who got things done. Armstrong liked his can-do optimism. It was refreshing, especially in comparison with some of the Chicken Littles at AT&T. To hear Hindery talk, all he had to do was pick up the phone and things got done. Phone pacts? *No problem.* How about a deal with Time Warner? *Consider it done.* Armstrong, who always was way too trusting, liked the sound of that. As for Hindery's unruliness—not a problem. Armstrong prided himself on being able to manage talent, especially thoroughbreds like Hindery. It never dawned on him that the SpencerStuart report, which had been put together on the basis of information that had been culled from Hindery's cable peers, just might be right. Which meant, by definition, that he was wrong. Confident to his core, Armstrong just assumed he could use his charm and management smarts to turn Hindery around. In hindsight, it was a very Big Blue-tinged way of looking at things.

Hindery, meantime, was dreaming. And as usual he was dreaming big. If he did a bang-up job running cable, who knows? Maybe he could become Armstrong's successor. John Zeglis had a similar plan in mind. He didn't relish the idea of a gunslinger like Hindery coming into AT&T at such a high level. But he also wasn't too worried. He'd read Hindery's background report. Just two words came to mind: *Damaged goods*. With his fast and loose ways, Hindery would be lucky to last a year. Dan Somers could already see that Zeglis and Hindery were headed toward a nasty showdown. But as usual he kept his thoughts to himself. As far as Somers was concerned, his job was to deliver TCI. It was up to Armstrong to manage the people who came along with it. People like Hindery.

And Armstrong? He never saw the storm clouds coming. After all the months of running himself ragged, he was just pleased—and relieved—to finally have a rescue plan in sight. He was also elated to finally have a solid management team in place. With people like Hindery, Zeglis, and Somers in his corner, really, how could he miss?

THE PRICE WAS RIGHT.

On Wednesday, June 24, 1998, AT&T announced that it had agreed to pay a whopping $48.3 billion, in cash, stock, and assumed debt to buy TCI. At that level, AT&T was paying around $51 a share for TCI's stock, a rich 40 percent premium to the $30 or so that TCI shares had been trading for in the weeks just prior to the announcement. Buried in the deal was a $5.5 billion cash payment for a number of extras, including Liberty's 39 percent stake, and 72 percent voting interest, in @Home.

The tagline on the front of the press kit that was given to reporters that day pretty much summed it up: "One cable, one company, countless possibilities." In buying TCI, AT&T was, in effect, buying its financial freedom, and in the process it was gaining access to some 33 million homes across America. Armstrong was practically glowing. "We have an exciting future," he said. "We can, and will, become an any-distance communications company, providing entertainment, telephony, and high-speed Internet access to our customers." Malone was just as bullish. "This merger is a tremendous growth opportunity for TCI shareholders and employees," the cable titan predicted. Indeed, the mere fact that some-body could finally talk about AT&T's future with impunity, in and of it-self, was something to cheer about.

The deal had a lot of moving parts. AT&T said it planned to roll its new cable TV and Internet assets into Consumer Services, which han-dled residential long distance. AT&T said it would set up a new track-ing stock for the unit, giving people a way to invest directly in the broadband assets. Once the deal closed, Hindery would become presi-dent of cable, reporting to John Zeglis.

Liberty Media went along as part of the TCI package, but in name only. Malone retained broad authority over Liberty's financing, day-to-day operations, and management. He was also free to chase deals, even those that competed headon with AT&T's interests. Liberty was set off as a tracking stock of AT&T. But it was mostly window dressing. The bottom line: Malone was in charge of Liberty. Period. As part of the transaction, AT&T agreed to write Liberty a check, essentially, for any tax benefits that accrued as a result of its association with TCI. The give-back was significant, equating to about $500 million annually for Lib-erty. AT&T tried to argue that it also benefited from the arrangement. That might have been true, at least on paper. But you sure didn't see Lib-erty writing AT&T a check, now did you?

Nobody looked better than Hindery. The deal was proof positive that TCI's ace carnival barker had been right all along. Even Malone, who'd pretty much seen it all in his 25 years in the cable business, was blown away by the selling price.

Other people were blown away too. But for different reasons.

On the day the TCI deal was announced, Bob Allen, AT&T's former chairman and CEO, was glued to his TV. Allen smelled trouble. Arm-strong's bullish predictions about the performance of TCI's cable plant were way too optimistic. It would take AT&T years, at least, to turn TCI's systems into sleek broadband conduits that were worthy of the AT&T name. He nearly fell out of his chair, however, when he read a story that quoted Armstrong bragging about the fact that he'd pulled the deal together in a matter of days. Allen let out a loud moan when he read that. "Oh, my God," he said to nobody in particular. "We've been had!"

A lot of cable TV executives shared his view. Some were openly incredulous at Armstrong's willingness to pay so much for TCI. It was a big collection, no question. But just because you owned a bigger trash heap didn't mean you were king of the hill.

Armstrong heard the snickers. But he really didn't care. Truth be told, he would have paid even more. As for the trash heap, like that old saw goes: One man's trash is another man's treasure. With TCI in his back pocket, AT&T finally had a fighting chance at a real future. Without it, well, that was another story. The one big caveat, of course, was that AT&T had to execute. Quickly and well. Otherwise, he'd just paid a ridiculous amount of money for a bunch of broken-down cable systems with no larger purpose.

The AT&T chief was keen to the challenge. "Our strategy for growth is in place," Armstrong intoned on the day the TCI deal was announced. Then he let one shoe drop: "If we execute to our full potential, we'll grow this business and reap the rewards of that growth." Being the optimistic sort of guy that he was, Armstrong didn't point out what might happen if AT&T *didn't* execute. Raining on his own parade just wasn't his style.

WHEN JERRY DeFRANCISCO found out that AT&T planned to buy TCI, he almost couldn't believe it.

Less than a month earlier he'd told his bosses that TCI and cable telephony probably wouldn't mix. Now, improbably, AT&T was making TCI the centerpiece of its bold phone-over-cable strategy.

Lew Chakrin called DeFrancisco into his office to deliver the news personally. DeFrancisco didn't say much. Neither did Chakrin. He had his marching orders. Chakrin had another surprise. DeFrancisco was being named the vice president of cable telephony. In short, it was now up to him to turn TCI's hodgepodge of networks into the engineering equivalent of a Bell telephone company. Again, DeFrancisco didn't say a whole lot. Just like Chakrin, he had his marching orders.

Chakrin told DeFrancisco that he needed to start pulling together a business plan immediately. Armstrong wanted to start selling AT&T-branded cable telephony as soon as the merger closed. That would take about a year.

The financial targets started filtering down from the CFO's office about a month later. And with each passing month the targets kept rising—precipitously and inexplicably. By the fall, DeFrancisco and his new team were being told that they needed to deliver 800,000 cable telephony customers by the end of 2000, ramping up to several million in the out years. In addition, AT&T was projecting that the cost of wiring up a single customer for cable telephony would be relatively modest, just $300 to $500 per home. Since the calculations were coming directly from the CFO's office, it was understood that those were the price points that AT&T needed in order to justify the deal to Wall Street.

DeFrancisco sort of scratched his head at that. He had no idea whether the targets were doable, or even remotely reasonable. And neither did anybody else at AT&T. During the TCI negotiations, nobody had actually bothered to go out and inspect TCI's systems. Instead, Somers and his deal team had simply relied on TCI's own assessments. In other words, AT&T was basically guessing.

DeFrancisco wasn't ordered to accept the ambitious projections for 2000 on the spot. Technically, he was asked. But he was asked in such a leading manner that it would have been almost impossible for any AT&T veteran to reject them.

How was he asked? Very carefully.

"We need to do this [800,000 cable telephony customers by 2000] to demonstrate that AT&T can deliver," Chakrin patiently explained in one such meeting. "Can you do that?" AT&T also wanted to launch cable telephony service in 10 markets—at least—within a year of the deal's closing to send a bold message to Wall Street. Could DeFrancisco and his team deliver on that aggressive schedule as well?

How to answer?

If DeFrancisco had felt free to speak his mind, he might have said exactly what he thought: that chances were probably slim to none that AT&T could deliver on such aggressive targets, especially given the questionable—indeed, the *unknown*—status of TCI's systems. TCI, after all, was composed of more than 600 separate cable systems, representing dozens, if not hundreds, of competing technical platforms. Its backroom functions, such as billing and customer support, were also a mishmash. Complicating matters further, Hindery was still swapping systems with other operators like baseball cards, so the network configurations were still changing.

The pressure on DeFrancisco was crushing. The press had already pounced on the fact that TCI's systems were among the worst in the industry. Tongues were also wagging that AT&T hadn't done its homework, and therefore didn't know what it was buying. Likewise, there was a lot of skepticism that AT&T could quickly transform TCI's systems into ones that could seamlessly support Bell-quality phone service. Naysayers were predicting that the overhaul of TCI would cost a lot more and take a lot longer than what AT&T was letting on. Inside AT&T, everybody was on pins and needles. Especially Armstrong.

So, Chakrin pressed, how about those business targets for 2000?

"Can you do it?"

DeFrancisco, a product of 25 years of AT&T training, carefully considered the question before him. Then he came back with an answer that was as cool and as precise as the Machine itself. The network chief told Chakrin that he could, indeed, meet the target *provided* the following three conditions were met: One, TCI's systems had to be uniformly upgraded and ready to go in conjunction with the rollout schedule. Two, ditto for TCI's backup systems, including billing and customer service. Three, AT&T's new local phone switches, which would be used to sort and route calls, had to be in place across the United States, thereby ensuring that AT&T could receive and hand off calls on the TCI networks. Implicit in the last item was a fourth condition: TCI had to have interconnection agreements in place with the Bells and other local phone companies, otherwise AT&T wouldn't be able to send and receive calls from other networks.

Failing that, DeFrancisco said, he could make no promises. Depending on the condition of TCI's plant, he said, rolling out AT&T-branded cable telephony to 800,000 customers could take months. Or it could take years.

There wasn't a whole lot that Chakrin could say to that. In classic AT&T style, he'd asked DeFrancisco an impossible question, and he received an equally impossible answer. DeFrancisco later wrote a memo outlining the three conditions in detail, just to make sure nothing got lost in translation. The memo got sent to all the senior officers, including Mike Armstrong, John Petrillo, and Dan Somers. DeFrancisco never heard back from anybody directly. But the 2000 target didn't go up anymore after that, so presumably his message got through.

A few months later DeFrancisco asked for permission to send out a technical crew to do spot checks of TCI's plant across the United States. DeFrancisco had some concerns about whether TCI's ongoing upgrades were being executed in a consistent fashion, and he didn't want any ugly surprises later. Word came back that Hindery had turned the request down flat. The TCI chief rightly pointed out that the time for due diligence was over. The deal was done.

10

THE SCENT GLAND
ON THE DEER

I JUST SENT YOU A FAX.

Those were the first words out of Leo Hindery's mouth. He was speaking to Tom Jermoluk, the chairman and CEO of @Home. It was 6 A.M.

"What is it?" a groggy Jermoluk asked, still fumbling with the phone in the darkness of his bedroom.

"Just read it," Hindery shot back. "I need you to get it back to me with comments by six thirty, because that's when we're putting it out [to the press]."

Still trying to wake up, Jermoluk shuffled over to his whirring fax machine and picked up the copy that Hindery had just sent him. According to the as-yet-unreleased press announcement, AT&T had just given Yahoo! a part of @Home's opening page to do with as it pleased. The upshot: When customers logged on to the @Home service, the first thing they'd see was a greeting from Yahoo!. In exchange, Yahoo! had agreed to promote AT&T's services exclusively on its Web site.

Now Jermoluk was awake.

He called Hindery right back and told him the deal was a non-starter. Giving the opening page to @Home's rival, on its face, was just stupid. Not only that, but it would trample all over @Home's partnership rights, which forbade one-off deals for anybody. As a publicly traded company, @Home was obliged to look out for the rights of its shareholders, not AT&T. Hindery, as TCI's president, had no standing to bargain for anything on behalf of @Home. Not even office supplies, let alone a big strategic deal. TCI was just an investor, not a controlling shareholder. And the fact that the AT&T–TCI merger was set to close in a few months did nothing to change that.

Hindery dug in his heels. "You have to agree to this," he loudly insisted, "because this is what we're doing."

Jermoluk refused to budge. If Hindery proceeded, the @Home chief said he'd put out a press release of his own—explaining why it made no sense whatsoever for TCI, a founding board member and a major shareholder, to be cutting a deal that gave 100 percent of the benefit to AT&T.

When Hindery continued to press, Jermoluk cut him off. "Do what you want," he snapped. "I'll see you in court."

The release never went out. The Yahoo! deal eventually cratered amid a lot of finger pointing on the powerful @Home board, which included representatives from Cox, Comcast, and Kleiner, Perkins, Caufield & Byers, the famous Silicon Valley venture firm. Most of the fingers, by the end, would be pointing directly at Hindery and his soon-to-be new boss, Mike Armstrong of AT&T.

THE IDEA OF LAUNCHING an Internet-access service for the cable TV industry had been dreamed up in early 1995 by John Doerr of Kleiner, Perkins. Anxious to find a home for his concept, Doerr, a legend in the venture capital community, turned to another legend, John Malone of TCI. Malone loved the idea, which aimed to marry the power of high-speed cable TV lines with the promise of broadband. From Doerr's perspective, a union with TCI only made sense. As the de facto leader of the U.S. cable industry, Malone held enormous sway over other major cable operators. The punch line, of course, was that a lot of TCI's networks were incapable of handling @Home's high-speed data service (not enough fiber). But since Malone wasn't the type of guy to let details stand between him and a big pile of money, he decided to work that part out later. The tour de force known as @Home was officially born.

Doerr also went to see Steve Case of AOL. He tried to get Case to become a ground-floor investor, arguing that AOL needed to establish a beachhead in the emerging broadband market. Case was skeptical. At the time AOL was the undisputed champ of dial-up, and broadband was so new that few people outside Silicon Valley had ever heard of it. Doerr told Case to ditch the blinders and get real. "You're at the top of the mountain now," he told the AOL chief. "But as soon as broadband takes off, AOL will be blown away." Case took a pass.

Cox and Comcast, the big cable TV operators, didn't hesitate to follow Malone's lead. The TCI chief had a rock-steady reputation for making smart money decisions, and Cox and Comcast didn't want to get left out. Neither company was convinced that @Home would take off. But since satellite TV was coming on strong, they figured it couldn't hurt to go along for the ride, just in case.

As a founding partner of @Home, TCI had hard control of the board. Cox and Comcast only had minority rights, but they weren't worried. According to the fine print of the partnership rules, TCI was required to roll out @Home services at a steady clip, with stiff penalties for nonconformance. Given the sad-sack state of TCI's cable systems, Cox and Comcast figured it would just be a matter of time before TCI defaulted, causing the balance of power to shift in their direction. It was a very smart hunch.

SINCE @HOME was a big bet on the future of broadband, Doerr thought it would make sense to bring in a network guru as its chief technologist.

Enter Milo Medin, a NASA engineer with a specialty in networked computing. Doerr tracked him down at NASA's Ames Research Center in Mountain View, located in the heart of Silicon Valley. Medin never called him back. Accustomed to having his calls returned promptly, Doerr put in a second call. Still no callback. Mystified by the rebuff, Doerr kept calling, over and over again. When he finally got Medin on the phone, an exasperated Doerr asked why he hadn't bothered to return any of his calls. Medin apologized, explaining that he'd never heard of Kleiner, Perkins, Caufield & Byers. When he saw the firm's name, he just assumed that Doerr was a lawyer trolling for new business.

Doerr met with Medin a few weeks later. In the meeting, Doerr excitedly sketched out how @Home's network would spin its Internet magic, delivering an experience to the home like no other. Each user, he explained, would be equipped with a cable modem and a T1 line, making for super-fast connection and surfing speeds. To hear Doerr talk, @Home was the missing link, a technology savior that would turn the Internet on its proverbial head.

Medin, who had built NASA's piece of the Internet, a project that had taken him on a global tour of 16 countries on six continents, including Antarctica and the Pacific Rim, listened patiently. Then he coolly explained why Doerr's cable plan would never work: In essence, Doerr was proposing to build a 10-lane on-ramp for a two-lane highway. @Home's network would crash at the first sign of a traffic overload. Instead of cruising the Net at blindingly fast speeds, @Home's customers could wind up waiting for hours just to get past the toll booth. Doerr was crestfallen. ("It was like I ran over his puppy," Medin later told some people.)

To make the @Home concept fly, Medin told Doerr that what he really needed was a "distributed" architecture, which would allow for the smooth flow of traffic across the network. Doerr was intrigued, and pressed Medin for more detail. How much would it cost to build a network like that to support, say, 1 million users? Medin thought hard, then ventured a guess: $120 million. Medin expected Doerr to recoil at the price. Instead, Doerr was outwardly relieved.

"That's all?!" Doerr shot back, clearly elated. "I thought you were going to say three-to-four billion, which would take a lot longer to round up!"

Medin was staggered. For $3 billion, you could build a space shuttle orbiter or a Nimitz class nuclear aircraft carrier. He was also confused. Even though he'd spent hours talking to Doerr, Medin still had no idea who he was or what, exactly, a venture capitalist did for a living. But he was about to find out. Doerr, who was as famous for his salesmanship skills as he was for his technology finds, picked up the pace from there. Within a few weeks of that discussion he would convince Medin to leave NASA and take a flier with @Home. The move would put Medin on the forefront of what was about to become a network revolution in America.

TOM JERMOLUK, known universally as T.J., had arrived at @Home by way of Silicon Graphics (SGI). Founded by Jim Clark in 1982, SGI was a hot maker of high-performance computer equipment. SGI's real claim to fame, however, was its dazzling special effects for Hollywood. SGI's computer-generated scenes of dinosaurs loping across the screen in *Jurassic Park* stunned audiences. For *T2,* the Arnold Schwarzenegger megahit, SGI used breakthrough technology to create one of the more memorable villains in movie history—an android that could reconstitute itself on the spot to penetrate concrete walls, steel bars, and even slide under a door. Viewers were impressed. So were investors, who sent SGI shares soaring.

As SGI's No. 2, Jermoluk had a high profile tending to day-to-day operations. In 1993 he was tapped to oversee SGI's partnership with Time Warner, which had decided to test the theory of broadband by building an advanced high-speed cable TV network in Orlando. Jerry Levin, Time Warner's chairman and CEO, was convinced that cable-modem services would trump dial-up services like AOL, and he aimed to prove it. SGI provided a lot of the test equipment, including the powerful set-top boxes that allowed consumers to navigate around the network. The SGI set-tops attracted a lot of attention, for their mind-bending performance as well as their mind-bending price, almost $9,000 apiece.

The Orlando experiment was widely derided in the press as an expensive vanity project. But it did succeed in confirming Levin's central thesis: People *loved* high-speed cable-modem services. Broadband allowed customers to surf the Net at speeds that were up to 50 times faster than pokey dial-up services, which relied on 100-year-old copper phone lines. People also liked the "always on" aspect of broadband, which gave users instant access to the Internet. All the media bigwigs paid visits to Orlando, including John Malone. As SGI's point man on the ground,

Jermoluk wound up taking on the role of technology ambassador and showed them around.

Doerr, never too far away whenever technological innovation was unfurling, took note. In 1994 he tried to recruit Jermoluk to head up an Internet startup that Kleiner, Perkins was about to launch: Netscape. Jermoluk was still enjoying his rocket ride at SGI, however, so he took a pass. The job went to Jim Barksdale, the former president of Federal Express. Marc Andressen, a former graduate student at the University of Illinois at Champaign Urbana, signed on as chief technologist. The heart of Netscape's business plan was Andressen's software masterpiece, Mosaic, a program with a graphical interface that made Web surfing a snap. Netscape went on to become a monster hit.

In 1996 opportunity knocked on Jermoluk's door again. The pitch, this time, came from John Malone.

Malone wanted Jermoluk to take @Home to the next level. His goal was simple: to make money. By revving things up, Malone figured cable operators could help spur the growth of broadband, thus lining their own pockets with billions of dollars in new revenue. @Home was key. Malone told Jermoluk that @Home was "the scent gland on the deer"— it was the reason that predators would come calling. ("Predators," Malone-speak for big strategic investors, were a very good thing.) It was a bullish statement, to say the least. At the time cable stocks were in the toilet, and @Home was basically a PowerPoint presentation.

The challenges were significant. @Home's original seed funding, about $12.5 million from Kleiner, was just about gone. The venture's cash-strapped cable backers were in no mood to step up with any more money, and it was unclear how the capital markets would treat @Home. There was also a lot of squabbling on the board. Cox and Comcast were already chafing under @Home's complicated governance rules, which favored TCI.

Jermoluk thought hard. Diving deep into cable wasn't exactly what he had in mind as his next career move. But this wasn't just any cable deal. It was a *Malone* deal. The idea of throwing in with Malone to build a business from the ground up appealed to his renegade sensibility. The timing was also right. By then Jermoluk had been at SGI for a decade, and he was ready for a change.

It was a good instinct. By then SGI's star had begun to fade on Wall Street, and some people were quietly blaming Jermoluk. That could be one reason why he wasn't Malone's first pick. Dave Dorman, who was at Pacific Telesis at the time, had actually been offered the job first. Malone and Doerr both pitched him on it. Dorman, a telecom veteran who had spent most of his career at Sprint, came close to accepting. But in the end he turned it down because he didn't think @Home's business model, which depended on unflagging support from its cable owners, was sustainable. (He was right.) As soon as Dorman bugged out, Malone and Doerr turned on a dime and went after Jermoluk.

After thinking it over for about a week, Jermoluk agreed to take the job. He'd passed on the Netscape opportunity, and he wasn't about to make that same mistake again. His appointment was announced on July 31, 1996. Jermoluk, who defined Silicon Valley cool, was characteristically laid back in talking about his abrupt career change. "I'm into small teams and building things," he said, referring to the broadband experiment he had just signed on to lead. "This is an exciting opportunity."

Back at @Home, the atmosphere was anything but laid back. Anticipation was building about @Home's long awaited debut, which had already been pushed back a few times due to technical problems. Determined to calm things down, Jermoluk hit the fast-forward button and vowed to meet the new launch date, now set for September. Right out of the chute, he hit a snag. @Home had planned to debut the service in two places in California: Sunnyvale and Fremont. But Sunnyvale, @Home soon discovered, hadn't been upgraded by TCI, so it couldn't handle the service. Sunnyvale was quietly dumped, leaving Fremont as the sole launch site. Medin, meantime, was working furiously to fine-tune @Home's technology, which still had a lot of bugs in it. It wasn't a rocket launch, to be sure. But in many ways it was just as complicated.

Nobody had a clue how the public would respond to a bleeding-edge service like @Home. It wasn't exactly a snap to use. Self-installation wasn't an option back then. Customers had to call up their local cable company—TCI in Fremont—place their order, and then wait for a special two-man technical crew to show up. The installation process was unwieldy and time-consuming. Technicians had to take the back off the

PC and manually install an Ethernet card and a data port. (Today both are standard items on PCs, but they weren't back then.) Then they had to install the @Home software, which could also be tricky. At $35 a month, plus a $150 installation fee, @Home was incredibly expensive. Traditional dial-up services like AOL, by comparison, only cost around $20 a month.

@Home launched in Fremont, as scheduled, in early September. An army of reporters turned out to commemorate the occasion. *Time* magazine dispatched a photographer to take pictures of the neighborhoods where the service was being offered. There was nothing to look at, mind you—just a bunch of houses in a California suburb. But the promise of @Home was exciting enough, apparently, to warrant a permanent reminder of the day. Matt Wolfram, @Home's senior press person, brought in a cherry picker so the *Time* photographer could get high enough in the air to get a good shot.

The launch, to almost everybody's surprise, went off without a hitch. The results, to nobody's surprise, were spectacular: People loved it. @Home, as promised, instantly transported customers into a digital Land of Oz where they could surf the Web with impunity. Downloading large files, even space-hogging video files, were a breeze. For Internet addicts, it was basically nirvana.

@Home's effusive reception in Fremont only further affirmed what John Doerr had been saying all along—that broadband would eventually crush dial-up services like AOL. Doerr by then was already bragging that @Home would have 1 million customers within a year. It would wind up taking @Home another three years to get there. But no matter. In Silicon Valley, especially during those heady days, perception was reality. And since the smart money on Wall Street was convinced that John Doerr had a crystal ball, *everybody* listened. Especially the predators.

IN THEORY, @Home was an independent company that was responsible for plotting its own course. But in reality it had to answer to a cabal of powerful cable companies that often had competing political agendas. Needless to say, this didn't make life easy for either side.

Control was a constant source of friction. In February 1997 @Home set plans to launch service in one of TCI's biggest markets, Chicago. TCI planned to announce the launch on Presidents' Day. Worried that @Home's big news might get buried or ignored, Wolfram called up a handful of reporters and tipped them off. As a result of his quick thinking, the launch got some nice write-ups a few days early. That, in turn, prompted other reporters to call. Wolfram was pleased by all the coverage, and he thought TCI would be, too.

He thought wrong.

Bruce Ravenal, who oversaw TCI's @Home investment, called up Wolfram—screaming. Trying to conserve cash, TCI had only upgraded a few neighborhoods around Chicago. Ravenal had deliberately tried to play down the launch for fear that local regulators might force TCI to upgrade the entire system. Incensed by the splashy coverage, Ravenal called up Wolfram's boss, Dean Gilbert, and ordered him to fire Wolfram. Gilbert called up Wolfram and delivered the bad news.

Shaken, Wolfram went straight to Jermoluk and told him what had happened. The @Home chief shrugged. "You don't work for TCI," Jermoluk told him matter-of-factly. "You work for @Home. So don't worry about it—you're not fired."

TCI's status as a controlling shareholder seemed to give it a heightened sense of purpose. TCI's purpose, unfortunately, seemed to be taking care of its own financial interests, not @Home's.

Early on, TCI tried to convince @Home to build a dumbed-down version of the service for PCs equipped with Intel's 386 microprocessors. TCI thought such a version might be appealing to consumers who hadn't yet upgraded their PCs, providing another revenue opportunity for TCI. @Home said no dice. The 386 had been regarded as cutting-edge technology in 1985. But by 1996 it had been eclipsed by newer chips like the Pentium, which offered processing speeds that were up to six times faster. Jermoluk pointed out that @Home's focus was on forward-looking technology, not *old* technology.

TCI also tried to push @Home to focus on rural America. The suggestion was clearly intended to help TCI, whose own systems were scattered in a hodgepodge of smaller markets. (At the time, many TCI systems had 50,000 or fewer subscribers.) TCI hoped to score points with regulators and win support in Washington, which regarded TCI with suspicion because of its poor track record on customer service. Jermoluk refused. At the time, most of TCI's rural systems hadn't been upgraded, so they couldn't support @Home, anyway.

Cox and Comcast also had some complaints. Their biggest one, by far, was the fee splits. Under the Master Distribution Agreement, or MDA, the cable operators had to share their @Home revenues in a 65–35 split, with the cable operators keeping the bigger piece of the pie. Cox and Comcast felt they deserved a much higher percentage of the split. They pointed out that the @Home service was riding on their upgraded cable TV lines. In addition, they were the ones selling the service and tending to customers. In short, they wanted to treat @Home just like ESPN, MTV, or any other programmer. Jermoluk was unimpressed. He countered that @Home wasn't just another part of the channel lineup, it was a whole new way to driving cable TV penetration. On top of that, the MDA, which laid out the fee splits, was iron clad. And nobody knew that better than Jermoluk, because he'd personally written most of it. Cox and Comcast refused to cede the point, and kept on arguing.

Most of the grousing was harmless posturing. For all its huffing and puffing, TCI recognized that @Home's value was inextricably intertwined with its ability to lead, not follow, the digital wave into the future. The bellyaching about @Home's fees was also predictable. Cable operators are always looking for ways to shave pennies off their operating costs. Or, better yet, get somebody else to pay the freight. The cable industry even has a term for it: OPM, short for Other People's Money. (Pronounced "o-pum") Using OPM is a way of life in the cable industry, and nobody did it better than Cox, and Comcast. With the possible exception of John Malone, who'd actually coined the term.

Jermoluk took it all in stride. Owing to the way he had come into @Home—on a pedestal, thanks to the hearty endorsements of John Malone and John Doerr—he had a lot of clout on the board. And he wasn't shy about expressing himself, especially when it came to protecting @Home's interests. But he also recognized that TCI and the other cable operators wielded a lot of influence, so he did what he could, within reason, to accommodate their needs.

———

IN THE SPRING OF 1997, a dark cloud settled over the cable television industry. Many cable stocks were trading at or near record lows. Everybody felt the financial pain, especially TCI. By then, Malone had already shut down TCI's capital program. Trying to conserve cash, he also delayed or canceled dozens of equipment orders. TCI's credit rating, meantime, was teetering on the edge of junk. Regulators were also complaining. TCI's service quality was eroding along with the morale of its battered workforce. Needless to say, TCI's upgrade efforts skidded to a halt. The problem, however, was that TCI needed to keep rolling out @Home at a steady clip. If it didn't, TCI ran the risk of losing its dominance on the @Home board. (Under the MPA, all the carriers had installation benchmarks they had to meet.) That, of course, was exactly what Cox and Comcast had been hoping all along.

Jermoluk, had his hands full. @Home was running on fumes, and he needed a big infusion of cash to take it to the next level. TCI and the other cable operators were in no mood to step up with additional funding. But they agreed to consider it, in exchange for a bigger piece of @Home. Jermoluk refused. Life was already tough enough with all the competing interests and political agendas on the @Home board. About the last thing he wanted to do was turn up the volume by giving even more control to his cable backers. But the problem remained: He needed more money.

Since it was clear that TCI and the others weren't going to help, he made a counterproposal: How about bringing in a couple of big strategic investors? Some of the @Home directors thought he was dreaming. Cable stocks were crashing. Not only that, but @Home's most visible backer, TCI, was struggling financially, and everybody knew it.

Jermoluk refused to yield. Owing to his many years at SGI, he had a lot of contacts at the country's biggest technology companies. Jermoluk was convinced he could leverage those relationships into easy money for @Home. TCI and the others didn't think he'd have much luck. But since Jermoluk was so insistent, they decided to let him try.

With that, Jermoluk put on his salesman's hat and hit the road in search of funding. He immediately went after @Home's suppliers, among others, using the venture's long-term growth potential as the hook. It was a smart move. After all, if @Home prospered so would they. It worked.

Before long, Jermoluk had managed to cobble together a small group of investors that included some of the biggest names in technology: Motorola, Sun Microsystems, and Bay Networks among them. In announcing the private placement, Jermoluk told his public relations staff to include as many numbers as possible in the press release so that reporters could easily calculate @Home's market valuation. There was a good reason for that. Motorola and the others, as it turned out, had agreed to buy a 4.5 percent stake in @Home for a rich $48 million. That left the broadband upstart with a staggering market value of $1.07 *billion*.

That caught *everybody's* attention.

As soon as the release hit the news wires, @Home was flooded with calls. Reporters, many of whom had dismissed @Home as little more than a technology experiment, were incredulous. Other reporters just couldn't believe it. Literally. David Banks, a veteran reporter for *The Wall Street Journal* in San Francisco, called up Wolfram just to make sure there wasn't a typo. When Wolfram assured him that the numbers were correct, Banks was stunned. "This valuation is outrageous," he told Wolfram. "You guys are out of your mind."

Banks had a point. @Home only had about 5,000 subscribers. Its @Work product for the business market had a grand total of just *five* customers. @Home was battling a spate of escalating service problems related to its cutting-edge technology. It was also unclear if @Home's cable backers, who were squabbling constantly, would be able to set aside their differences and work together collegially. @Home's biggest benefactor, TCI, was in financial distress. There was also the matter of @Home's profits: There weren't any. @Home was bleeding red ink like crazy, and probably would be for years.

But all that said, @Home's market valuation, was, indeed, $1.07 billion. And that suddenly made the cable TV experiment known as @Home a broadband giant of epic proportions.

@Home quietly filed for an initial public offering, or IPO, that May. By taking @Home public, Jermoluk hoped to raise even more cash and also capitalize on the market's growing enthusiasm for broadband. Investors who perused the IPO filing got their first glimpse of @Home's finances. As with any startup, the numbers were ugly. For the first quarter ended March 31, 1997, @Home revealed that it had racked up losses of

$11.7 million, and revenues of $806,000. For the calendar year 1996, its first full year of operations, @Home recorded a loss of $24.5 million, and revenues of just $676,000. Still, if you believed John Doerr and John Malone—and a lot of people did—the venture's upside potential was enormous.

THE FIRST PREDATOR showed up in June. And it was a big one.

In a bombshell announcement, Microsoft said that it planned to invest $1 billion in Comcast. The cable giant, which had been trying for years to get its hooks in the cable TV business, basically said what John Malone had been preaching for years: that the cable TV pipe was the superhighway to the future. Microsoft said the TV and PC were about to merge, and it didn't want to miss out on the coming gold rush. Wall Street, which had been pummeling cable stocks into submission, did a collective gasp at the audacity of the move—and promptly sent cable stocks soaring. Investors' rush to embrace cable said as much about the psychology of Wall Street as it did about the promise of broadband. Even if you really didn't believe in convergence, Microsoft's strong endorsement was impossible to ignore.

The timing, for @Home, couldn't have been better. By the time its IPO came up the following month, in July, cable stocks were red-hot.

The opening price was set at $10.50. That was well over the $7 that had been expected. In the face of heavy demand, @Home increased the number of shares it planned to offer by a full 1 million, for a total of 9 million shares. It was a smart move. On the first day of trading, @Home's shares *opened* at $24 7/8, a 130 percent increase over the IPO price, and never looked back. The shares whipsawed up and down in heavy trading throughout the day, finally closing at $17. More than 12 million shares traded hands. By the time it was all over, @Home had raised $94.5 million in new capital, leaving it with a market value of $2 billion. Not bad for a company with no profits, few customers, and only a cursory game plan.

RIGHT AFTER THE IPO, @Home went into a serious building mode. Jermoluk would later refer to it as @Home's "good period."

And, indeed, it was. Flush with cash and imbued with a renewed sense of purpose thanks to the run up in cable stocks, @Home started the painstaking task of turning its blue-sky concept into a real business. @Home secured its first real office space—a two-story building in Redwood City, California, in the heart of Silicon Valley. The building, a pre-World War II space, wasn't fancy, to say the least. It had concrete walls, and fistfuls of electrical cords hung from the ceiling like jungle vines. To pump up the urban feel of the place, Jermoluk encouraged employees to paint graffiti on the walls. They responded by filling the walls with a gallery of artistic designs, using chalk, spray paint, and a rainbow of felt-tip pens to leave their indelible marks. Jermoluk loved it. To him, @Home's stark space was the perfect counter-punch to the plush paneled offices of its cable TV owners. It also spoke volumes about @Home's ethos, which was firmly rooted in Silicon Valley and its hip, edgy ways.

Jermoluk, a native Hawaiian with a shock of blond hair, went out of his way to play up the cultural difference. He purposely eschewed the big corner office in favor of a regular cubicle. He kept his custom-painted surfboard propped up in the corner for fast runs to the beach. Hewing to the Valley's tradition of throwing beer bashes for employees, @Home rolled in the kegs every Friday afternoon. Jermoluk, who was worth millions by then, swilled beer along with everybody else.

Jermoluk reveled in doing things his own way. Which is to say, *not* the cable way. He used the company cafeteria for employee meetings. (In the early days, he used to hold the meetings in his cubicle, surfboard and all.) During these all-hands meetings, Jermoluk would haul his lanky frame on top of the Coke vending machine so he could see everybody. After a while, it became his de facto podium. Employees loved it. When *Dateline,* the NBC newsmagazine, showed up to film a segment about @Home, the piece showed Jermoluk cheering employees along from his perch on top of the Coke machine. @Home's cable backers were appalled. Jermoluk was delighted.

By then @Home was one of the hottest startups in Silicon Valley, and everybody wanted to go along for the ride. As @Home's payroll grew, so did the internal debates about the direction of the company. With so many influences—the company was home to an odd mixture of Internet, media, and cable types—staff meetings were lively. Media types were quick to envision a futuristic service with all sorts of cool digital add-ons; @Home's engineers were just as quick to push back with long discourses on the challenges of trying to turn blue sky into a marketable product. The debates raged on for hours at a time.

Hindery, meantime, was running hard to whip TCI into shape. By then he had been promising Wall Street that TCI would lead, not follow, the cable industry into the Digital Age. But the hard reality was that TCI needed a miracle—or deep-pocketed investor—to help speed things along.

Anxious to reel in AT&T as a strategic partner, Hindery came up with an idea: @Phone. The plan called for AT&T to use TCG's local networks to offer AT&T-branded local phone service across the country. AT&T, in turn, would help TCI upgrade its cable TV networks in major markets. There was just one hitch: Hindery didn't have the authority to do the deal. TCG was jointly controlled by TCI, Cox, and Comcast, so there were other shareholders' rights to consider.

Jermoluk went nuts when he found out. (Cox and Comcast were just as upset. But since they didn't want to butt heads with Hindery, they let Jermoluk deal with it.) When Hindery refused to budge, Jermoluk took his complaints directly to Malone. By then Malone had already had an earful from Cox and Comcast, so he wasn't surprised by the call. Malone quickly sided with Jermoluk, thus ending the @Phone debate. The episode would mark the beginning of a running feud between Jermoluk and Hindery.

IN JUNE 1998, AT&T announced plans to buy TCI for $48 billion. Embedded in the purchase price was a $5.5 billion cash payment for a number of other assets, including Liberty's 26 percent stake in @Home. Since TCI had 58 percent voting control, AT&T appeared to be buying a swing vote on the powerful @Home board.

But like they say, appearances can be deceiving.

Unbeknownst to AT&T, the real power brokers on the board were Cox and Comcast. TCI by then had fallen behind on its customer targets, triggering a penalty in the form of expanded "veto" rights for Cox and Comcast. The upshot: Cox and Comcast could neutralize TCI's voice—and now AT&T's voice—on almost any given issue. The power shift, ironically, had occurred while the AT&T-TCI talks were still in progress. Hindery, who was leading the talks for TCI, was understandably not anxious for AT&T to find out. Jermoluk claimed Hindery instructed him to not mention the change to Armstrong. The @Home chief told Hindery he wouldn't lie if Armstrong asked him a direct question, but he said he wouldn't go out of his way to clue him in, either.

Jermoluk, truth be told, didn't really care that AT&T was about to overpay for TCI's diminished @Home rights. He also didn't care if Hindery hung himself trying to double-talk AT&T. But what Jermoluk did care about—deeply—was how AT&T's acquisition of TCI might affect @Home's long-term business interests. Things were already complicated enough with all the competing political interests of TCI, Cox, and Comcast. It was anybody's guess what would happen to @Home's big, dysfunctional family once AT&T showed up.

It didn't take long to find out.

On the day the AT&T-TCI deal was announced, AOL put out a press release saying that it looked forward to getting "unfettered access" to all of AT&T's cable systems. That was a straight shot across the bow of the cable industry, because whatever rules applied to AT&T were, by definition, going to extend to the rest of the cable industry. Cable operators shuddered. Until then, they'd managed to contain the open access argument pretty well. But now that AT&T was part of the cable TV club that was going to be a lot harder. Why? Size. Even TCI, as big as it was, didn't have the heft or reach of an AT&T. But the two together had enough visibility and clout to influence the balance of power in the emerging broadband world. AOL smartly recognized the shift, which was one reason Case had been so fast to pounce.

Armstrong, schooled in the ways of Big Blue, had a different view. At IBM, open architectures were standard. They were also regarded as a customer-friendly way of doing business. The AT&T chief basically applied the same logic to the cable TV industry: so long as the terms and conditions were right, he thought open access wasn't such a bad idea. The problem, however, was that AT&T, owing to its new status as No. 1 cable operator, suddenly had a lot of influence over the rest of the industry. Any stance it took on open access, by definition, was going to affect everybody else. And all his well-intentioned, Blue-tinged explanations didn't change that bruising fact. Comcast and the other operators were keen to the problem, which was one reason they were practically having heart palpitations. About the last thing they needed, or wanted, was to have the new leader of the U.S. cable industry speaking out in favor of open access—in any form.

Sensing a rare opportunity, the Bells came out swinging. So did AOL. Before long, lobbyists for both camps had descended on Washington like a swarm of cicadas—and the shrill sounds of their insistent demands for open access were deafening.

In mid-December, the drama took a turn. With the open-access issue still raging in Washington, Jermoluk quietly set plans to merge @Home with Excite, the big Web portal. By merging Excite into @Home, Jermoluk hoped to create a Web giant that could challenge AOL. Hindery went crazy when he found out. In addition to drawing the attention of regulators, he was worried that AOL and the Bells would use the Excite deal to push their political agendas in Washington. That, in turn, might hurt AT&T once the TCI deal closed. (The deal would close a few months later, on March 9.)

Jermoluk didn't care. His No. 1 priority was growing @Home's market value, not watching AT&T's backside. As far as he was concerned, AT&T was the one that had created the open access mess, and it was up to AT&T to clean it up. Cox and Comcast weren't wildly in favor of the Excite deal. But they didn't try to block it, either, especially since John Doerr was pushing it. The $6.7 billion merger was formally announced on January 19, 1999. Just as Hindery had predicted, AOL and the Bells used the news as an excuse to step up their drumbeat in Washington.

THINGS CAME TO A HEAD the following month. The showdown took place at the Pro-Am Celebrity Golf Tournament in Pebble Beach, California.

Armstrong and John Petrillo were coming in for the tournament, which was being sponsored by AT&T. Armstrong had never spent much time with Jermoluk. He thought the relaxed atmosphere of the famed golf course, with its spectacular views of the rocky California coast, might provide a nice setting to talk. Jermoluk had another agenda entirely.

The trio agreed to meet at AT&T's hospitality suite, which was located near the first fairway. Jermoluk arrived prepared. The Silicon Valley grapevine was rife with rumors about a pending deal between Yahoo! and AT&T, and Jermoluk wanted answers. A few minutes into the conversation, Jermoluk fixed an icy stare in Armstrong's direction and asked him point blank if AT&T was in talks with Yahoo! Armstrong seemed taken aback by the question, and immediately reassured him that no deal was in the works. Petrillo did the same. Jermoluk had little choice but to put the Yahoo! matter aside and move on to other business. His uneasiness, however, persisted. As it turned out, there was a good reason for that.

On Monday morning at 6 A.M., the call came in.

Hindery told Jermoluk that AT&T was less than an hour away from announcing a big strategic deal with Yahoo! The agreement would give half of @Home's opening page—the part reserved for AT&T's local content—to @Home's archrival. Jermoluk was livid, and threatened to sue. The release never went out.

With Armstrong's assurances still ringing in his ears, Jermoluk called an emergency meeting of the entire @Home board. Hindery tried to get Jermoluk to reconsider. He refused.

The special session was held in New York about a week later. All the heavyweights showed up: John Malone of TCI; John Doerr of Kleiner, Perkins; Brian Roberts of Comcast and Jim Robbins of Cox; and, of course, the soon-to-be AT&T team of Mike Armstrong and Leo Hindery. As soon as the TCI-AT&T deal closed, Hindery would jump the fence and become AT&T's new cable chief. Everybody in the room was keenly aware of that fact.

Jermoluk arrived loaded for bear. As soon as he walked into the conference room, he distributed four-inch-thick binders that laid out, in excruciating detail, why the Yahoo! deal didn't work—legally, strategically, contractually, or commonsense-wise. The first page was emblazoned with "Leo's Deal" in big, bold letters. (As if anybody was unclear as to whom Jermoluk blamed.) The report was scathing. In addition to stomping all over @Home's partnership rights, Jermoluk argued that the transaction would demolish @Home's value in the marketplace.

Hindery tried to defend himself. He didn't get much help. Even Armstrong, who was arguably the one person in the room who could have saved his hide, refused to come to his rescue. Pressed to explain, Armstrong told Jermoluk and the other board members that he'd never given Hindery the authority to do the deal. All he'd ever done, he swore, was to ask Hindery to explore the *possibility* of a deal. That's it. Nobody had much to say to that. The suggestion that Hindery would blast off on his own didn't strike a lot of people around the table as particularly unusual. The person who seemed the most surprised, by far, was Armstrong.

The cable execs at the table tried to be respectful. After all, Hindery was about to become the president of AT&T's new cable business. Nobody wanted to rattle his cage too much for fear that he'd retaliate later. The sole exception was Jermoluk. He'd despised Hindery ever since he'd tried to jam through the @Phone deal, and the Yahoo! episode had only confirmed what he'd always believed—that Hindery was a loose cannon who needed to be taken out.

John Malone, who was still Hindery's boss, didn't say a whole lot, But all you had to do was take one look at the stone-serious expression on his face to know that he wasn't too happy. By then he'd been getting an earful about his No. 2 for months, and he was tired of it. Malone used to tell people that Hindery reminded him of a kid he knew back in college: To eke out a passing grade, the kid would go from professor to professor, hat in hand, and say "So-and-so won't fail me if you don't." The ruse worked for a while; then people got wise.

Hindery had a similar style. To jam through a deal quickly, Hindery would convince somebody to merely "consider" a deal, then use that as leverage to get the next guy to agree, and on down the line. In reality, nobody had really agreed to anything. But by leading people into believing that the "deal" was set, Hindery could, on occasion, move things along at a rapid clip.

Malone had been burned by the gambit himself. On the TCI deal, Malone had found it almost impossible to figure out what was in process, and what was actually done. After a while, he started riding close herd on Hindery just to stay in the loop. Malone asked Jerry Kern, his longtime lawyer, to do the same. Bruce Ravenal also joined in on the Hindery Watch. Before long, they were all spending way too much time just trying to manage Hindery.

Malone was hugely grateful to Hindery for all his work on behalf of TCI and its shareholders. And he was particularly impressed by that selling price, $48 billion. But by the time the TCI deal was done, Malone had largely, and sadly, concluded that it was probably time for Hindery to go. He told Jermoluk in a private moment that one of the best things about the TCI deal—besides the rich selling price, that is—was getting rid of Hindery. Burning bridges and breaking glass was fine so long as you didn't plan to stick around. But it wasn't Malone's style. Jermoluk, as you might expect, didn't disagree.

11

MediaOne—
GOING FOR BROKE

I T WAS FRIDAY, March 19, 1999. John Malone was out taking a
look at a cattle operation just north of Denver when he got a call on
his cell phone. What the caller had to say caused Malone to stop
dead in his tracks.

Comcast was planning to buy MediaOne Group, the big Denver-
based cable operator, for a staggering $60 billion. The negotiations were
expected to wrap up over the weekend. Assuming there were no last-
minute hitches, the megamerger would be announced early Monday
morning.

As soon as the conversation ended, Malone put in an urgent call to
Mike Armstrong. The AT&T chief was crestfallen. He'd just spent $48
billion to buy TCI's bragging rights to being the biggest cable TV operator in America. Once Comcast merged with MediaOne, however, it
would rival AT&T in size. Standing in Comcast's shadow wasn't exactly
what he had in mind.

"What should we do?" Armstrong asked, his voice laced with concern.

AT&T's options were limited. It only had one deal currency: its
famed "T" common stock. "T" was owned by thousands of small, risk-
averse investors. If AT&T tried to make a run for MediaOne and things
went haywire, the stock price could get crushed. Comcast's investor base
had a completely different profile, so it didn't have that problem.

Malone didn't have to think twice.

"Nothing," he shot back. "They have a currency. We don't. Let it go."

IF ONLY ARMSTRONG had listened.

Instead, the AT&T chief did what almost anybody in his position would have done under the same circumstances—he conferred with his senior management team. His two top advisors were hardened deal makers with a soft spot for cable. Asking Dan Somers and Leo Hindery if they wanted to take out Comcast was like asking a kid perched on the front step of a candy store with his nose pressed to the glass if he wanted to go in: The answer was yes, yes, and yes.

Comcast's deal was announced Monday morning. It was March 22. Brian Roberts, Comcast's president, luxuriated in the limelight of what was clearly the crowning achievement of his career. "This is a breathtaking moment in the history of Comcast," Roberts said in a prepared statement. The merger, he bragged, would create "the world's largest broadband provider." The message wasn't lost on anybody: AT&T was about to become an also-ran.

Hindery wasn't so sure about that.

The TCI president had saddled up at AT&T thinking he was going to be sitting atop the biggest cable TV operation in America. Now Comcast was threatening to undercut AT&T's—and by association Hindery's—clout. He didn't take the intrusion lightly. Known as King Leo in the cable industry, Hindery took pride in his mantle as the cable industry's top power broker. He wasn't ready to hand over his crown just yet. And he certainly wasn't willing to give it to a pup like Brian Roberts.

It wasn't just a grudge match, however. Hindery had hoped, eventually, to buy MediaOne, then use it as bait to get Comcast and the other big operators to sign long-term phone deals with AT&T. Without MediaOne in his back pocket, Hindery worried that the phone pacts might be a tough sell.

Dan Somers, AT&T's chief financial officer, wasn't concerned about Comcast, the staggering price, or almost anything else, for that matter. To him, it all came down to simple arithmetic. To beat Comcast, all AT&T had to do was come back with an offer of at least $60 billion, pump it full of cash and other incentives, then let her rip. All in all, it was a very Dan Somers way of looking at things.

Privately, Somers wasn't so sure that MediaOne was critical to AT&T's larger strategic goals. He also wasn't sold on the idea of doing two back-to-back blockbuster deals—too much room for mayhem. And if AT&T didn't really *need* MediaOne, why put the balance sheet—not to mention investors—through all that angst? But Somers didn't say any of this out loud. The way he looked at it, it wasn't his job to tell the AT&T chairman what to do. If Armstrong wanted to make a run for MediaOne, he'd walk through walls to make it happen.

Armstrong's first instinct was to let MediaOne go. Comcast had beaten AT&T to the punch fair and square. The timing also wasn't so great. The $48 billion TCI deal had just closed, and it was going to take a lot of work to transform TCI into something that was worthy of the AT&T name. Wall Street was watching—and waiting. So were regulators. This was no time to be taking his eye off the ball. There was also that sticker price: $60 billion. That was a big nut, even for AT&T. Armstrong wasn't interested in getting into a bidding war. Maybe it was better to just sit this one out.

Amos Hostetter strongly disagreed. The co-founder and former chairman of Continental Cablevision told Armstrong flat out that he'd be foolish to let Comcast walk off with the MediaOne prize. MediaOne was a once-in-a-lifetime opportunity. He also thought that Comcast's bid price of $60 billion sorely undervalued MediaOne's rich cache of assets. So don't wait, Hostetter urged, or you'll be sorry.

In hindsight, Armstrong would have done well to send the cable billionaire packing. The problem? Hostetter's interests were fatally, and fundamentally, at odds with those of AT&T. Hostetter and his family owned about 13 percent of MediaOne's stock, so he stood to *personally* benefit if AT&T stepped up with a richer offer.

John Malone's advice, on the other hand, was coming from an entirely different direction. Malone's wealth was tied up in AT&T, so he was concerned about anything that might put downward pressure on the stock price. And as Malone was keenly aware, nothing can drive down a stock price faster than being on the wrong side of a bidding war. A bidding war, of course, was exactly what Hostetter was hoping for. Because if MediaOne's stock price went through the roof, so, too, would the value of his personal net worth.

Hostetter put on quite a show. In pushing AT&T to make a run for MediaOne, he talked passionately, and endlessly, about the fact that investors would lose their voice if Comcast triumphed. But the real issue, many suspected, was *Hostetter's* voice. Comcast had two classes of stock: a high-voting version for the founder and his family members, and another for everybody else. Since Hostetter was in the "everybody else" category that meant he was going to get stuck with low-voting Comcast shares once the deal closed. That's not to say that Hostetter wasn't genuinely concerned about Comcast's voting structure. But that is to say that he had a huge personal stake in the outcome.

Revenge, in all likelihood, was also a motivator. In 1996 Hostetter agreed to sell Continental to MediaOne, then called U S West Media Group, for a cool $4.7 billion in cash and stock, and the assumption of $7 billion in debt. Hostetter had founded the company in Boston in 1963, and he was adamant that it not be moved. Unfortunately, he never bothered to put this bedrock requirement in writing. Instead, he relied on the handshake promise of MediaOne's chairman and CEO, Charles "Chuck" Lillis, to honor his wishes.

Big mistake. Right after the transaction closed, Lillis quietly started laying plans to move Continental's headquarters to Denver, where MediaOne was based. Lillis felt he had no choice. Even though he'd just spent $12 billion to buy Continental, it was clear to him that Hostetter had every intention to carrying on in a business-as-usual fashion. To a certain extent the whole thing was just a battle of egos. But since Lillis was the CEO and Hostetter wasn't, there was never any doubt as to who was going to win that war of wills.

In a last-ditch attempt to stop the move, Hostetter flew out to Denver and made a personal plea to the MediaOne board. It didn't do any good. Hostetter resigned shortly thereafter. Most of his Boston-based managers followed him out the door. Hostetter, a prideful sort who wasn't used to losing, refused to paint his resignation as amicable. Instead, he issued his own press release, citing "irreconcilable differences" for his abrupt departure. Lillis wasn't mentioned by name. But behind the scenes the aggrieved billionaire left no doubt as to whom he blamed.

BY THE TIME Comcast announced plans to buy MediaOne in the spring of 1999, Hostetter had been stewing over his ugly parting for the better part of two years. And he finally had a chance to settle the score.

On March 25, just three days after Comcast's announcement, he sent a letter to MediaOne complaining about the deal's terms. Hostetter also asked for permission to be let out of a standstill agreement so that he could try to land a higher bid. "Although time is limited, I believe that you have a duty under these circumstances to permit me to seek superior value and terms," Hostetter wrote in his letter. MediaOne gave Hostetter the green light about a week later, on March 31. The very next day, Hostetter picked up the phone and called AT&T.

For Hostetter, the idea of turning the tables on Comcast in such a high-profile fashion must have bordered on delicious. In taking aim at the Comcast deal, he was openly challenging the wisdom of the same MediaOne board that had dismissed him so lightly two years earlier. And he was challenging the wisdom of Chuck Lillis, in particular, who had engineered the deal.

The news that Hostetter was breaking ranks and throwing in with AT&T was greeted with cheers over at MediaOne. And nobody was more pleased, perhaps, than Lillis. After all, if AT&T stepped in with a big counteroffer, that only meant one thing: MediaOne's selling price was going up.

Hostetter wasn't the only one who didn't think much of Lillis. A former academic-turned-businessman, Lillis had a high-handed manner that grated on a lot of cable TV executives. Lillis's habit of sermonizing about the cable business—to veterans who had grown up in the cable trenches—probably didn't help. All that said there's no denying that Lillis had a good bead on the future trajectory of the industry. Convinced that upgraded cable TV lines would eventually trump the Bells' copper pipes, Lillis used to talk up the promise of broadband to every opportunity. Since most cable veterans had no idea what broadband was, nobody paid him much mind. They just assumed that Lillis, who never seemed to tire of hearing himself talk, was blowing more hot air. They figured wrong.

Lillis also turned out to be a savvy deal maker, as demonstrated by his handling of Comcast and AT&T. By the summer of 1998, Lillis had largely concluded that he needed to grow MediaOne's footprint to make it a major force in the emerging world of broadband. His top strategist, Doug Holmes, agreed. Together they started calling on America's top cable operators. They met with Cox, Adelphia, and Century, among others. Nobody wanted to sell. Brian Roberts of Comcast wasn't interested in selling either. But he was interested in buying. Lillis wasn't so sure he wanted to sell to Comcast. His preferred buyer, by far, was AT&T. Why? MediaOne and AT&T both believed in the promise of cable telephony. AT&T's corporate governance was also similar.

If Lillis had been an old-line cable operator, he probably would have just picked up the phone and given AT&T the lowdown. But Lillis thought that wouldn't have been cricket. Moreover, he thought AT&T had ample time to make its move. By then Wall Street bankers had been telling MediaOne for months that AT&T was coming, but nothing had ever happened. Cable values, meantime, were peaking and Comcast was offering a rich 32 percent premium for MediaOne's shares.

What to do?

Lillis decided to take the money. It was a cagey move. If AT&T didn't show up, MediaOne still had a rich offer of $60 billion on the table. But if AT&T did show up, it would be forced to negotiate off that $60 billion baseline. So the floor, in effect, was set. All that said, MediaOne's deal team was convinced that AT&T would come calling. And for two very good reasons: Amos Hostetter and Leo Hindery.

Holmes assumed that Hostetter would go a little crazy at the mere thought of losing his big stick—his voting rights. Hindery was the clincher. By then Hindery had been telling almost anybody who would listen that he thought Lillis was a piece of crap for reneging on his handshake deal with Hostetter over Boston. As far as Holmes was concerned, the teaming of Hostetter and Hindery, two prideful cable veterans with an axe to grind with Lillis, was just about perfect.

To draw AT&T into the battle, Lillis insisted, over Comcast's objections, on including a clause in their merger agreement that allowed MediaOne to entertain "superior" offers for a period of time. Roberts got the hint. He was so concerned about AT&T sneaking in and stealing his prize that he tried to get the window set at just five days. Lillis refused, insisting on a full 45. Roberts also wanted a $3 billion breakup fee. Lillis agreed to half that amount, $1.5 billion. That was okay by Roberts. The way he looked at it, even AT&T, as big as it was, would have to think twice about breaking up his dream deal if it had to cough up that kind of cash on top of the huge purchase price. He couldn't have been more wrong about that.

BACK AT AT&T, the running feud between Leo Hindery and John Zeglis was turning ugly. Armstrong, always anxious to help, did what he could to smooth things out between them. That only made a bad situation worse.

Hindery, on paper, was supposed to report to Zeglis, who in turn reported directly to Armstrong. Hindery had agreed to the arrangement while the TCI deal was being negotiated. But as soon as the deal was signed, Hindery started balking. Armstrong was disappointed by Hindery's about-face. But in hindsight he only had himself to blame: Zeglis knew almost nothing about the cable TV business. Hindery, in sharp contrast, was a veteran of the cable TV wars. He was also famously difficult to manage. Nobody who knew the two men, even remotely, figured they'd work together very well. Except Armstrong, that is. Confident of his ability to manage people, the AT&T chief felt sure that he could win them over with time. Once they got into their new jobs, he assumed they'd set aside their personal differences to focus on the larger goal—saving AT&T. It was a very idealistic—some might say Big Blue—way of looking at things.

Working relations between Zeglis and Hindery broke down almost immediately. Part of that owed to their personal styles, which just didn't mix. Zeglis, reflecting his Midwestern roots and Harvard schooling, was polished and studied. Hindery, by contrast, was an explosion of energy and emotion. Whereas Zeglis embraced the Machine's plodding sense of order, Hindery despised it. Even their manner of dress was a study in opposites. Zeglis, an avid sailor and outdoorsman, cut a trim figure in his impeccably tailored suits. Even his beat-up leather briefcase exuded preppy cool. Hindery, a former stock car driver, embraced NASCAR chic. On his off-time, he often wore golf shirts emblazoned with company logos. The two men did have at least one thing in common, however: Sir Winston Churchill: They were both ardent admirers.

Zeglis and Hindery managed to be civil to each other in public. Behind the scenes, however, it was a constant food fight. Hindery openly bristled at Zeglis's constant attempts to manage him. Zeglis, in turn, found Hindery's cocky manner to be disrespectful, both to him, personally, as well as to the larger AT&T organization. Hindery's habit of ducking out of meetings, or refusing to attend them at all, didn't help. Adding to the psychodrama, both men aspired to succeed Armstrong as AT&T's chairman and CEO.

Armstrong, ever optimistic, hung in there. Trying to get Hindery and Zeglis to communicate better, he called them both into his office to talk things through—over and over again. He also took the two warring executives out for long, languid dinners. The outcome, in both cases, was exactly the same: So long as Armstrong was present, Hindery and Zeglis were congenial with each other. As soon as he wasn't, however, the backbiting turned fierce. In exasperation, Armstrong even turned to John Malone for advice. Malone told him what he *didn't* want to hear: That Hindery was basically unmanageable.

Just before the TCI merger closed in early March, Hindery moved in for his signature squeeze play: He told Armstrong point-blank that the reporting arrangement with Zeglis wasn't going to work. Moreover, he wasn't sure how long he would last if the arrangement wasn't changed. Armstrong got the message: Hindery wanted to report directly to Armstrong. Otherwise he was walking.

Armstrong was in a tough spot. By then he'd been telling Wall Street for almost a year that Hindery would be overseeing AT&T Broadband, which housed the Internet and cable assets. If Hindery walked, Armstrong was worried that he'd be left with a huge cable operation to manage—and nobody to manage it. In addition, a lot of TCI employees were loyal to Hindery. So it was possible that others would follow him out the door. The stakes were sky-high. No less than the future of AT&T was riding on the outcome of the cable strategy. Armstrong didn't want to take any chances.

A few days later, Armstrong called Zeglis into his office and delivered the bad news: Henceforth, Hindery would report directly to the chairman's office. Zeglis was crushed. He had hoped to use Broadband to prove his executive mettle, paving the way for him to go on to something much bigger—like the CEO's job. Now it was threatening to turn into a huge embarrassment.

Armstrong tried to soften the blow. He quickly reminded Zeglis that he would still have operational responsibility for Consumer Services and International, two major divisions that accounted for more than 60 percent of AT&T's annual revenues. Zeglis, schooled in the AT&T art of the pregnant pause, listened quietly. After a moment, he finally spoke. "It's okay," Zeglis said, the emotion draining out of his face. "I can live with it." He reinforced the same message to Armstrong a few days later. "Don't worry," he told Armstrong. "I can live with it. It's really okay."

But it *wasn't* okay. Armstrong's decision to back Hindery over the staid but solid AT&T veteran was, for Zeglis, the final indignity. By then Zeglis had been playing the role of the good lieutenant for more than a year, subjugating his pride and political ambitions for the greater good of AT&T. To go through all that only to have Armstrong give his backing to a loose cannon like Leo Hindery was beyond galling. He would not forget it.

HINDERY WASN'T THE ONLY one who was having trouble fitting in at AT&T. Bob Annunziata, the former head of Teleport, was also struggling. In classic AT&T style, the organization did what it could to make him feel at home—right up to the day the Machine chewed him up and spit him out like a paper shredder gone awry.

At a senior management meeting in October 1998, Annunziata openly marveled as Frank Ianna, the president of AT&T's Network Services unit, boasted that it only took AT&T 48 days to activate new phone lines for business customers. MCI's installation times, by comparison, were running at around 50 days, he proudly noted. All around the table, heads nodded in admiration. Except one, that is—Annunziata's.

"Mike, I don't know about you," Annunziata boomed, addressing his comments directly to the AT&T chairman, "but every meeting I go to [with customers] I'm getting my ass kicked."

His razor-sharp point wasn't lost on anybody: 48 days was completely unacceptable. His criticism carried a lot of weight. Annunziata was the new head of Business Services, and his religion was customer service. Annunziata threw out a challenge: How about slashing installation times to just 15 days for customers who were "off net"—not already on the Teleport network—and just five days for existing "on net" accounts. Even if Ianna's group couldn't meet the 15-day target, at least it would give AT&T an aggressive goal to shoot for. No pain, no gain, right?

Wrong.

AT&T didn't do things that way. Installation times were calculated on the basis of years of experience—there was nothing willy-nilly about them. Any new policy or procedure had to be carefully vetted and re- searched. To just make up a new policy on the spot like that was, well, it just wasn't done.

Armstrong loved it. To the dismay of many senior managers, Annun- ziata's proposal was later adopted for the entire Business Services organi- zation. In a nod to tradition, the directive was given an AT&T-style handle: "The 5–15 Rule." Needless to say, the Machine ground up a couple of gears on that one.

As a manager, Annunziata was smart, confident, and bursting with new ideas. In short, he was exactly the kind of executive that the bureau- cracy despised. At AT&T, slow and steady had always been preferred to fast and aggressive. Humility, or at least the appearance of humility, was also valued. It was no mistake that a lot of AT&T chairmen over the years had hailed from the Midwest. The heartland of America has always been known for its polite but plodding ways. That was AT&T.

Annunziata, a New Yorker by birth and in spirit, was the polar oppo- site of Midwest. He wasn't a big fan of meetings. And he particularly dis- liked the marathon sessions that defined the AT&T experience. After sitting through a few presentations with 50-plus slides—another AT&T hallmark—Annunziata called a time-out. Hoping to get his employees to focus on meaningful communication as opposed to pointless postur- ing, he fired off a memo saying that henceforth all slide presentations would be limited to just 10 slides. The Machine listened, and responded accordingly.

When the lights dimmed and the first slide hit the screen at the next meeting, Annunziata couldn't believe his eyes. Just as he had instructed, the presenter only had 10 slides, but each one had been divided into *four* quadrants, for a total of 40 points of discussion. Annunziata roared out loud with laughter. Nobody else seemed to get the joke. After that, the slide shows in his department got a lot shorter.

AT&T's NEW CABLE BUSINESS, meantime, was also having some adjustment issues.

As TCI's longtime technology chief, it was up to Tony Werner to oversee the massive upgrades that were critical to the deployment of AT&T-branded phone service. Shortly after the TCI deal had been announced, he started getting deluged with calls from AT&T's various division heads. One of the calls came from Frank Ianna, who had broad responsibility for AT&T's global network. Ianna suggested they set up a conference call to talk about TCI's networks. Werner agreed, and promptly arranged the meeting.

The next day, Werner and his team spent almost two hours bringing Ianna and his group up to speed. Over the course of the wide-ranging discussion, Werner and his managers shared a host of confidential details about TCI's technology plans. By the time the meeting wrapped up, Werner felt that he was off to a good start with his new partners at AT&T.

Or maybe not.

The very next day, Werner got a call from Mark Dzuban of AT&T Labs. Dzuban told Werner he wanted to set up a conference call between their two teams so they could talk about TCI's networks. Dzuban said his boss, Dave Nagel, also wanted to sit in.

Puzzled by the déjà vu nature of Dzuban's request, Werner pointed out that he'd given a briefing on that exact subject to Ianna and his group just 24 hours earlier. Dzuban exploded. "Why are you talking to them?" he demanded.

Werner was floored by his reaction, and quickly explained. Dzuban, however, was suspicious, and obliquely insinuated that Werner was just trying to sidestep Nagel's office. That was the last straw.

"Look," Werner shot back. "Ianna called. He seemed to be in a position of authority, so I talked to him. It was that simple."

But as Werner and other TCI execs were discovering, *nothing* at AT&T was ever simple.

Why all the fuss over TCI's technology plans? Just two words: funding levels. At AT&T, a person's political power was inextricably tied to the amount of revenue that his or her division generated. Ipso facto, more revenues equated to more power, bigger titles, better perks, etc. With budgets for in-house projects plummeting along with AT&T's fortunes, AT&T execs were scrambling to latch on to TCI. It was all part of the Machine's survival code, which, beneath its courtly surface, encouraged executives to eat or be eaten.

The attitude was a by-product of the AT&T culture, which had a strict social order. A person's stature was indicated by his or her "level," or "band." Jobs were ranked A-E. At the very bottom were the "A" employees, indicating low-level office help and the like; "E" was reserved for directors. Above that were the officers, including the CEO, CFO, and so on.

Titles were critical. Officers got to pick out their own furnishings and artwork. Everybody else had to pick out of a book that was sectioned off by—you guessed it—job level. The fixation on offices was deeply embedded. When TCI first agreed to merge with Bell Atlantic in 1993, Malone and other TCI executives were appalled at the sight of Bell employees scurrying around TCI's headquarters putting dibs on different offices.

AT&T titles were rife with larger meanings. Within the fishbowl of AT&T, there was a world of difference between a "marketing vice president" and a "vice president of marketing." The differentiator? If the functional description of the job—marketing, in this case—preceded the title, that meant the person was one of many with the same job. (Example: marketing vice president.) If, however, the title preceded the functional description, that meant the person was the only one with that particular job, indicating a very senior-level person. (Example: vice president of marketing.)

Mindless? Of course. Time consuming? You bet. But that was the AT&T way.

Perhaps not surprisingly, outsiders often struggled with AT&T's maddening emphasis on form over function. On one occasion, Milo

Medin of @Home was invited to talk with AT&T employees about the future of technology. Walking in the door, Medin happened to notice a big "C" on a placard at the entrance of the auditorium. When he asked somebody to explain, he was told matter-of-factly that it meant nobody below a C level—designating a middle- to senior-level manager—was allowed to attend. Medin, who had grown up in the egalitarian world of engineers and computer scientists, was dismayed. Nobody at AT&T gave it a second thought.

In addition to insulating employees from each other, the culture's preoccupation with invisible boundaries also hampered the organization's ability to step back and see the bigger picture.

Consider the Fiber Mystery.

On another occasion Medin went to Atlanta to meet with AT&T's network engineers. @Home's traffic was growing rapidly, and Medin hoped to secure long-term capacity from AT&T. A few minutes into the meeting, Medin inquired about the status of AT&T's vaunted fiber network—fiber-optic glass lines that are capable of carrying massive amounts of voice, data, and video content. AT&T rarely talked about how many miles of fiber it had installed, or even where they were. On AT&T's Web site there was only a very general description. And no map.

Pressed by Medin, one of the AT&T engineers reluctantly put up a slide that showed AT&T's entire fiber deployment. According to the map, AT&T had a staggering amount of fiber installed—around 35,000 miles. Qwest, which had one of the biggest fiber networks in the country, only had about 18,000 miles. The engineer proudly pointed out that AT&T had the largest fiber network of any carrier in the United States.

Medin was puzzled, and promptly asked why AT&T had never bothered to advertise that fact. The AT&T engineers had no idea. They were only responsible for the network, they explained.

Moving on, Medin quickly deduced that AT&T had 16 "channels," signified by a different color on a single fiber, installed at key points throughout the United States. But he could also see that fully half the network was sitting idle.

"Great," Medin told the group, zeroing in on the eight idle channels, "we'll take these."

Silence all around the table.

"What's wrong?" Medin asked. "The channels don't work?"

"No, they work."

Stone silence.

"They're not available?"

"No, they're available."

More silence.

"So what's the problem?"

After some gentle prodding, one of the AT&T engineers finally spilled the beans: AT&T's customer service systems had never been upgraded to handle "trouble tickets"—customer complaints—on those eight channels. As a result, they simply weren't being used—by anybody.

Medin was aghast. For want of a simple software upgrade, quite literally, half of AT&T's fiber capacity was sitting idle, robbing the company, potentially, of tens of millions of dollars in lost revenues.

With some prodding from Medin, the engineers later asked Basking Ridge to push AT&T's software division to do the needed upgrades so that the eight channels could be put into service. AT&T complied, and was rewarded for its efforts with a $100 million contract from @Home.

ARMSTRONG DECIDED TO go for broke.

Somers, Hindery, and Hostetter were all convinced that AT&T needed to make a mad dash for MediaOne, if only to make sure that Comcast didn't trump AT&T in the marketplace. Gene Sykes, a Wall Street heavyweight who was the head of Goldman Sachs's media practice, also supported the deal. In the face of that kind of experience and intellectual firepower, Armstrong decided to ignore the butterflies in his belly and make his move.

Determined to topple Comcast, AT&T came back with its counteroffer. And what a staggering offer it was: $62 billion. About a third of it, $20 billion, was in cash. The rest was in stock and assumed debt. At $62 billion, AT&T was offering to pay a rich 26 percent premium for MediaOne's shares, which were trading for around $69. The bid represented a 17 percent premium over the value of Comcast's all-stock offer, which had shrunk in value thanks to downward pressure on its stock price. To give MediaOne some extra comfort about the stability of its currency, AT&T agreed to put a "collar" around its stock price. If AT&T's stock price fell out of the collar before the deal closed, the telecom giant said it would kick in even more cash—up to $3.6 billion on top of the $20 billion it was already offering—to make up the difference. AT&T also agreed to give MediaOne shareholders full voting rights. That was a straight shot across the jaw of Comcast, which had only offered low-voting shares. And no collar.

Wall Street was stunned by AT&T's extreme generosity. So was Comcast. "It's simply breathtaking," one Comcast executive said on the day the offer was unveiled.

MediaOne agreed, and on May 6, 1999, it formally accepted AT&T's offer. Comcast, which had tried in vain to round up a strategic investor to help beat back AT&T, terminated its merger agreement the same day.

As a consolation prize for busting up its deal, AT&T agreed to sell Comcast nearly half—2 million—of MediaOne's 5 million customers, including 1.5 million subscribers in the Philadelphia market that Comcast had lusted after for years. In return, Comcast agreed to sign a big phone pact with AT&T. The one caveat was that AT&T had to get two other big cable operators to do the same. Comcast also collected a $1.5 billion breakup fee.

As for Amos Hostetter, he made out best of all. In addition to getting a 26 percent boost in the value of his MediaOne holdings, the aggrieved billionaire got to keep his voting rights. He also got a big dose of revenge: As soon the merger closed, AT&T said Hostetter would become the new non-executive chairman of AT&T Broadband—based in Boston, of course. In addition, he got a coveted seat on the AT&T board. The circular nature of Hostetter's sweet payback was so improbable, yet so complete, that it bordered on Shakespearean perfection.

AT THE TIME it probably didn't seem like much of a risk.

In packing its MediaOne offer with every kind of financial sweetener, AT&T was saying, in effect, that it strongly believed the U.S. financial markets would continue their march into the stratosphere. Somers and

Hindery, who had worked shoulder-to-shoulder to reel in MediaOne, told some board members they thought the chances were small—10 percent tops, to some recollections—that AT&T's stock price would lose any value before the transaction closed. Translation: The collar was just window dressing.

Their bullishness wasn't unique. After all, this was the heady spring of 1999. The Internet bubble was growing, the financial markets were humming, and the telecom sector was turning white-hot. It was a time of frothy hopes and even frothier business plans. Wall Street lapped it up like a cat pouncing on spilt milk. So did everybody else, for that matter.

But what if the markets tanked, the telecom sector cooled, the Internet bubble burst, and AT&T's stock price dropped through the floor? To be sure, it probably seemed like a one-in-a-million chance that everything could crater at once. But what if it did? Nobody on the AT&T side bothered to answer that scary question. They were too busy celebrating.

12

A GIANT LEAP
OF FAITH

E VEN BEFORE AT&T decided to make a run for MediaOne, there were worrisome signs that AT&T's financial projections were way too optimistic. Privately, in fact, some people thought they bordered on pure fiction.

The first sign of trouble had bubbled to the surface in 1998. That fall, the budget for 1999 was hand-delivered to the various business heads for their review. One of the recipients was Bob Annunziata. He had just been named the new president of AT&T's $23 billion Business Services group. According to the 1999 budget, his group was expected to grow by 11 per-cent—more than $2 billion—on a year-over-year basis.

Annunziata scratched his head at that. Revenues had only grown by a modest 4 percent in 1998. The former Teleport chief was pretty confident that he could push the division to grow by 8 percent in 1999. But the very idea that he could almost triple the growth to 11 percent was absurd. Moreover, he saw nothing in the internal numbers to suggest that such a target was reasonable, or even remotely doable.

The problem, of course, was WorldCom. The Clinton, Mississippi, based carrier had just merged with MCI, and the combined company was blowing the doors off everybody. A lot of that owed to WorldCom's chairman and CEO, Bernie Ebbers. A scrappy entrepreneur with a drawl as thick as Mississippi mud, Ebbers was determined to topple AT&T as the No. 1 brand. And he was making good progress.

Third-quarter results had just been released. WorldCom reported rock-steady revenue growth of 10 percent in its core-long-distance business, and 19 percent growth overall. AT&T's results, while in line with expectations, were a mixed bag. Revenues in Business Services grew by 4.7 percent, helping to offset its 2.9 percent decline in residential long distance. Total growth: just 4.3 percent overall. Granted, AT&T had a much bigger base of customers—66 million versus MCI's 20 million. But it was also becoming clear that the newly reconstituted MCI was a runaway train.

Annunziata was impressed, but also a little puzzled. MCI seemed to be impervious to price wars and guerrilla marketing tactics. Prices were going down, not up. Yet WorldCom kept gaining, mostly at AT&T's expense. Annunziata, however, was far more concerned with AT&T—the 1999 revenue targets for Business Services, in particular. As best he could figure, Dan Somers, the CFO, was trying way too hard to keep pace with WorldCom.

AT&T's annual budgets had always been driven from the top down. The approach was rooted in history. During its monopoly heyday, the long-distance business was remarkably predictable. Ttraffic would spike up and down with the seasons and holidays. (Mother's Day could always be counted upon to generate huge call volumes.) But for the most part, traffic patterns were consistent. As a result, the CFO's office could pretty easily predict traffic patterns and plan the budget accordingly. Then it was up to the division heads to manage their expenses so that they delivered.

The arrival of discount calling changed everything. All of a sudden, people started calling anytime, anywhere. AT&T's traffic models, which had been assembled over decades of steady-as-she-goes calling patterns, went right out the window. By the late 1990s, and certainly during Somers's reign, AT&T was being forced to guess, more or less, about its year-ahead projections. And Somers was incredibly optimistic about what AT&T could achieve, and in what time-frames.

Annunziata wasn't. All his data, as well as his gut instincts, told him that Business Services didn't have a prayer of growing by 11 percent in 1999.

The 11 percent figure, as it turned out, had also caught Armstrong's eye. He was well aware that business revenues had only grown by 4 percent in 1998, and he was curious as to how Annunziata was planning to almost triple the growth in just 12 short months. Now he understood: He wasn't. Annunziata said he could hold his own against MCI, but 11 percent growth was preposterous. Annunziata told Armstrong that the revenue target for his division would have to be rolled back to a more realistic level. The AT&T chief didn't disagree.

With Armstrong's blessing, Annunziata delivered the same message to Somers. It was an unusual demand—unheard-of, in fact. By challenging his targets so openly, Annunziata was telling Somers, in effect, that his financial projections were junk. Curiously, Somers didn't even attempt to engage Annunziata in a discussion about why he thought the revenue targets were so flawed. Nor did he go back and review his original forecast, which had been based on thousands of data points, to see where he might have gone wrong. Instead, Somers simply did as he was asked. With that, the 1999 revenue targets for Business Services were quietly rolled back to 8–9 percent, just as Annunziata had requested.

AS THE YEAR 1999 began, AT&T found itself hard at work on another big deal. The would-be partner, in this case, was Time Warner.

The stakes were high. Time Warner was the second-biggest cable operator in America, with access to more than 20 million households in such prime markets as New York and Orlando. AT&T wanted to use Time Warner's cable TV networks to offer AT&T-branded local phone service across the country. Leo Hindery, who was set to become AT&T's cable chief as soon as the TCI deal closed, hoped to use Time Warner as leverage to get other cable operators to step up. If he could knit together enough deals in enough markets, Hindery figured he could get AT&T direct access to more than 80 percent of the 108 million cable households in America. That was more than enough to give AT&T a good running start at the Bells.

Hindery had started talking up the phone pacts on the day the TCI merger was announced. And he kept on talking. And talking. In interview after interview, Hindery waxed on effusively about the pacts, describing them as the linchpin of the entire AT&T cable strategy. Along the way, he managed to create the impression that a big deal with Time Warner was imminent.

Behind the scenes, there was a lot of gnashing of teeth. John Petrillo, AT&T's strategy chief, was doing his best to push things along, but progress was slow. By early 1999 AT&T and Time Warner had agreed on a broad framework. But they were still quibbling over important details, including capitalization requirements, fee splits, and, most critical of all, bandwidth allocation—the amount of network capacity that AT&T would have at its disposal.

Both sides had legitimate concerns. Time Warner didn't want to hand over its cable networks to a potential rival without having the terms of usage closely defined. AT&T, for its part, didn't want to get so hemmed in so tight that it couldn't evolve its services along with technology. In the digital world, after all, "phone service" was the same as an Internet connection, was the same as a video transmission—just a series of computer-generated 0s and 1s. Neither side wanted to wake up 10 years later and find itself at the mercy of the other.

Adding to the pressure, AT&T was starting to get caught up in a public relations disaster of its own making. *The Wall Street Journal* was beginning to draw a bead on the fact that AT&T had yet to sign even a single big phone deal. Cable operators were also starting to wonder. Time Warner was mum, but that only added to the mystery. Armstrong continued to come across as upbeat and confident in his public comments. But he was feeling the heat.

Anxious to calm things down, Hindery convinced five small cable operators to sign phone deals. The deal was squishy, to say the least. All five of the companies were TCI affiliates, so they had a vested interest in keeping Hindery happy. One of them, InterMedia Partners, was Hindery's old company from San Francisco. Another, Peak Cablevision, was headed by TCI's longtime CFO, Donne Fisher. In its press release, AT&T said it expected to own anywhere between 51 percent and 65 percent of the joint ventures, and pay one-time fees to the operators that would total, in the aggregate, "tens of millions of dollars." The gambit backfired. Instead of assuring investors, the announcement threw a spotlight on the fact that AT&T had yet to sign even a single, credible phone accord.

AT&T and Time Warner continued to haggle. By late January the two sides had managed to work out a broad framework for their partnership. But they were still far apart on a number of important details, including the critical question of bandwidth allocation. Even so, Armstrong thought the details were firm enough to go ahead and make an announcement. Jerry Levin, Time Warner's chairman and CEO, wasn't too wild about the idea of announcing a deal before a definitive agreement had been signed. But he also knew that Armstrong was under a lot of pressure, so he went along with the plan.

On February 1, 1999, AT&T and Time Warner triumphantly announced a 20-year strategic accord on phone service. Armstrong was effusive. "Together with TCI and agreements with five TCI affiliates, the Time Warner joint venture will enable AT&T to reach more than 40 percent of U.S. households over the next four to five years," he declared. Levin was less ebullient, but he did point out that the partnership was proof that "fiberoptic cable networks are the surest, quickest route to the digital future."

Under the terms of the deal, the venture was to be 77.5 percent owned by AT&T and 22.5 percent owned by Time Warner. AT&T said the new partners planned to pilot phone service over Time Warner's upgraded cable TV lines in one or two cities by the end of the year, and begin broader deployment in 2000. The deal managed to take some pressure off AT&T, at least for the moment. By then AT&T had been promising for months that it would have phone pacts in place covering 50 million households by the end of 1999. Thanks to the Time Warner deal, AT&T appeared—finally—to be on track to fulfill that crucial promise.

Wall Street cheered the news, sending AT&T shares up by more than $1.00 to close at $93.50. With Time Warner in the bag, the assumption was that the other big cable operators would quickly follow. In their joint press release, AT&T and Time Warner noted, almost as an aside, that they expected to sign a definitive agreement for their phone accord within 90 days. It would turn out to be the longest 90 days in history.

ON THE SAME DAY that the Time Warner deal was announced, Gary Winnick, the chairman of Global Crossing, was working hard to convince Bob Annunziata to dump AT&T and join him at Global.

Winnick offered Annunziata $30 million to come on board as the CEO. His pay package included an eye-popping signing bonus of $10 million, and free first-class travel for him and his family anywhere in the world. Winnick also threw in a Mercedes-Benz for Annunziata's wife.

Annunziata had walked away from Teleport with more than $25 million in his pocket, so he wasn't exactly hurting. But a $30 million pay package was impossible to ignore. Armstrong was contrite. He'd only appointed Annunziata to the Business Services job a few months earlier, and he had expected him to stick around, at least for a while. But the AT&T chief also couldn't blame him. Not at those prices.

"What would it take to get you to stay?" Armstrong asked. It was inherently understood that AT&T couldn't match the money. Or even the Mercedes. But maybe there was something else in the AT&T portfolio that appealed to Annunziata?

Indeed, there was.

Annunziata wanted the No. 2 job at AT&T—the chief operating officer's job.

Since Armstrong had already made it clear that he considered himself to be the de facto COO, Annunziata deliberately avoided using that term—COO. He danced around it by saying he wanted "operations"— meaning Business Services, Network Services and AT&T Solutions—to report directly to him. Those three divisions formed the operational heart of AT&T.

Armstrong was incredulous. Annunziata was serious.

"I can get things done in 20 minutes that are now taking two weeks," Annunziata insisted. Translation: He wanted the COO's job, and he wanted it now. If Armstrong agreed, Annunziata would take a pass on Winnick's $30 million opportunity—as well as the Mercedes-Benz— and stay put.

It was a sincere offer. Annunziata had spent 17 years at AT&T early in his career, and he still loved what the company represented—to

America, to the industry, to his own personal journey in life. And it broke his heart that the company was faltering so badly. Annunziata could also see that Armstrong was struggling. The AT&T chief didn't seem to be making much of an impact on the dense culture, or almost anything else, for that matter. AT&T was still the same lumbering giant he'd always remembered. And it was driving him crazy.

AT&T's arrogance was as strong as ever. During one meeting, Annunziata happened to ask a senior sales executive to name his top customers in Mexico. Annunziata was trying to figure out how to increase AT&T's share of the market, and he thought big customers would be a good place to start. The AT&T executive didn't have a clue. Annunziata got the same blank response when he asked another manager in another meeting to cite AT&T's biggest traffic hubs in the United States. The guy had no idea. If Armstrong would agree to make him the equivalent of the COO, Annunziata felt sure he could clean up that sort of stuff in a New York minute.

Armstrong was impressed, to a point. He used to tell people that there were two ways to deal with hungry executives like Annunziata: You could get upset over their arrogance, or you could embrace their ambition. Armstrong, a sunny sort by disposition, nearly always chose the latter.

The AT&T chief considered Annunziata's offer, and came back with a counter: He'd give Annunziata Solutions, but not Network Services. Frank Ianna had been in the top job at Network a few months earlier. Armstrong didn't want to start reshuffling the deck so soon. Privately, however, Armstrong had other, bigger concerns. Trying to manage the competing interests and agendas of Zeglis, Hindery, and Somers was challenging enough without adding yet another strong-headed executive like Annunziata to the mix.

Armstrong's reluctance to accept Annunziata's offer spoke volumes about his own managerial blind spots. Point of fact, the AT&T chief wasn't managing any of his top staffers particularly well—*especially* Zeglis, Hindery, and Somers. The addition of an experienced, bull-nosed operations chief like Bob Annunziata probably would have helped. So why didn't Armstrong bite? Ego, in all likelihood, was a big factor. The AT&T chief felt like he had the asylum under control, and he didn't want to bring in anybody who might be perceived as undercutting his authority. On top of that, he was utterly convinced—why, it was never clear—that his top executives would eventually start rowing in the same direction. All in all, it was a very Big Blue way of looking at things.

Hal Burlingame, the human resources chief, tried to get Armstrong to reconsider. But Armstrong refused. Annunziata finally left AT&T in early February to take the job with Global Crossing. Wall Street appreciated the loss, even if Armstrong didn't. The news sent AT&T shares down by 1 3/8; Global's shares soared by 4 1/4 to close at 57 7/8.

BY THE TIME Annunziata left, AT&T was gearing up to launch cable telephony services across the United States.

The rollout plan was ambitious, calling for AT&T to launch service in 10 markets during the first 12 months. Remarkably, the plan had been based largely on TCI's verbal assurances about what its networks could do, and in what time frames. That would turn out to be a big mistake.

In late 1998, AT&T set up a cable telephony pilot in Fremont, California. That was where @Home had also made its debut. The TCI deal was scheduled to close in March, and AT&T hoped to get all the bugs worked out so it could start turning up markets immediately thereafter.

It was during this honeymoon period that AT&T executives got their first good look at TCI's shoot-from-the-hip style. For managers weaned in the staid but precise ways of AT&T, it was a real eye-opener.

On one occasion, Armstrong called up Hindery with a seemingly simple request: He wanted TCI's customer service center in Fremont to operate flawlessly during the launch, with zero dropped or abandoned calls.

Hindery's effusive response? No problem.

It was an exceptional answer, to say the least. In the cable industry, achieving a 100 percent performance rate was virtually impossible. Even the best cable operators in the country, like Cox, dropped a few calls an hour. While TCI's customer service record was improving, it was still considered an industry laggard. Armstrong, however, was so pleased by Hindery's response that nobody at AT&T dared to quibble.

TCI executives also showed an unnerving ability to recreate reality on the spot. In one meeting, Armstrong asked a TCI executive point-blank if TCI's Dallas system, which was supposed to launch right after Fremont, would be ready on time. The executive's response: Absolutely. We can even launch earlier, if you'd like.

As soon as Armstrong left the room, however, the TCI executive turned to an AT&T manager who had witnessed the entire exchange and told him that he actually needed to shift the launch to another location in the sprawling Dallas suburb. The reason: TCI's plant wasn't ready. The panicky AT&T manager quickly pointed out that AT&T didn't have an interconnection agreement for that part of Dallas, so a move wasn't possible. (Interconnection agreements set out the terms for handing off local phone calls.) The TCI executive shrugged, totally oblivious, or at least unconcerned, that he had just told a giant whopper to the AT&T chairman. After that, AT&T project managers started being a lot more precise when they asked questions.

The TCI deal closed on March 9, 1999, paving the way for AT&T to move ahead immediately with its rollout plans.

Or maybe not.

TCI's idea of "upgraded," as it turned out, didn't always jibe with "upgraded" in AT&T's precise world. Part of the problem owed to the makeup of TCI itself. The company consisted of 600 different systems, representing dozens of technical platforms and billing systems. It wasn't uncommon for an individual market to consist of a dozen or more systems. Chicago, for example, was composed of 90 different systems that had been knit together over the years. Fremont had nine. Adding to the challenge, Hindery was still swapping cable systems with other operators trying to finalize TCI's "footprint," so new problems were popping up all the time.

The unique nature of telephony only added to the rising tensions. Unlike cable, which allows for more creative engineering, telephone companies have exacting standards for just about everything—from the decibel level of dial tones to the temperature inside central switching offices. Even employee *name tags* are regulated. (The strings that hold the actual name tag are considered a choking hazard.) There are hundreds of rules related to wiring. Different types of wires are assigned different colors—no mixing and matching allowed. Even basic functions, like grounding, which refers to the manner in which wires are bundled together, are spelled out in exacting detail. (If improperly grounded, power can back up into the lines and damage sensitive phone gear, or even worse, it can back up into the telephone receiver and deliver a nasty shock to a customer.) AT&T's checklist was endless.

From TCI's perspective, AT&T's attention to such mindless details was, well, mindless. The way TCI veterans saw it, the things AT&T was asking TCI to redo—color-coding on wiring, name tags, installing enough backup power for a moon launch—had no real impact on the mission at hand. AT&T veterans, perhaps not surprisingly, saw TCI's propensity to cut corners as further proof it didn't understand, let alone appreciate, the unique nature of the telephone business. It was a cultural disconnect that would only get worse with time.

For these and other reasons, AT&T's first market, Fremont, wound up being pushed back—three times. The service finally launched in May, almost four months behind schedule. AT&T's experience in Fremont would not be unique.

AS SOON AS the TCI merger closed, Hindery switched sides and joined AT&T as the new president of Broadband. One of his first moves was to try to get Broadband as far away from AT&T as possible.

Under Jerry DeFrancisco, AT&T's cable telephony team had been based in Basking Ridge. Hindery wanted to move the entire operation to Denver, which was where TCI was based. DeFrancisco balked. He felt that Broadband needed to have a continued presence in Basking Ridge, to ensure that it received support from the company's mid-level tiers, which was where a lot of the work at AT&T got done. Hindery disagreed. The group, sans DeFrancisco, relocated to Denver.

Hindery brought in Curt Hockemeier, a former Teleport executive, to replace DeFrancisco. Hockemeier had been working with John Petrillo on the Time Warner phone pact, and he welcomed the change of pace. It was a good fit. Hockemeier had more than 20 years' experience in the cable business. He knew Hindery from his days with Cox and Teleport, so he had no starry expectations—about Hindery or the condition of TCI's cable systems. He just assumed that they were in far worse shape than what AT&T, or even Hindery, was letting on.

Hockemeier gamely offered everybody on DeFrancisco's 40-person team a job in Denver. A few accepted. Most didn't. With that, AT&T's aggressive push into the local telephone business—sans telephone people—began in earnest.

Broadband's (formerly TCI's) cable crews, perhaps not surprisingly, didn't know beans about phone service. So they had to be trained, starting with the basics. Owing to the finicky nature of phone service, it sometimes took installers several hours, and several visits, to wire up a single home. The process itself was painstaking: New wiring had to be installed along with special battery packs, which supplied power in the event of an electrical outage. (The Bells' networks have independent power. Cable TV networks don't, which is why you lose cable service, but not phone service, during electrical power outages.)

Over the years, TCI had spent as little as possible to maintain its networks, and it showed. Construction was spotty. It wasn't uncommon for noise from hair dryers, garage-door openers, even microwaves to creep into the lines, creating disruptions to the cable service. Because the systems varied so much, lessons learned in one market couldn't necessarily be applied to the next. So Hockemeier was always starting from scratch—over and over again—with each new market he entered. Needless to say, it slowed things down a lot.

TCI's backroom systems—billing, provisioning, and customer support—were a mess. In Fremont, orders for phone service were taken by hand, then faxed over to TCI's customer service centers. The manual system was slow but necessary because TCI's customer service reps weren't yet trained to deal with phone service. (Like everything else in the exacting world of telephony, phone orders have to be filled out in a precise manner, using specific codes for different services and functions.) TCI didn't get much help from the Bells. In the early stages, about half of AT&T's new phone orders were being incorrectly provisioned— phone parlance for the transfer of lines from one carrier to another. Customers sometimes wound up with the wrong phone number, wrong calling features, or, worst of all, no phone service at all.

In an interview with *The Wall Street Journal* that July, Armstrong allowed that the transformation of TCI's networks was challenging. But, he added rather hopefully, "it's not so daunting that it's not doable."

But doable in what time frame?

AT&T's financial targets were still calling for it to have 800,000 cable telephony customers by the end of 2000, ramping up to several million in the out years. Estimated cost to wire up a customer for telephone service: just $300 to $500 per home. Hockemeier took one look at the ambitious targets and uttered just one word: "Stupid." Even if all the technical problems could have been magically fixed with the wave of a wand, there was the pure physicality of the installation process to consider. TCI only had a handful of crews that were capable of installing cable telephony, and they were only turning over two jobs a day, at most. As for the $300–$500 installation figure, that wasn't even close.

At his very first budget presentation, Hockemeier lowered the boom: Assuming there were no major setbacks, AT&T could reasonably expect to have 400,000 cable telephony customers in hand by the end of 2000. That was *half* the number that had been promised by DeFrancisco. There was more bad news: The cost to wire up a single home for cable telephony wasn't going to be $300–$500. It was more like $800–$900, at least initially.

Hockemeier wisely made no reference to the earlier projections. Instead, he just walked Armstrong and the other senior executives through his business plan, taking care to explain his new projections and the underlying methodology that had produced them. John Petrillo, who had leaned on Lew Chakrin, who had leaned on Jerry DeFrancisco to extract the original, inflated targets, didn't say a word. Neither did Dan Somers, who had developed the 2000 budgets based on his best, and with hindsight, obviously flawed, projections about the future performance of TCI's cable television business.

Armstrong didn't say much. He was taken aback by the dramatic difference between Hockemeier's projections and the original targets that had been laid out more than a year earlier. But he also respected Hockemeier's cable expertise, so he didn't argue.

"Curt, that seems like a very thoughtful presentation," the AT&T chairman said, trying to sound a positive note. "Now go make it happen."

BY THE TIME the first cool autumn breezes started kicking up around the manicured grounds of Basking Ridge, Leo Hindery's career at AT&T was over.

Hindery knew a lot about the cable TV business, no question. And he worked like a dog, for sure. A renowned workaholic, Hindery routinely started his day at 5 A.M. and often didn't turn in until close to midnight. But he also burned too many bridges and broke too much glass. His seeming inability to separate fact from fiction—or just wishful thinking—was the clincher.

It was never clear to AT&T executives if Hindery stretched the truth on purpose, or if he just dwelled in a very gray world where black wasn't always black, and white wasn't always white. But what is clear is that Armstrong, who had put so much faith in Hindery early on, grew disillusioned with him. Then he grew to distrust him. And from that point on it was no longer a matter of *if* Hindery was going to leave—it was just a matter of when.

That Hindery turned out to be a square peg in a round hole at AT&T should not have come as a surprise. AT&T's own background report on him had drawn a bead on that possibility early on. The doomed Yahoo! deal was another graffiti scrawl on the wall of fate. Explaining himself before the @Home board, Hindery had been insistent that Armstrong had given him approval to cut the deal on AT&T's behalf; Armstrong had been just as adamant that he had done no such thing. It must have been quite a sight to see: a TCI president accusing the AT&T chairman of lying, and vice versa.

Weaned in the large and forgiving ways of IBM, Armstrong chose to look the other way. It was a delusional pattern of relating between the two men that would play itself out during Hindery's fast-and-furious run. By the end, Armstrong would no longer be looking the other way. But he would be looking in the mirror.

QUESTIONS ABOUT HINDERY started bubbling to the surface not long after the TCI deal closed in 1999. In mid-March, Hindery proudly informed the AT&T board that he had managed to land a big phone deal with Chuck Dolan, the powerful chairman of Cablevision Systems Corp. Board members were impressed.

John Malone was suspicious. He'd known Dolan for years. And he couldn't believe that the Cablevision chief, who was a notoriously tough bargainer, would agree to anything until the Time Warner accord was finished.

Following his nose, Malone offered Hindery his hearty congratulations. Hindery puffed up at that. He was running out the door to meet Dolan for lunch, and asked Malone if he'd like to come along. Malone said he'd be delighted, and off they went.

Over lunch, Hindery proceeded to recount for Dolan, and a now-mesmerized John Malone, what he had just told the AT&T board. Dolan looked at Hindery like he was nuts. "Leo," Dolan asked, clearly perplexed, "what in the world ever gave you the idea that I'd do a deal like that?" Hindery turned beet red, and quickly changed the subject. For the rest of the lunch, nobody said a word about the non-existent phone deal that Hindery had just touted to the AT&T board.

After lunch, Hindery tried to explain the mix-up to Malone. Dolan, he insisted, had reneged on his word. He also suggested that Dolan's about-face was partly Malone's fault, saying the only reason he'd backpedaled was because Malone had been present—why, it wasn't exactly clear. Malone sort of chuckled to himself at that. AT&T never did get a big phone deal with Cablevision, or any other big cable TV operator, for that matter.

In the end, the thing that really did in Hindery's career at AT&T had nothing to do with cable. Or even phone accords. It was the constant surprises. Some people even had a name for them: Hindery Specials.

Soon after the TCI deal closed, Hindery cut a landmark retransmission deal with NBC that included carriage for high-definition television (HDTV) signals of NBC-owned stations. In a press release announcing the deal, Hindery waxed on effusively about what a proud day it was for AT&T. Jim Cicconi, AT&T's general counsel, went into work early that day and happened to catch Armstrong in his office. Cicconi, who had just been reading about the deal in *The Wall Street Journal*, offered his hearty congratulations. A stricken look shot across Armstrong's face.

"Oh," Cicconi said, catching himself. "You didn't know about it, did you?" The AT&T chief didn't even try to put on airs: "No," he fired back.

Hindery also cut a major sponsorship deal with NASCAR. Embedded in the arrangement was a two-year, $5 million sponsorship with Mike Borkowski, a driver on NASCAR's Busch circuit. Hindery, a one-time stock car driver himself, was an avid supporter of the sport. The terms of the $80 million deal had been worked out by Matt Bond, who had been working under Hindery's orders. Bond just assumed that Armstrong knew what was going on. He assumed wrong.

Additionally, Hindery cut a nine-figure deal with Michael Ovitz, the head of Creative Artists Agency, to develop programming for AT&T. Armstrong found out after the fact, and forced him to cancel it. Ovitz, who was one of the top power brokers in Hollywood at the time, graciously agreed to let AT&T off the hook.

But those were nothing compared to the Motorola Mystery.

Somers was having dinner with a couple of cable executives in New York when he got a call on his cell phone. Somers tried to keep his cool, but the other people at the table could tell that something was terribly wrong by the way he was sputtering. ("He did *what?* For *how* much?") Hindery, he soon learned, had just committed Broadband to buying up to 2 million cable TV set-top boxes from General Instrument and 1 million cable modems from Motorola. Value of the deal: up to $1 billion. The legal department had just received a document seeking signatures for an initial $250 million commitment, and AT&T's lawyers didn't know what to do with it. Under AT&T's bylaws, any expenditure in excess of $50 million had to be approved by the board.

A story (by this author) about the pending deal soon appeared in *The Wall Street Journal*. It put AT&T in an extremely awkward position. As far as AT&T was concerned, there was no deal because the board hadn't approved the transaction. Yet the president of Broadband was insisting otherwise. Motorola was also in a tough spot. It didn't want to run the risk of offending AT&T, which was a longtime customer. But it also didn't want to trounce on Hindery.

Armstrong was livid. He was also deeply embarrassed because it left the impression that he couldn't control his own executives, and didn't know what was going on inside his own company. And, in fact, both of those things were true.

The only one who seemed to be feeling no pain was Hindery. He thought the transaction was a win-win for everybody. Hindery later insisted that he'd kept Armstrong informed all along, and even claimed to have a stack of memos proving as much. Armstrong had no clue what he was talking about. The AT&T chief said the episode was just another example of Hindery using "piss hole communications"—idle banter in the bathroom or in the hallways—as a lame excuse to ram through another Hindery Special. As for Hindery's claim that he had a stack of memos giving him approval to proceed—irrelevant. AT&T's bylaws required purchases of that magnitude to have board approval. Period.

The thing that finally did in Hindery, remarkably, was a speech. He was out on the West Coast addressing a group of investors when he started to dump on AT&T, and on Armstrong in particular. Always a colorful speaker, Hindery used florid language to depict AT&T as a sick company, and Armstrong as a weak and ineffective leader. Off to the side, a young man from AT&T's investor relations department was writing down every word. Right in the middle of his spiel, Hindery finally told him to "stop writing all this down." The IR person responded by dutifully writing down Hindery's exact words to "stop writing all this down." Those handwritten notes later got faxed to Armstrong at his home in Connecticut.

That was it.

Armstrong was outraged that Hindery would dare to be so openly disrespectful of him, and so openly disrespectful of AT&T. He decided right then and there that Hindery's career at AT&T was finished.

Armstrong's tough reaction drew some criticism at the time. Some said he was just being thin-skinned. Others said he was being churlish, even small. But dig a little deeper. This wasn't about AT&T. Or even Armstrong's management. It was about something much bigger and, to Armstrong, at least, something far more important. It was about trust. It was about loyalty. It was about supporting your team, no matter what. By then Armstrong had been bending over backward to accommodate Hindery for the better part of a year. He'd also given Hindery the benefit of the doubt, over and over again, and made excuses for him until he was blue in the face. And in return Hindery had seen fit to disgrace him, and the company he represented, in a throwaway speech at an investors' dinner. Thanks a lot, pal.

Armstrong faxed Hindery's comments over to Hal Burlingame and told him what he had in mind. Burlingame who'd been listening to a growing chorus of complaints about Hindery for months, wasn't surprised—either by Hindery's lapse or Armstrong's reaction. He agreed that it was time for Hindery to go.

Before Armstrong could carry through on his plans, however, Hindery pulled *another* blooper. The scene of the crime, this time, was Trinity College in Hartford, Connecticut. Hindery was there on a speaking engagement when a reporter in the crowd happened to ask a question: Is AT&T in talks with AOL? Rumors were swirling that AT&T was trying to work out a deal around the @Home assets. Hindery issued a flat denial. His comment got picked up on the newswire, and broadly disseminated across the United States.

It was an honest answer, but also an unfortunate one. AT&T was, in fact, talking to AOL. Hindery just didn't know about it. Armstrong was secretly meeting with Steve Case, AOL's then-chairman, to discuss a number of possible collaborations. The talks never went anywhere. Even so, Hindery's response created a problem because publicly traded companies can't mislead investors. AT&T later put out a short, cryptic press release explaining itself: The release made it clear that AT&T was, indeed, talking to AOL. Hindery just didn't know about it.

Hindery was furious that Armstrong would even think about going behind his back like that. Hindery prided himself on being a guy in the know, and the fact that he'd been shut out on something as important as an AOL deal left him looking a little flat-footed. (In his memoir, Hindery identified this episode as the reason he was ready to leave AT&T.) Hindery later accused Armstrong of being disrespectful, which in itself was pretty rich. It probably never occurred to him that Armstrong probably felt the same way about Hindery's handling of the Motorola deal— and the NBC deal, and the NASCAR deal, and so many others.

When Hindery finally got back to New York, Armstrong called him into his office and lowered the boom: He was out. Hindery, for once, didn't have too much to say.

TOM JERMOLUK, the @Home chief, literally let out a whoop when he heard the news about Hindery. "Ding, dong, the witch is dead!" Most people in the cable industry weren't that openly effusive. But almost nobody was surprised.

Hindery's departure was announced on October 6, 1999. In the press release, AT&T used the standard line that Hindery was leaving "to pursue other interests." It also noted that Hindery would continue to act as a strategic advisor to Armstrong on cable issues. "I look forward to working with Leo in his new role," Armstrong said in a prepared comment. Hindery returned the favor, saying, "It has been my pleasure to work for Mike Armstrong and with AT&T." On that rather insincere note, the curtains came crashing down on the short but colorful Hindery era.

13

THE PERFECT STORM

C HUCK NOSKI smelled trouble.

It was November 1999. Noski was having breakfast with Mike Armstrong at the Hyatt Hotel in Greenwich, Connecticut. Armstrong explained the situation: Leo Hindery, the CEO of Broadband, had just been pushed out, and Dan Somers, AT&T's CFO, was headed out to Denver to take his place. The AT&T chief wanted Noski, who was Hughes's president and chief operating officer, to take Somers's place. They'd been talking off and on for a while, but Hindery's sudden departure had accelerated things.

It was an intriguing opportunity. AT&T, after all, was a grand American icon. Noski also liked the idea of working with Armstrong again. But one thing kept eating at him; the tracking stock. There was a lot of speculation in the press that AT&T might issue a new tracking stock for its wireless division. Though nothing was final, the betting was that AT&T would proceed shortly.

Noski was concerned. On the upside, trackers allow people to invest in, or track, the performance of a particular group of assets, hence the name. On the downside, the stocks tend to release a lot of testosterone. All of sudden, executives attached to divisions with their own tracking stocks start feeling like they're running their own show. Noski had seen the behavior time and again at Hughes, a longtime tracking stock of General Motors. When Armstrong was the CEO, he used to schlep to Detroit periodically and try to convince GM to spin off Hughes as a standalone company. The GM leadership—Jack Smith was in charge at the time—always found a polite way to turn him down. But the exercise consumed vast amounts of time and energy on both sides.

If Armstrong decided to issue a tracker for AT&T Wireless, Noski was afraid it might pave the way for a breakup of the entire company. Once Wireless had its own tracking stock, it would just be a matter of time before it started pushing for a full spin-off. And once that happened, it would just be a matter of time before the other divisions started pushing for their freedom, as well. Noski told Armstrong that he was willing to come to AT&T to help him execute on the cable strategy. But Noski also made it clear that he had no interest in coming to AT&T just to break it up.

Armstrong waved off his concerns. The tracking stock, he explained, was merely a financial instrument to help unlock the value of AT&T's wireless assets. Once Wireless had its own tracking stock, the hope was that its value would soar, generating capital for future expansion. As for the notion of spinning off Wireless entirely—not in the cards. AT&T's strategy was predicated on the "one company, one brand" concept, Armstrong explained. So a spin-off would actually be antithetical to AT&T's larger strategic goal.

Armstrong's answer seemed to satisfy Noski. That, in turn, delighted Armstrong. By then he'd been trying to lure Noski away from Hughes for over a year, and he was ecstatic at the prospect of having Noski back by his side again.

Not many people knew it, but Armstrong tried to recruit Noski a lot earlier. He got stopped short by Jack Smith, the chairman of General Motors. Armstrong's separation contract didn't allow him to poach from Hughes for two years without GM's consent. Hoping to get a pass, Armstrong called up Smith in 1998 and made his pitch. "We really need this guy," he plaintively explained. Smith was unmoved: "So do we." Noski stayed put.

Noski wasn't especially anxious to leave Hughes. He'd been at Hughes for almost 10 years, save a short detour to United Technologies in 1997, and he still enjoyed the work. But he found Armstrong's sales pitch to be compelling. Thanks to the TCI and MediaOne deals, Armstrong figured he had the right assets. It was just a matter of putting all the pieces together and making them run like a Swiss timepiece. Noski liked the vision. He also liked Armstrong. The two of them had worked well together at Hughes, and the idea of teaming up again struck a comfortable chord.

BY LATE NOVEMBER AT&T was a jumble of activity. By some accounts, it was orderly chaos. To others, however, it was just chaos.

The $62 billion MediaOne deal was in the bag, but it was wending its way through the regulatory process and wasn't expected to close until the spring. Concert, a big global partnership with British Telecommunications PLC, had also been announced, but the final terms were still being worked out on two continents. There was a lot of squabbling on the @Home board. AT&T was constantly fighting with the other cable operators about the venture's strategic direction. Nobody was happy with the venture's performance. @Home's network was crashing constantly, causing a lot of angst among customers and investors.

The Wireless tracking stock, as Noski had feared, was a go. The news was formally unveiled in New York City on December 6. More than 800 investors and analysts showed up for the all-day confab, which was held at the Waldorf-Astoria. AT&T kicked off the meeting by announcing that it planned to create a separate tracking stock for Wireless as a prelude to an initial public offering in the spring. AT&T said John Zeglis would become the chairman and CEO of Wireless, reporting to Armstrong.

Dan Somers was making his last official appearance as CFO, so it was a big day for him, as well. AT&T said henceforth he would be the permanent president of Broadband. He'd only had the appointment on an interim basis following Hindery's abrupt departure, so the conversion was significant.

The real showstopper, however, was the earnings guidance. Somers said AT&T was confident that Business revenues would grow revenues by 9–11 percent in 2000. That got *everybody's* attention. The original forecast had called for growth in the 8–9 percent range, which was slightly above the 7 percent that the division had delivered in 1999. Business Services also got a new leader: Rick Roscitt, the former head of AT&T Solutions. Roscitt replaced Michael Keith, who had been pushed out in part because he failed to meet his financial targets.

Broadband was another bright spot. Somers promised that the division, which clearly constituted AT&T's future, would deliver revenue growth of 12–14 percent in 2000. Somers's enthusiasm was almost palpable. By 2001, he boasted, Broadband would have "millions" of cable telephony customers, and by 2004 it would grab a third of the Bells' local phone business in markets where they competed head-on. It was an astonishing show of confidence, especially considering the long list of operational challenges that Broadband was still struggling with back in Denver. Wall Street loved his rosy optimism.

The investors' conference was the capstone of a run of good news. About a week earlier, Jack Grubman, a star analyst with Salomon Smith Barney, had reversed his famously bearish view and issued a "buy" recommendation on AT&T stock. He also affirmed AT&T's contention that it could realize returns of 30 percent on its cable properties. AT&T shares edged up on the recommendation, setting the tone for the week leading up to the Waldorf lovefest.

Grubman's reversal was met with cheers around Basking Ridge. Nobody cheered louder than Armstrong. By then the AT&T chief had been grousing for months that Grubman wasn't giving his company a fair shake. One person to whom he complained was Sandy Weill, the chairman of Citigroup, which owned Salomon. Weill sat on the AT&T board, and was an ardent Armstrong supporter. Armstrong, who sat on the Citigroup board, returned the compliment.

The fact that Armstrong would even think to raise the Grubman issue to a sitting board member like that raised some eyebrows. It shouldn't have. As the chairman of Hughes Electronics, Armstrong once wrote a letter to then-President Clinton urging him to transfer jurisdictional licensing power for U.S. commercial satellite launches from the State Department to the Commerce Department. Armstrong thought the licensing process under State was taking so long that it was leaving U.S. manufacturers at a competitive disadvantage. By shifting the authority to Commerce, Armstrong thought the entire satellite industry would benefit. Clinton declined to get involved.

Critics later tried to use the missive as an example of Armstrong's cluelessness. But a more practical explanation is that Armstrong was just following his salesman's nose. To his way of thinking, America was being unfairly hobbled in the race to commercialize space, and he wanted to let the top decision maker, President Clinton, know how he felt. Exceptional? Of course. Over the top? Maybe. But it was also pure, unadulterated Armstrong. A salesman to his marrow, he just couldn't resist making his pitch. Never mind that the guy he was pitching happened to be a sitting U.S. president. Armstrong took the high ground, insisting he'd only been trying to do what was best for his industry, best for his country, and best for his company.

NOSKI STILL WASN'T sure if he wanted to take the job with AT&T.

Cautious by nature, Noski tried to do his homework. He had long conversations with Dan Somers, the outgoing CFO. He also had come-to-Jesus sessions with John Petrillo and John Zeglis. He even button-holed a few AT&T directors. Everybody said the same thing: AT&T was poised for a seismic transformation, one that could, quite literally, change the world. As AT&T's CFO, Noski stood to have a big influence. Noski, who was not without ego or ambition, found that idea appealing.

Noski was reluctant to uproot his family and move East. He'd done it once before a few years earlier, and he still winced at the memory. In July 1997, Noski agreed to become the CFO of United Technologies, which was based in Hartford, Connecticut. Noski gamely moved his family across the country, forever ending—or so he thought—his long love affair with California. He'd only been in the job about two months when he abruptly quit to take the No. 2 job at Hughes—president and chief operating officer. With that, Noski uprooted his family again and headed back West. His fast job-hop raised a lot of eyebrows around United Technologies. Noski, for his part, rarely talked about the episode.

After a lot of consideration—and no shortage of lobbying by Armstrong—Noski agreed to take the job with AT&T. His family, however, stayed put in Los Angeles.

Noski's appointment was announced on December 9, 1999. He did an interview with *The Wall Street Journal* that same day. In the interview, Noski made it clear that he had strong feelings about the CFO's role. "I don't always agree with Mike Armstrong, and Mike doesn't always agree with me," Noski told the *Journal* rather matter-of-factly. "We think differently, but we are very complementary." In other words, he was no Dan Somers.

Noski's belt-and-suspenders style drew some notice around AT&T. Connie Weaver, the head of AT&T's Investor Relations department, pulled Noski aside and gave him some friendly advice. Among telecom investors, she pointed out, Scott Sullivan, the high-flying CFO of WorldCom, was considered the gold standard for financial executives. Sullivan had a reputation for being brazenly optimistic about World-Com's prospects. Noski got the message—and promptly ignored it. "Thanks," he told Weaver, "but I've got my own style, and I think I'll stay with it."

The AT&T board was welcoming of Noski. But some directors also made it clear that Somers, with his can-do spirit and aggressive style, had set the bar high. George Fisher, the chairman and CEO of Kodak, went even further, telling Noski that he thought Somers was going to be a tough act to follow. Fisher had no idea how right he was.

IT DIDN'T TAKE Noski long to figure out that AT&T was a country at war with itself. And Armstrong was the benevolent king that everybody was shooting at—constantly.

The first hint of trouble bubbled to the surface in December. Dave Dorman, a respected telecom veteran, had just been hired as the CEO of Concert, which was AT&T's global partnership with British Telecommunications. The $10 billion deal was set to close in early January. Dorman's polite southern manner belied his razor-sharp instincts for business. And he was none too happy about Concert's financials. From what he could discern, the transaction was going to hit AT&T's bottom line hard. The problem? When the transaction had been announced a year earlier, AT&T had promised that it would be accretive to neutral—not dilutive. Noski, who'd only been at AT&T a few weeks himself, agreed, and promptly alerted Armstrong. The AT&T chief promised to bring up the matter with John Zeglis, who was leading the Concert negotiations.

A few days later, Noski received an urgent call from Zeglis. The AT&T president was upset. Armstrong had just informed him that Concert's terms had to be changed. That was a problem. The partnership agreement was jammed with tax instruments, in-kind contribution requirements, and scores of other financial details. Somers had just finished negotiating the final terms in an emergency session at Kennedy Airport. Sir Peter Bonfield, British Telecom's CEO, had made a special trip over on the Concorde to wrap things up, in fact. To overhaul the contract now, Zeglis explained, would require a major effort on two continents. And Christmas was just around the corner.

Noski was unmoved.

Exasperated, Zeglis made one last-ditch try. "Dan and Mike get to do dilutive deals," he pointed out rather plaintively, "so why can't I?" "Dan" was a reference to Dan Somers. "Mike," of course, was Mike Armstrong.

Noski was dumbfounded.

"John," he began, picking his words carefully, "I don't know how to respond to that. But AT&T made public statements that Concert wouldn't be dilutive, so the deal has to be structured to deliver on that promise."

Why so insistent? Investors valued AT&T on its EPS, or earnings per share. And in general investors don't like surprises. If the company announced that Concert would actually be dilutive instead of neutral, AT&T's stock price could get pounded.

Zeglis relented. British Telecom wound up contributing an extra $250 million to make the numbers work to Noski's satisfaction. Less than a week later, in early January, the Concert deal closed. Buried in AT&T's release was a single line noting that the partnership was expected "to lead to neutral to modest earnings growth in 2000," just as AT&T had promised.

THE NEW YEAR brought even more surprises. Most of them were bad.

One Friday afternoon in late March, Dan Somers, John Petrillo, and Marilyn Wasser, AT&T's corporate counsel, came striding in to the executive offices in Basking Ridge. It was around 4 P.M. As they made their way to Armstrong's office, they were literally giving each other high-fives in the hallway.

The source of their jubilation? @Home. Somers, working with Petrillo and Wasser, had just convinced Comcast and Cox to give up their blocking rights on the board. In exchange, AT&T had agreed to guarantee them $48 a share—for a total of $2.9 billion—for their @Home shares. These so-called puts could be exercised by Cox and Comcast starting in 2001. The deal, which still needed to be approved by AT&T's board, stood to leave AT&T with hard control of the venture.

Noski had no idea what was going on, so he walked over to see what all the commotion was about. He got an earful. Somers, who by now had been joined in his high-five fest by Armstrong, excitedly told Noski what he had just worked out. Right away, Noski started getting a sinking feeling in the pit of his stomach.

Over the weekend, Noski tore through the term sheet trying to figure out what, exactly, AT&T had just gotten itself into. The signs didn't look good: Under the language of the contract, AT&T was committed to a hard $48 target. If @Home's stock price rose, AT&T would wind up with a relative bargain. But if @Home's stock price dropped, AT&T would be stuck. The deal had no protection against downward fluctuations in the market. If @Home's stock price tanked, AT&T would still be obliged to step up and pay the full freight: $48 a share, or $2.9 billion. @Home's shares were gaining ground thanks to the Internet boom. But what if the Internet bubble burst? Somers told Noski not to worry. That only made Noski worry even more.

Cox and Comcast, meantime, were doing some high-fives of their own. They were tired of arguing with AT&T over the strategic direction of @Home, so they were happy to finally have the opportunity—at a firm $48 a share—to say good riddance.

Tension on the @Home board had started building right after the TCI deal closed. The strain didn't owe to any one thing—it was a combination of escalating irritations on both sides. @Home's abysmal performance in the marketplace only made things worse. On a positive note, @Home's stock price was continuing to climb even as its technical problems mounted. But that was of little solace to AT&T and the other cable operators, who were being besieged by thousands of angry customers.

Armstrong had assumed that AT&T's presence on the @Home board would result in a flurry of big phone pacts. If anything, however, it was having the opposite effect. The more time cable operators spent with Armstrong and his crew, the more they were convinced they wanted nothing to do with AT&T. Armstrong's flexible stance on open access—resisted by cable operators everywhere—didn't help.

By late 1999, AT&T had basically given up on the Time Warner phone accord that had been announced with such fanfare in February. It was also making little headway with other cable operators. Frustrated by the lack of cooperation, Armstrong finally threatened to "overbuild" his cable brethren with "fixed wireless." Bad move. In the cable world, overbuilders—companies that compete head-on with cable operators inside their franchise areas—are accorded the same respect as, say, pond scum. When Armstrong tossed out the overbuild threat at one meeting, Dave Woodrow of Cox took the bait. "You can't even get your own cable networks to work," he chided. "How are you going to get [fixed wireless] to stay up?" Armstrong instantly recoiled, insisting he hadn't been trying to threaten anybody.

As 1999 pushed into 2000, the political crosscurrents were turning into a riptide. By then Tom Jermoluk, @Home's chairman and CEO, had resigned. (Tired of all the infighting, Jermoluk wisely cashed out his @Home shares—about $300 million worth—and walked.) His successor, George Bell, the former head of Excite, was largely a marketing guy, and it showed. Under Bell, @Home's network problems skyrocketed. In some markets, the service would crash for hours at a time, snarling traffic and eating e-mail with abandon. Customers howled. Cable operators were helpless. Under the partnership agreement, @Home had sole responsibility for the network, including technical support. Complicating matters further, AT&T and its fellow board members were arguing constantly about @Home's strategic direction. AT&T wanted to use @Home to further its phone ambitions. Cox and Comcast, which had blocking rights over big decisions, felt that the interests of @Home—

not AT&T—should be the real driver. Cox and Comcast also had no interest in stepping up with more money. AT&T, by comparison, felt that a major overhaul of @Home's network was in order. That, of course, was going to cost a lot of money. As winter gave way to spring, the mad dance escalated.

By March of 2000, Somers, who was still out in Denver riding herd over Broadband, had seen enough. He decided to fix the @Home problem once and for all.

Late that month, he summoned Cox and Comcast to the law offices of Wachtell Lipton in New York for an emergency meeting. When Dave Woodrow of Cox and Larry Smith of Comcast showed up, Somers had a term sheet waiting for them. Somers told the startled pair that AT&T was sick and tired of getting blocked. He was also tired of all the network problems—it was making AT&T look bad. So here's the deal, Somers told them: "We're buying you out." If they refused, AT&T wouldn't provide any additional capital. AT&T also wouldn't renew its carriage commitments. That was sure to pound @Home's stock price. In other words, Somers said, winding up for his knock-out punch: "You guys can have the whole fucking thing."

Woodrow and Smith quickly retreated to a nearby office to consider their options. AT&T's term sheet had no prices, just blanks waiting to be filled in. After talking it over, they quickly came back with a counteroffer: Cox and Comcast would buy out *AT&T.*

Somers turned them down flat. "No way," he said. "That's not happening." It was a good thing, too, because Woodrow and Smith were bluffing. Woodrow and Smith had no interest in buying out AT&T's stake. (Moreover, neither one had authority to make such an offer.) They just wanted to get a fix on how dead-set he was to do the deal. Somers' unequivocal answer told them exactly what they needed to know.

With that, the game kicked into high gear. Over the course of the afternoon, Somers and his team went back and forth with Woodrow and Smith, now joined by their respective attorneys. The next day they haggled some more. Somers finally forced a showdown: He gave Woodrow and Smith exactly 30 minutes to come back with a final proposal. Otherwise he was walking—and he wasn't coming back. "We'll write this stuff off," Somers chided, practically daring them not to meet his deadline. "We don't give a shit. We'll build our own high-speed network if we have to."

One more time, Woodrow and Smith retreated to a nearby office to discuss their options. It was a clutch moment. Even if Somers didn't make good on his threat—and they weren't so sure he was bluffing—@Home's days were clearly numbered. Relations on the board had been deteriorating for a while. If they were forced to share the @Home board with AT&T now, it was going to be a nightmare. That was the bad news.

The good news? "Dan's in the room."

Somers had a sterling reputation for offering rich premiums and drop-dead-gorgeous terms to sellers on cable deals. As a result, "Dan's in the room" had become a battle cry of sorts. If Somers was in the room, meaning he was leading negotiations for AT&T, that meant the guys on the other side of the table—Cox and Comcast, in this case—were probably going to clean up.

Woodrow and Smith considered Somers's offer: $27 a share. @Home's stock was trading for around $18, so the offer, on its face, represented a pretty good premium. Should they take it?

That's about the time Brian Roberts, Comcast's wily president, showed up. Roberts was heading out for a family vacation in Martha's Vineyard, and he'd stopped by on his way. Roberts took one look at the $27 offering price and uttered just two words: "Double it."

Woodrow and Smith were stunned: $54 a share? Woodrow told Roberts there was no way.

"Yeah, but don't forget," Roberts replied, a smile washing across his face, "*Dan's* in the room." Grins broke out all around. "We've got him," the Comcast chief instructed, "so let's get him good, and let's get outta here!"

Somers almost fell out of his chair when he saw the $54 price tag. But just as Roberts had predicted, he didn't back down. Somers quickly came back with a counteroffer of $42. Roberts suggested splitting the difference, and that's what they ultimately agreed on: $48.

The deal done, Somers gathered his troops and made a beeline to Basking Ridge to deliver the good news to Armstrong in person. That was on Friday. By Monday, Marilyn Wasser had scheduled a telephonic board meeting so the directors could give their final approval.

Chuck Noski was the lone questioning voice on the call. He pointed out that the transaction, while attractive from a control perspective, was not without risks. If the financial markets turned, there was no downward price protection: AT&T would be on the hook for the full $2.9 billion. Even though the financial markets were humming right then, Noski warned, things could always change.

Somers picked up the beat. By taking hard control, he countered, AT&T could decisively move ahead with its plans—no more squabbling with Cox and Comcast about @Home's strategic direction. No more arguing with @Home engineers about how to fix its crushing network problems. No more arguing, period. As for the financial markets, not to worry. The NASDAQ, a trading index that tracks technology stocks, had just passed 5,000, an all-time high. Somers closed by saying he felt highly confident about the deal, and highly confident about the future of @Home. There was very little discussion after that. The board unanimously approved the @Home deal.

The next week Noski went to see Armstrong and had a heart-to-heart talk. He was still upset about the open-ended nature of the @Home agreement. But he was even more upset about the manner in which the deal had been jammed through. He told Armstrong that if he ever got surprised like that again, he would quit. Not the way I do business, he told Armstrong. And it's not the way *you* should do business, either, he added. Armstrong apologized, and promised that it would never happen again. (Somers always contended that Noski know about the deal.)

The @Home deal with Cox and Comcast was announced on March 28, 2000. The NASDAQ, which had reached its all-time high just two weeks earlier, would begin its slow descent around the same time. Within a year, it would be flatter than a pancake.

AS THE OPERATING results for the first few months of 2000 started trickling in, it became clear that AT&T might have difficulty meeting its full-year financial targets.

Long distance, as usual, was the problem. Volume wasn't the issue.

On any given day, AT&T could count on millions of people using its vaunted long-distance network. That was the easy part. The not-so-easy part was trying to figure out the *price* of those minutes. The price was determined by many factors. Wholesale or retail? Were the minutes part of a flat-rate calling plan? Or was the customer paying full boat, meaning he wasn't subscribing to any sort of discount calling plan? Bulk sales to wireless carriers picked up some of the slack. But the question was still the same: How much will the *long-distance* part of those calls cost? On the plus side, wireless calls ate up a lot of minutes; on the downside, a lot of those minutes were practically free. Most cell phone carriers buy their minutes in cut-rate blocks, then turn around and sell them for pennies. That's why Verizon, Cingular, and the others can afford to offer such cheap, flat-rate calling plans. Good for customers, no question. But not so good for AT&T.

Such was the situation that Chuck Noski found himself in during the early part of 2000. To all appearances, AT&T was on track to meet its first-quarter financial targets. But the picture was a lot fuzzier with respect to the full year. Noski talked to Armstrong about his growing concerns. They decided to review AT&T's operations, just to make sure everybody had a plan in place to meet the year-end targets. It was a delicate situation, to say the least. AT&T had just increased its targets a few months earlier. Even worse, it had done so before a standing-room-only audience of 800 investors at the Waldorf-Astoria in New York.

The politics were crushing. Rick Roscitt, the new head of Business Services, made no bones about the fact that he thought his targets were too aggressive. In classic AT&T style, some of the other division chiefs were immediately suspicious. Was Roscitt really convinced that he couldn't meet his targets? Or was he just trying to re-baseline his business so that he'd look like a hero later? The more Roscitt talked, the more the others piled on.

Howard McNally and Bob Acquilina, the co-heads of Consumer Services, were also complaining. Like Roscitt, they'd gotten appointed to their positions after their targets had been issued. Their predecessor, Gene Lockhart, had stepped up to the numbers. But now he was gone. Some sniped that Lockhart had only agreed to the targets because he knew he would never have to deliver on them. This hypothesis is totally unsubstantiated. But it is reflective of the mindset that gripped AT&T at the time.

Noski was also in the crosshairs. Some AT&T veterans thought he was grandstanding. He'd only been AT&T's CFO for a few months. By questioning AT&T's targets so aggressively, and so quickly, he was essentially casting aspersions on his predecessor, Dan Somers. Was Noski really *that* concerned? Or was he just trying to look like a Boy Scout to win points with Wall Street? Some people couldn't help but wonder.

By then there was a buzz in the market about the upcoming IPO of AT&T Wireless. The offering was expected to raise around $10 billion, making it a the largest IPO in U.S. corporate history. The exact date of the IPO hadn't yet been set. But the expectation was that it would occur in the late spring. This was February. It was a tricky situation. If AT&T lowered its year-end guidance before the IPO it would surely disrupt the offering. But if AT&T waited until after the IPO date, it might be accused of withholding information from investors.

As the spring wore on, the internal reviews intensified. Day in and day out, Noski and Armstrong sat side-by-side and listened as a parade of business heads lamented the rapid deterioration of AT&T's business, even as they continued to insist that their own divisions were right on track. To Noski's astonishment, nobody admitted to the possibility of missing his targets, or even allowed for a whiff of doubt.

During one review session, Nick Cyprus, the company's controller, tried to walk the senior management team through AT&T's financial projections. The numbers looked dismal. One by one, all the business heads started taking Cyprus to task for AT&T's lousy showing. Cyprus had nothing to do with ginning up the numbers mind you. He was simply reporting the figures that had been given to him by the very same business heads who were now attacking him. After a few minutes of watching his controller get eviscerated, Noski lost it.

"This is the dumbest fucking thing I've ever seen in my life," Noski railed before hurling a few other choice words in the direction of AT&T's stunned, and now silenced, business chiefs. Nobody needled Cyprus after that. Frank Ianna came up afterward and gently patted

Noski on the back. "Many of us are not surprised at your reaction," he told the still steaming CFO. "We're just surprised it took you so long to finally blow up."

Exasperation with Noski, meantime, was building. Some AT&T veterans thought he had a lot of nerve trying to tell them how to manage their businesses. After all, Noski had only been at AT&T a few months. And he was a telecom newcomer, to boot. As AT&T veterans were well aware, the company had a long history of rallying in the third and fourth quarters to meet its year-end financial targets. And a lot of senior executives were convinced that AT&T could still rally if Noski would just calm down and step out of the way. Armstrong, for his part, wasn't so sure that Noski was right on this one. It was still early in the year, so AT&T had plenty of time to make good on its promises to Wall Street. But he also wasn't about to buck his ace CFO, who was clearly bothered by the lack of clarity into AT&T's future.

AT&T's operational review ground on through the spring, blowing right through the IPO date—April 26. By the end of the month, Armstrong was still hopeful that AT&T could cling to its targets. Noski wasn't. The crucial moment finally came on the evening of May 1. During a marathon executive session in Basking Ridge, AT&T's senior leadership rolled through the numbers. By the time the session wrapped up, the decision had been made. AT&T would have to take down the 2000 guidance. It was a painful decision, especially considering that the guidance had been taken *up* to a round of applause on Wall Street just five months earlier.

AT&T put out a press release the very next morning, May 2. The news was glum: AT&T said revenues for 2000, which had originally been forecast to grow by 8–9 percent, would only grow by 6–7 percent. Revenues in Consumer Services would fall by 5–7 percent, as opposed to the 3–5 percent originally estimated. Business Services, which had been touted so highly just a few months earlier, also had disappointing news. Instead of growing by 9–11 percent, as Somers had promised, it would only grow by 8 percent. The overall impact of the reductions on earnings: about 13 cents a share. The targets for Wireless which was growing revenue by 30 percent a year, and Broadband were unchanged. The timing of the release—about a week after the wireless IPO—was unfortunate. AT&T insisted it hadn't been trying to delay the news until after the IPO, but some investors weren't so sure about that.

Wall Street went nuts.

Shocked and angered by this nasty surprise, investors pummeled AT&T's stock, sending it down by 14 percent to close at $42. The Bronx cheer shaved more than $22 billion off AT&T's market value, marking one of the biggest single-day declines in U.S. history. The plunge shook the entire telecom sector, sending billions more in market value straight down the drain. Inside the hushed offices of AT&T, Armstrong and his executive team were reeling. Noski, who'd spearheaded the campaign to lower the guidance, suddenly looked like the Grinch Who Stole Christmas. And he was about as popular, too, in some circles.

ANXIOUS TO CALM things down, Noski and Armstrong hit the road to talk to big institutional investors. They got a chilly reception.

Brad Vogt, a portfolio manager for Capital Research, made no attempt to hide his upset. "We're really disappointed," a clearly distressed Vogt told Armstrong. The comment stung. In addition to being AT&T's largest shareholder, Capital Research was one of the most respected investment houses in media. And it had enthusiastically supported Armstrong's cable strategy from day one.

Never one to concede defeat, Armstrong quickly acknowledged that AT&T had some big challenges ahead. But he also insisted that the company was finally on the path to redemption. Noski, who was singing off the same song sheet, did his best to sound upbeat. But in the face of AT&T's dramatic reversal, there wasn't much he could say. AT&T's numbers spoke for themselves. And what they had to say—about Armstrong's leadership, the slide of long distance, and, indeed, the whole rocky ride into cable—wasn't very good.

Over the next several days, Armstrong and Noski put in repeat performances with a half dozen investment houses in New York and Boston. The drill was pretty much the same everywhere they went. By the end of their emergency good-will tour, they were like two bedraggled carpetbaggers who had worn out their welcome. And almost nobody was buying the paper-thin excuses they were peddling.

Investors weren't the only ones who were rattled. The nation's big credit-rating agencies, which controlled the flow of blood to AT&T's main artery—which is to say, ready access to the capital markets—were also upset. And that could only mean one thing: trouble.

Up until then, AT&T had managed to maintain a good—though not great—relationship with the rating agencies. The tension, however slight, owed to Dan Somers. Though he had always been well regarded among the rating agencies, he was also known as a CFO who didn't like to be challenged or disappointed. Moody's knew that all too well. Right after the TCI deal closed in early 1999, Moody's had lowered AT&T's credit rating by just a notch. The reduction stood to cost AT&T just $3 million a year in added interest expense for every $1 billion in debt. Somers, however, was livid. During a meeting with Moody's, Somers expressed his displeasure by pounding on a table with his fist while shouting, "We are a double-A company!" as shocked analysts looked on. At the time, AT&T was meeting its earnings guidance, so nobody really cared. But to be pigheaded *and* miss his targets was completely unacceptable.

Now it was Moody's turn to vent.

When Noski showed up to talk about AT&T's lowered guidance, Bob Ray, the lead analyst on AT&T, was waiting. He pulled Noski into a side room to talk. Ray was steamed. He didn't accuse Somers of lying outright, but he came close enough. Given AT&T's dramatic about-face, Ray said it seemed clear to him that Somers hadn't been as "forthcoming" as he should have been. And he was unhappy about that. *Really* unhappy. Translation: Because of Somers' handling of the 2000 financial projections, AT&T suddenly had a big credibility problem with Moody's. And that meant, by definition, that Noski suddenly had a higher hurdle to clear.

The implications were enormous. AT&T was already hustling to keep up with its interest payments, which were running around $2 billion a year at the time. And that was with a top credit rating. If Moody's slashed AT&T's rating, those fees would soar. Even worse, it could hobble AT&T's ability to go back out to the market for additional funding. If that financial artery got shut down or severely constricted, AT&T was dead.

Noski was in a tough spot. He couldn't exactly trash Somers. But he didn't feel inclined to defend him, either. So Noski did the only thing he felt he could do under the circumstances—he said as little as possible about the earlier, flawed projections, and just tried to reassure Ray that AT&T was finally on the case.

EVEN AS NOSKI was trying to make peace with Wall Street, John Malone was fiddling around with some numbers on his own. And he didn't like what he was seeing.

The MediaOne deal was a complete disaster for AT&T's balance sheet. Somers had projected that AT&T's debt would only go up by about $4 billion, or around 10 percent, once the deal closed. Instead, it was going to almost *double* to a gut-busting $65 billion. About half of that was going to be tied up in short-term debt. The bulk, around $28 billion, was going to be balled up in commercial paper that would have to be paid back in less than a year. For months Malone had tried to steer board discussions around to the debt. His questions were always leading, never accusatory. Polite, not pointed. And he never pressed in a fashion that suggested he was panicked. Now he wished he had.

The commercial paper was a noose around AT&T's neck. When MediaOne was in play in the spring of 1999, Somers had set up a revolving bank facility so AT&T could demonstrate to the MediaOne board that it had financing in place. (Think of it in terms of a house mortgage: The seller isn't going to budge until the buyer has financing nailed down.) It was a smart move. With a bank line in place, a company can issue commercial paper—which is basically a corporate IOU—in less than an hour. Conventional loans, by comparison, can take weeks to finalize.

That said, paper is not without its perils. The payback periods are exceedingly short—just 2 to 270 days. (Some paper rolls daily.) For that reason, a lot of CFOs are skittish about taking on too much paper. If the financial markets turn, a company can find itself in a bind real fast.

Somers wasn't worried. After all, AT&T wouldn't have to draw down on its bank lines until after the MediaOne deal closed. That would take a year, giving AT&T plenty of time to "term out" its commercial paper into a conventional loan. In the meantime, funds would be flowing in from a variety of sources to offset the $62 billion purchase price of MediaOne. Or at least that's what Somers was hoping.

The sale of MediaOne's "non-strategic assets," which included stakes in cell phone carriers, cable TV companies and other media properties around the world, was key. Somers figured they would fetch $18 to 20 billion, after taxes, once they hit the auction block. He also assumed that AT&T could sell MediaOne's 25.5 percent stake in Time Warner Entertainment (TWE) for $13 to 15 billion. The venture, which had been created in the early 1990s, included most of Time Warner's cable TV systems, as well as HBO, Warner Bros., and Road Runner, the high-speed Internet access service. Jerry Levin, who was Time Warner's CEO at the time, had been trying to unwind the partnership for years. Somers figured he'd jump at the chance to buy out AT&T.

Assuming buyers stepped up as expected, AT&T stood to rake in $31 billion in cold hard cash, at the minimum. Somers planned to use that money to offset the final purchase price by more than 50 percent. The upshot: Instead of paying $62 billion for MediaOne, AT&T, in effect, would only wind up paying around $31 billion. All in all, it was an incredibly clever financing plan. Assuming, of course, that things worked out as expected.

The problem?

Nothing worked out as expected.

The biggest spoiler, by far, was timing. Unfortunately for Somers—and especially for AT&T—this was no longer the heady spring of 1999. It was now the worrisome spring of 2000, and the financial markets were turning. The Internet bubble was deflating with a vengeance along with investors' confidence in the debt-ridden telecom sector. Even though the NASDAQ had just zoomed past the 5,000 mark—a record—it was losing air fast.

The MediaOne financing plan unfortunately didn't allow for bad breaks. It had been predicated on the rather optimistic assumption that the world's financial markets would continue to stay strong. It also assumed that AT&T's stock price, which had been pushed to new highs thanks to optimism over the cable strategy, would continue to go up—or at least not go down. Improbably, it had also assumed that one of the wiliest CEOs in media, Jerry Levin, would roll over and play nice just because AT&T asked.

On the one hand, you had to admire Somers's bullish optimism. Only so many CFOs would have been willing to roll the dice like that. On the other hand, he was using AT&T's future, essentially, as table stakes. Somers didn't arrive at these rosy-hued conclusions all by himself, of course. He had plenty of help from his Wall Street advisors, led by Gene Sykes of Goldman Sachs.

The whole plan was a bust. In the end, MediaOne's international assets didn't bring in $18 to 20 billion. They brought in $12 billion. And AT&T was never able to unload its 25.5 percent stake in TWE. Levin later told AT&T that he'd be willing to pay $5 to $6 billion, tops. But failing that, Levin told Armstrong and Noski that he was happy as a clam to sit tight and carry on. After all, Levin coolly noted, "partnerships *are* the way of the cable industry." And this was from a guy who'd been trying—for years—to unwind TWE. Armstrong and Noski were stunned. They were also stuck. AT&T had no leverage to force a sale. Nor could it sell the stake to anybody else.

The famous MediaOne "collar" was the clincher. Because AT&T's stock price had fallen so much in the intervening period between the announcement of the deal and the closing, the collar had been triggered, forcing AT&T to step up with an additional $3.6 billion in cash. That was on top of the $20 billion in cash that AT&T had already promised. And that was on top of the $1.5 billion that it had already given to Comcast for breaking up its deal.

To be sure, an extra $3.6 billion in the context of a $62 billion deal wasn't that much. But when you piled it on top of everything else that had gone wrong or careened off the tracks, AT&T's financial house of cards, which had been held together with little more than spit and hope, started to crash. Instead of cruising to the MediaOne closing with a cool $20 billion in cash in its back pocket, AT&T was suddenly looking at the prospect of having to borrow an extra $20 billion just to stay afloat.

Under normal circumstances, AT&T could have bailed itself out by tapping into its backup bank lines. But that wasn't an option, either. Hoping to save a few million in banking fees, Dan Somers had reduced the lines—twice, actually—right before he took off for Denver in the fall of 1999. The two reductions left AT&T with a sole backup facility of just $10 billion. That was about $15 billion shy of what AT&T needed right then.

Because of AT&T's shaky financial position, Moody's and Standard & Poor's told Noski he couldn't go back out to the markets for long-term financing. He also couldn't turn to the banks. Not unless AT&T wanted to see its credit rating get whacked, that is. Moody's and S&P really had no choice. After all, lenders look to them for straight advice on the creditworthiness of potential debtors. Moody's and S&P couldn't very well look the other way while AT&T merrily refinanced. Noski could have said nuts to the agencies and gone out anyway. But those lenders were only going to turn around and ask Moody's and S&P for updated credit reports, putting Noski right back where he started.

THE PERFECT STORM. That, in financial terms, is what Noski was dealing with. There were no pitching seas to roll the boat. No Hollywood movie to tell the sad tale. But the Perfect Storm it was, an improbable confluence of financial calamities so exquisite—and so deadly—that it threatened the very solvency of one of the longstanding bedrocks of corporate America.

Against all hope, reason, and expectation, AT&T was suddenly staring straight into the jaws of a major liquidity crisis. Nobody dared to utter the "B" word out loud. But as of the summer of 2000, bankruptcy wasn't so far fetched. For a century-old survivor like AT&T, it marked yet another historical first, of sorts. The last time AT&T was in that much trouble, Alexander Graham Bell was still on the payroll. Perhaps even more stunning, AT&T had managed to achieve this ignominious feat in just 12 short months. On that rather urgent note, AT&T's long, hot summer of discontent began.

14

CASH CRUNCH

M IKE ARMSTRONG was incredulous that AT&T could have painted itself into such a tight spot.

"Holy shit!" the AT&T chief blurted when Noski dropped the bomb about AT&T's looming financial crisis. "How'd *that* happen?"

It was a valid question. The very idea that AT&T could actually run out of money was foreign to him, as, indeed, it should have been. With a decent planning job by his former chief financial officer, Dan Somers, and a few lucky breaks, AT&T wouldn't have been in such a fix. But that didn't happen, and now the world's most famous phone company was stuck up to its headlights in mud.

John Malone, never one to say "I told you so," tried not to rub it in. "AT&T ain't broke," he told a glum-looking Armstrong after the June board meeting broke up. "You're just having a cash crunch. This is only a serious problem if it's allowed to fester."

But saying that AT&T was "just having a cash crunch" was like telling a man clutching his chest that he was "just having a heart attack." Unless proper emergency steps were taken quickly, the patient, in both cases, could wind up in a bad way real fast.

OUT IN DENVER Dan Somers was pushing hard to put his imprint on Broadband. And unfortunately for AT&T, he was having lots of success.

Somers's appointment to the Broadband job was controversial from the very start. John Malone and Amos Hostetter, in particular, didn't think he had the management heft to pull it off. In addition to having a weak résumé, Somers had no standing in the cable industry. That was a lot more important than most people realized. In the United States, cable is actually a very small club. Malone was a charter member. So was Hostetter. So was Jerry Levin of Time Warner, Chuck and Jim Dolan of Cablevision, and Brian and Ralph Roberts of Comcast.

Somers was an outsider. Even worse, he was an outsider with "AT&T" tattooed on his forehead. Cable and phone companies had a long history of mutual distrust, so the AT&T affiliation only made things harder for him. Somers's dealmaking skills were also starting to come under the microscope. Malone was still smarting over Somers's handling of the MediaOne deal, and he had no interest in giving him even more influence over AT&T's future by sticking him in the driver's seat at Broadband. Hostetter largely concurred.

Armstrong also had his doubts, which was one reason he'd secretly tried to find somebody else to take the job. His top pick was Steve Burke, Comcast's cable chief. But Burke wasn't interested. Talks with Bill Schleyer, the longtime cable guru at Continental, also went nowhere. Somers, meantime, had his hand up for the job. *Way* up. On the plus side, Somers loved the cable TV business. He also understood AT&T. Most important of all, perhaps, he was a devout believer in the phone-over-cable strategy that was so critical to AT&T's future. Armstrong appreciated Somers's enthusiasm. He was also under the gun to name somebody fast to fill Hindery's shoes. On that wobbly note, Somers got the job.

SOMERS'S ARRIVAL IN Denver in the fall of 1999 was met with mixed emotions. On one hand, a lot of the TCI executives were sorry to see Hindery go. But on the other hand, people were generally hopeful that Somers might be able to improve Broadband's relations with Basking Ridge. Thanks to Hindery's escalating political battles with Armstrong, relations had begun to turn rocky, and the expectation was that Somers could help smooth things out. Given his background, people just naturally assumed that Somers would be able to inject some much-needed financial discipline into the business. They also assumed that he understood the nuts-and-bolts of the cable TV business, which, like any industry, has its own lexicon and way of doing things.

Shortly after his arrival, Susan Marshall, who was TCI's—now Broadband's—liaison with @Home, scheduled a meeting with her new boss to bring him up to speed. During the briefing, she reviewed @Home's network issues, capital plans, customer service problems, and more. @Home was having a lot of technical problems, so Marshall tried to be as detailed as possible in her explanations.

As the review ground on, however, it became apparent that Somers was having difficulty keeping up. His eyes seemed to be glazing over at some of the technical descriptions, and he kept asking her to repeat things over and over again. Flustered, Marshall took the conversation down a notch. That didn't seem to help much, so she took the conversation down another notch. Somers was still confused. After about an hour, both sides decided to call it quits. As soon as the meeting was over, Somers came staggering out of his office, clutching his head as if in pain. "She gave me a headache!" Somers wailed out loud, directing his comments to nobody in particular. "I didn't understand anything she said!"

All around the hallway, heads snapped around like slingshots. Tony Werner, Broadband's chief technology officer, happened to be standing nearby. He wasn't quite sure what to think—the mere sight of the new president clutching his head and moaning that was a little off-putting. He assumed that Somers was just having a dramatic reaction to what might have been an overly technical session.

Werner ambled over to Somers and offered to review the material again with him. Werner was accustomed to explaining the ABCs of cable networks to investors, so he was good at boiling down complex technical concepts into bite-size pieces that laymen could digest. With that, the duo headed back into Somers's office for round two. Two hours later, *Werner* was the one with the headache. No matter what he said, or how he said it, it didn't seem to stick.

A few days later Werner happened to be talking to Dave Nagel, the head of AT&T Labs, and mentioned the episode. When Werner explained Somers's symptoms—glazed eyes anytime the talk turned too technical, superficial questions, no depth of understanding about cable, no recall on things that had just been explained—Nagel didn't seem surprised.

"Not only is Dan not detail oriented," Nagel explained rather matter-of-factly. "He's detail *averse.*"

Somers' cable expertise quickly drew notice from TCI veterans. A lot of people marveled at his ability to make big calls on things that he seemed to know very little about. Take set-top boxes. TCI had always been a dedicated user of equipment from General-Instrument (GI), a cable set-top maker based in Pennsylvania. The affiliation owed to John Malone, who had worked at a division of General Instrument early in his career. As TCI's president, Hindery continued to beat the GI drum. As soon as Hindery got pushed out, Scientific-Atlanta (SA), which was GI's chief rival, was on the phone to Somers.

Somers thought it might be wise to start integrating other types of gear into Broadband's systems. The idea made a lot of sense on paper. The problem, however, was that the technical platforms of GI and SA weren't compatible. That's why cable operators had always tended to use one or the other, but not both. Somers, however, was insistent. He soon ordered up a market test in Atlanta, where Broadband owned some local cable systems.

When Werner got wind of what Somers was planning, he grew concerned. To make such a play fly, SA would have to switch out Broadband's existing GI gear and run a parallel system. Switching out the technology platform of a live cable system was no small challenge. It has to be executed perfectly, or else it can cause a lot of disruptions to customers' existing cable, data, and phone services. Switch-outs are also expensive because other gear—in the cable head-end and elsewhere—has to be pulled out and replaced so that everything stays in sync.

Somers agreed that it might make sense for SA to come out to Denver to talk through the details for Atlanta. A meeting was hastily arranged.

SA put on quite a show. During the slide presentation, SA's sales representatives put up a series of charts that claimed, among other things, that people would buy more pay-per-view services if SA's equipment was used. They also asserted that Broadband wouldn't have to make as many service calls. The idea that customers would purchase more pay-per-view services just because an SA box was sitting on top of the television was inventive, to say the least. That was like saying that a person would surf the Web more often if he was using a Dell computer as opposed to a model from IBM. It also wasn't entirely clear how SA's gear could have a positive impact on customer service.

Somers, however, was elated. "See!" he kept telling Werner and the others as each fantastic claim was thrown up on the screen. "I told you this was a good idea!"

Werner and his team held their tongues. But afterward one of them pointed out to Somers that "just because SA puts a bunch of numbers on a slide" doesn't mean that its claims were true. Somers refused to yield, and told Werner to put together an equipment contract so that the Atlanta trial could proceed. Werner did as he was asked. But he included specific clauses that held SA's feet to the fire on its various claims, including higher pay-per-view rates and reduced service calls. SA was unwilling to commit to those claims in writing, however, so the project never went forward.

Somers had lots of ideas for improving Broadband's business. But sometimes they just weren't very well thought out.

"Non-pay" cable customers—people who receive their cable TV service illegally—have always been a headache for the cable industry. Somers had a brainstorm: How about setting up a piracy SWAT team? Broadband could dispatch trucks to drive around the United States and track down non-pays. Once identified, they could be converted into paying subscribers. If the SWAT teams could convert just one out of every five illegal customers, thought Somers, Broadband could increase its profits by millions of dollars annually.

It was a clever idea in theory. But in practice it just didn't make much sense. A lot of "non-pays" are actually just honest, law-abiding customers who've had their service disconnected improperly by cable technicians. Somers also wasn't taking into account the cost of such a program, which, given its national reach, had the potential to become quite expensive. As for the idea that Broadband could bump up its profits by millions of dollars annually, hard to say. Somers never bothered to conduct an actual market test, so there was no way to verify his underlying business assumptions. He was basically guessing.

Somers was just as creative when it came to figuring out how to do more with less money. Fortunately for him, his finance team had no interest in cutting corners to get there.

Somers at one point asked his staff to look into the possibility of implementing a "pay as you play" program for Broadband. The practice, which was being used by Lucent and other big vendors, allowed buyers to take possession of new equipment, but only pay for it when the gear was actually installed. Another vendor-financing technique allowed companies to take possession of equipment, but not book the obligation immediately.

Broadband's finance department balked, arguing that the techniques didn't comport with standard accounting rules. Somers didn't press, but some people were alarmed that he would even inquire about such things. (WorldCom would later get in trouble for using similar accounting tricks.) One person put in a discreet call to Basking Ridge to nose around. Don't worry, came the fast reply. Somers is no crook—he's just a crummy accountant. The answer, while a relief, was hardly comforting.

Somers's unfamiliarity with the cable TV business shone through in other ways. He hardly ever talked about his cable experiences in the United Kingdom. And he rarely mentioned his old cable company, Bell Cablemedia, by name.

The behavior struck a lot of people as odd. As a group, cable executives like to show off for each other. Get a bunch of them together in the same room and before long, more likely than not, they'll be swapping war stories from the cable trenches. Not Somers. On the rare occasions when he did speak up, he tended to talk mostly in broad strokes. After a while, people started asking him detailed questions about the nuts and bolts of the cable TV business just to see how he'd respond. Time and again, Somers would sidestep his inquisitor by throwing out round-robin answers that were short on substance but long on wind. After a while, some people became convinced that Somers actually knew very little about the cable TV business.

The experience of Curt Hockemeier was typical. Hockemeier, who had more than 20 years' experience building cable TV networks for Cox and Teleport, was responsible for rolling out AT&T-branded cable telephony across the United States. So his work went right to the heart of AT&T's $110 billion cable strategy.

Every week, like clockwork, Hockemeier would schlep into Denver from wherever he happened to be working to give Somers a detailed progress report. During these briefings, Hockemeier would enumerate all the problems that his crews had encountered in the field that week— network outages, cut cable lines, phone snafus, and the like. And every week, like clockwork, Somers would sit there stone-faced, not saying a word. Week in and week out, he offered not a word of criticism. He also offered no suggestions, no helpful commentary, no feedback, period. Hockemeier couldn't help but feel that he was talking to himself. Other cable executives had similar experiences.

After a while a lot of seasoned cable executives, including Hocke-meier, started feeling like they didn't belong at Broadband. So they left. Somers used the exodus as an opportunity to bring in his own hires. He brought in Mike Huseby, a longtime Arthur Andersen auditor, as Broad-band's chief financial officer. He brought in another Arthur Andersen consultant, Joe Began, as his chief information officer. Other hires hailed from banking, wireless, and even a national bakery. Everywhere, so it seemed, but the cable TV business. The influx of non-cable talent only seemed to reinforce the notion that Somers didn't know very much about the business he was trying to manage.

By mid-2000, Chuck Noski was arriving at some hard conclusions. Broadband had committed to growing its revenues by 12–14 percent in 2000, but it was clear from the monthly performance numbers that it was going to have a hard time staying on track. Noski didn't want any ugly surprises later, so he decided to go out to Denver and have a heart-to-heart talk with Somers. He took along Nick Cyprus, the AT&T controller, and Connie Weaver, the head of AT&T's Investor Relations department.

The trio met for a closed-door session with Somers and his chief financial officer, Mike Huseby. The atmosphere was charged. By then Noski was asking all the business heads, including Somers, to submit monthly progress reports. By forcing all the divisions to verify their numbers every 30 days, Noski hoped to get a better bead on AT&T's overall performance.

As far as Somers was concerned, however, Noski was just sticking his nose where it didn't belong. By merely raising the question of whether

Broadband could deliver on its targets, Noski, by inference, was questioning whether his team could deliver. Somers didn't take the intrusion lightly. He also didn't want his Denver team to feel that it could under-deliver by simply making excuses to Noski. That was just an invitation to fail.

Noski opened the meeting. He tried to take the high ground, but buried in his messaging was a sledgehammer with Somers's name on it. Given the sliding fortunes of AT&T, Noski said it was imperative for him to be able to communicate accurately with Wall Street. (Translation: Somers didn't do that as AT&T's CFO, so now Noski was having to patch things up with investors.) In order to do that, however, Noski said he needed to have an open, honest, and continuing dialog with all the divisions, including Broadband. In that spirit, Noski told Somers and Huseby that he wanted to hear their unvarnished thoughts about Broadband's performance. So don't hold back, Noski urged. Just give me your very best judgments about the business.

It was an earnest request, but also redundant. Asking Dan Somers to speak his mind was like asking a charging bull to aim for the red flag: *No problem.* Leveling a steely eye in Noski's direction, Somers told him exactly what he thought: that he was fully committed to meeting his original targets of 12–14 percent in 2000, and had every intention of delivering. Moreover, he continued, vaulting over to the subject that was really eating at him, Broadband was his business to manage—not Noski's. He didn't like Noski's habit of calling up Huseby to grill him about Broadband's monthly numbers. Huseby answered to him, not Noski. *So back off Chuck, I know what I'm doing.* With that, Somers leaned back in his chair, adding an air of finality to his verbal slapshot. The razzing was free. And intended.

Noski came right back at him.

"Dan," he began, gearing up for his return volley, "this is not about commitment. This is about soberly assessing Broadband's performance." "Moreover," Noski continued, skidding into scoring position, "my job as the CFO is to understand and assess where we are financially, and to be able to express that coherently to the board and to Wall Street. Your job as the president of Broadband is to work the business as hard as you can, and make your plan." In other words, Noski was attempting to do what Somers *should* have done when he was sitting in the CFO's seat—get a clear bead on AT&T's finances so he didn't have to go back to Wall Street later with bad news. The razzing was free. And intended.

The face-off ended on a terse but cordial note. Each understood where the other was coming from. Noski would not be bullied—not by Somers, not by anybody. Somers would not be micromanaged—not by Noski, not by anybody.

After that, the quality of financial information flowing from Broadband to the CFO's office in Basking Ridge would improve a bit. Broadband's performance, however, would not. By the end of the year, Somers would fall short on the revenue and earnings targets that he had defended so aggressively, setting the stage for an even rougher 2001.

JUNE 2000 WAS a critical month for AT&T.

The MediaOne deal, which had been making its way through the regulatory approval process for more than a year, was close to being done. Behind the scenes, Noski and his team were still poring over AT&T's finances. Everybody was a little tense.

Early that month, a conference call was held with MediaOne's senior executive team. One topic of discussion concerned MediaOne's non-strategic assets. In keeping with AT&T's wishes, MediaOne was moving quickly to sell off those assets, which included One-2-One, a wireless operator in the United Kingdom; Telewest, a U.K.-based cable operator; and a 6 percent stake in Vodafone, a global wireless provider. A lot was riding on the outcome. Somers and his bankers had calculated that the assets would fetch $18 billion to $20 billion. AT&T planned to use those proceeds to offset MediaOne's $62 billion purchase price.

The sales, unfortunately, weren't garnering nearly as much money as Somers had predicted. In addition, the tax bite was huge—around 40 percent of the gross sales price. So the net proceeds were being whittled down quickly. The money, about $8 billion at that point, was being held in a special account that was set to transfer over to AT&T just before the merger closed.

Doug Holmes, MediaOne's senior strategist, delivered some bad news: There was a snag with one of the overseas assets. The problem had the potential to reduce the final selling price by as much as $100 million. The price differential was large enough that Holmes thought it might be prudent to delay the close until the problem could be solved.

Marilyn Wasser, AT&T's corporate counsel, cut him off.

"What is critical is that we get this deal closed," she firmly instructed. "So if it costs us $100 million, then it costs us $100 million."

Holmes let out an audible gasp.

Back at AT&T, nobody said a word. Wasser was a longstanding member of AT&T's senior management team. She had ready access to Armstrong and the AT&T board. She was respected, even revered, at the highest levels of the company.

After a brief silence, a junior finance person from the AT&T side finally cut in: "Now, Marilyn," he said, trying to add a light air to what was obviously an embarrassing situation for everybody. "I don't think you really meant what you said . . ."

On that shaky note, the silence was broken. The conversation continued, with no mention of Wasser's steely directive.

To be sure, $100 million was beans in the context of a $62 billion deal. But it was still $100 million. Even more importantly, perhaps, it was $100 million that AT&T didn't have to spare right then. Why so cavalier? The short answer: because that's how AT&T did things. And not even a cash crunch of epic proportions could put a dent in that 100-year-old mindset.

The MediaOne executives just shook their heads. It seemed inconceivable to them that AT&T would be so casual, even indifferent, to a $100 million shortfall. But that wasn't their problem. If AT&T was willing to eat the money, MediaOne was happy to let it. As it turned out, however, nobody had to eat anything. The problem cited by Holmes was ultimately worked out, and the MediaOne deal closed without delay on June 15, 2000.

BY THE SUMMER of 2000 it was clear to many AT&T veterans that the John Zeglis who sat atop AT&T Wireless was not the same John Zeglis who had staunchly defended AT&T's interests for more than two decades. The new version was even tougher. Some said he was also meaner.

Shortly after the AT&T Wireless tracking stock was issued, Armstrong sent out a memo in which he outlined his expectations for the two organizations, AT&T and AT&T Wireless. In the memo, he urged employees to be respectful of the fact that there were now two classes of stock: the original "T" stock, which represented the old-line long-distance business as well as the new cable assets, and the new "AWE" stock, which only tracked the wireless business. Both issues traded alongside each other on the New York Stock Exchange. Wireless had its own strategic goals, business plans, and shareholders. But the two companies still lived under the same roof, so to speak, in that they shared a common name, corporate staff, governance, and balance sheet. Armstrong's message was simple but clear: AT&T and Wireless need each other to be successful, so let's all get along, guys.

Zeglis didn't see it that way. As far as he was concerned, AT&T Wireless was independent in spirit and in mission. Their business objectives were also wildly different. AT&T was tethered to long-distance and cable; AT&T Wireless was a pure-play wireless company. They also had two sets of shareholders. In short, it was a brand-new world. And in the new world order Zeglis's allegiance was to AT&T Wireless, not AT&T.

Zeglis soon gathered his troops and gave them a message: If and when an actual issue crops up, we'll deal with it. But until that time arrives, carry on as usual. (Translation: Ignore Armstrong's memo.)

A lot of people were shocked—even outraged—by Zeglis's hard line. In hindsight, however, the only thing that is surprising is that so many people were surprised.

Zeglis was a street fighter. A street fighter in proper pinstripes. But a street fighter nonetheless. The tougher the challenge, the better he liked it. Take the Telecommunications Act of 1996. He'd labored over every word of the infamous 14-point checklist that set out the terms and conditions under which the Bells could enter the long-distance business. Thanks to Zeglis's poison pen and almost endless capacity for mind-numbing detail, the checklist turned out to be the military equivalent of a Sherman tank in full combat mode—it was almost impossible to penetrate. Though the Bells had boasted that they would blow through the checklist in a matter of months, it would wind up taking them close to five *years*.

Everybody at AT&T had loved Zeglis's take-no-prisoners style when he was general counsel. As the head of Wireless, however, his combativeness sometimes left people a little breathless. Negotiating with AT&T over Wireless's long-distance contract, Zeglis haggled over every term, every footnote, every penny. Jim Cicconi, who had succeeded Zeglis as general counsel in 1998, felt the heat. Every time he tried to pin down his former boss on some contract detail, Zeglis would come back swinging. Cicconi and the other AT&T execs were stunned. They hadn't expected a layup. But they hadn't expected a street rumble, either. Cicconi tried to keep his sense of humor. "Where you stand," he later quipped, "sometimes depends on where you sit."

Part of Zeglis's attitude owed to the hand that he'd inherited. AT&T Wireless was the No. 2 wireless operator in America. But it was fast becoming an also-ran. The company, which had been formed out of the old McCaw Cellular systems, only had about 9 million subscribers. Its networks covered areas with just 114 million people. Verizon Wireless, which was the No. 1 carrier, was about double its size. And the field was getting even more crowded with the entry of Cingular, a joint venture of BellSouth and SBC Communications.

AT&T Wireless also had a screaming technology problem. Its networks were based on TDMA (time division multiple access) a wireless standard that AT&T inherited when it bought McCaw back in 1994. (Craig McCaw, the founder of McCaw Cellular, was the one who actually picked the TDMA platform.) On the plus side, TDMA was less expensive than its sister technology, CDMA (code division multiple access). But TDMA didn't have nearly as much capacity, which was a big problem given the hyper-fast growth trajectory of digital wireless. A third standard known as GSM (global system for mobile communications) was the de facto international standard. The three technologies weren't compatible. So customers on one service, say Verizon, couldn't use the same cell phone if they decided to switch to AT&T Wireless, and vice versa.

Zeglis soon arrived at two hard conclusions: He'd have to spend heavily to rapidly expand the network, and he'd have to dump TDMA and convert to a new technology, probably GSM because of its global appeal. Both initiatives were going to be hugely expensive. But if he could make fast tracks on both, Zeglis was convinced he could turn the company into a real contender.

AT&T was in no position to help. Thanks to the MediaOne deal, its debt load had shot up to a gut-busting $65 billion. So it couldn't even think about taking on more debt to help fund Wireless's expansion. Cash was also scarce. The culprit, once again, was MediaOne. Nobody had yet broached the idea of reducing, or even eliminating, the annual dividend. But given AT&T's dire financial straits, that wasn't out of the question. (The idea of slashing the dividend would not be proposed until later in the summer.)

Zeglis didn't care. His only concern was AT&T Wireless. Turning a blind eye to AT&T's financial pain, Zeglis brazenly informed the board that he might need as much as $7 billion to fund his aggressive construction program. Some of the directors were shocked by the size of his request, especially considering AT&T's mounting financial pain.

A few directors were openly suspicious. By then Zeglis had been pushing the board to distribute the rest of the wireless tracking shares, arguing that it would give the unit a lot more autonomy in the marketplace. (At the time only about 15 percent of the shares were publicly traded; the other 85 percent were still owned by AT&T.) Some people thought Zeglis was trying to make his needs look more extreme than they actually were to force the board's hand. After all, if the capital needs of AT&T Wireless got outsized enough, AT&T would have no choice but to set the unit free. Zeglis only added to his growing reputation as a hostile agent by reminding people, over and over again, that AT&T had a legal obligation to do whatever it took to ensure Wireless's success. The implied threat wasn't lost on anyone.

The conspiracy theory made for a good story, to be sure. Zeglis had a reputation for being Machiavellian to his core. So the idea that he would use his cunning to work his way out of AT&T for good resonated in some circles. But even if that was true—so what? As the CEO of AT&T Wireless, Zeglis was doing exactly what he should have been doing right then—he was trying to get his company ready for the future. Zeglis's conclusion that he needed to grow the footprint was spot-on. Likewise, his decision to dump TDMA in favor of GSM was also smart. As for his fat number—$7 billion—that was just experience talking. Given AT&T's declining fortunes, Zeglis figured the board would never approve his initial request, no matter what it was. So he decided to aim high and hope for the best.

As for the accusation that he was trying to force the board's hand—absolutely. John Zeglis, like every other power player at AT&T, was skilled at working the system to get what he wanted. But at the end of the day, the final decision about funding rested solely with the AT&T board. If the board was that unhappy with his political grandstanding, all it had to do was say no.

In the end, however, the board didn't tell Zeglis no. Instead, after a lot of gnashing of teeth on both sides, it gave him permission to spend $2 billion to tend to the wireless business. But the board's approval came with a string attached: Zeglis had to cover most of the cost on his own. He could find a big strategic investor, sell assets, or do some creative combination of the two. But AT&T had nothing to give, so he was basically on his own. Ironically, the board's decision would wind up giving Zeglis exactly what he had wanted all along: complete freedom from AT&T.

THE TUG-OF-WAR over funding touched a raw nerve on the board. But nobody was more offended, perhaps, than Chuck Noski. As the point person responsible for fixing AT&T's ailing balance sheet, it befuddled him as to why someone of Zeglis's bearing and stature would turn on the very company that had nurtured him for so long. Hoping to get things on a better track, Noski decided to go see Zeglis in person to talk things over.

The meeting was held in Zeglis's office. Noski got right to the point. He told Zeglis that he was disappointed that they hadn't managed to forge a more constructive working relationship. He also reminded Zeglis of their very first conversation—a three-hour breakfast at the Hilton Hotel in Short Hills, New Jersey. During that meeting, they'd agreed to work shoulder-to-shoulder to help Armstrong take AT&T to the next level. They'd also promised to maintain an open, honest dialog.

Zeglis listened to what Noski had to say, and then carefully waded in. "I'm sorry if there was some misunderstanding," Zeglis coolly replied.

All in all, it was the Harvard Law School equivalent of flipping up the middle finger, without actually performing the deed. Zeglis wasn't about to offer any apologies. He was sick and tired of watching AT&T blow through promise after promise to Wall Street, and he was determined to make sure Wireless didn't fall into the same trap. He also found Noski's sequential, by-the-book way of doing things to be tedious. As a lawyer, he understood it. As a businessman, he despised it. Wireless was lashed to a red-hot industry where the battle lines were being redrawn every day, and he didn't intend to fail. Zeglis also didn't like being lectured by a guy who had—what, six months?—under his belt at AT&T. It offended him, in fact. Noski was a short-timer who was still commuting in to Basking Ridge from Los Angeles every week. Zeglis, by comparison, had devoted his life to AT&T. *So take your righteous indignation down the hall to somebody who might care, pal, 'cause I'm not buying.*

Zeglis, never one to confront an adversary head-on, didn't say any of this out loud. Instead, he did what he usually did anytime he disagreed with a political opponent: he said as little as possible.

Zeglis's efforts to find a big strategic investor stepped up a notch after that. It didn't take him long to hit pay dirt.

As luck would have it, DoCoMo, one of the biggest communications companies in Japan, was looking for a U.S. partner. DoCoMo was offering serious money—as much as $10 billion. But there was a catch: AT&T had to spin off Wireless as a separate, publicly traded company. DoCoMo had extended the same offer to AT&T a few months earlier, in April. Armstrong wasn't interested. At the time the Wireless tracker was about to hit the market, and he was adamant about keeping the company in AT&T's portfolio.

Back then, however, AT&T didn't know that it was within spitting distance of a major liquidity crunch. Now it did.

DoCoMo's demands hadn't changed very much. It was still willing to step up with a ton of dough—around $10 billion. But AT&T had to agree to spin off the wireless division as a separate company. DoCoMo also wanted Wireless to commit to the international GSM standard. As a show of good faith, it wanted the company to convert 13 markets to GSM by mid-2004. If the division failed to deliver, AT&T Wireless had to give back DoCoMo's money, all $10 billion of it.

What to do?

At another point in its long, illustrious life, AT&T probably would have told DoCoMo to take a hike. Wireless represented one of AT&T's best hopes for the future. The unit was growing revenues by 30 percent a year, providing a nice counter-balance to AT&T's core long-distance business, which was deteriorating by the quarter.

But AT&T didn't have the luxury of thinking so logically right then. It was strapped hard for cash, and DoCoMo was offering a bundle. That was money that could be used to pay down the debt, which was threatening to break AT&T's financial back. To be sure, one might argue that lopping off your future to secure your present is a dangerous, short-term game. But as any near-drowning victim will tell you, any floating device will do when you're sucking seawater and going down for the third time.

AT&T took the money.

A few directors were so relieved that they openly heaped praise on Zeglis. "We really needed this, and you brought it home," an effusive Amos Hostetter told Zeglis in front of the entire board. In classic AT&T style, the high praise was delivered with a big dollop of suspicion on the side. Zeglis by then had been pushing the board for months to hurry up and distribute all of the tracking shares to the public. To have DoCoMo suddenly come back with a hard demand for a full spin-off, which was exactly what Zeglis wanted, struck some people as way too coincidental. But those concerns quickly gave way to the sober reality that AT&T was desperate for cash. And DoCoMo was offering a pile of it—$10 billion for a 16 percent stake in Wireless.

Not everybody was happy about the DoCoMo deal. Dave Dorman, for one, hated the idea. He was convinced that the absence of a wireless business would seriously hobble AT&T in the marketplace. (And he was right.) Noski finally took him aside to walk him through the numbers. Since the DoCoMo deal had already been signed, there wasn't much Dorman could do about it. (Dorman was named AT&T's president on

November 28, 2000; the DoCoMo deal was announced two days later.) Even so, his nagging concerns about AT&T's future remained.

John Zeglis was elated. In addition to getting his funding nailed down tight, he got back something that was arguably even more precious to him—his pride. After 25 years of sweating the details for AT&T and getting almost no recognition for his efforts, at least not the kind that mattered to him, Zeglis was finally poised to break out on his own, and under a hail of good wishes from the board, no less. For a guy who'd devoted his entire career to winning—at the regulatory game, at the Bells game, at the AT&T political game—it must have felt pretty damn good. Like that old saw goes, success really *is* the sweetest revenge.

THE DISCUSSION ABOUT breaking up AT&T was ignited, remarkably, by a single question: How can we separate Consumer Services from the rest of AT&T?

It was a simple query on its face. But it was busting at the seams with larger implications. After all, if you were going to separate Consumer Services, why stop there? This was March 2000. The Wireless division was already headed to a full spin-off. Then it would be Broadband's turn. Before long, AT&T would be like the famous disappearing Cheshire cat from *Alice in Wonderland*. Only instead of just a smile being visible, only the famous AT&T brand name would be adrift in the air.

The driver was Wall Street. AT&T was still valued by Wall Street on its "earnings per share," or EPS, which was being dragged down by consumer long distance. If AT&T could find a way to corral Consumer, so the thinking went, then its EPS might improve accordingly.

On paper, at least, the idea had merit. AT&T's three other divisions—Wireless, Broadband, and Business Services—were still growing. But those gains got wiped out once you added in Consumer, whose revenues were eroding by more than 10 percent a year. The board considered a range of options. It could sell Consumer outright, do a joint venture with another carrier, or just carve up AT&T and sell off the pieces. The debate went on for months. As the summer wore on, the board got comfortable with the idea of separating off Consumer. That was the beginning of the end of AT&T.

Nobody used the "B" word: "breakup." But everybody inherently understood where the conversation was leading. Noski coaxed the board along. If the pieces of AT&T's puzzle were reworked, he pointed out, a lot of the debt could be offloaded to the high-flying parts of the business that could more easily afford it. Wireless was growing revenues by 35 percent a year. (The DoCoMo deal had yet to happen.) Broadband, while not growing as fast as everybody had hoped, was still delivering solid double-digit improvements, so its future looked bright.

Armstrong blinked.

Hard.

If AT&T got carved up, his "One Cable, One Company, Countless Possibilities" strategy was dead. Armstrong couldn't stomach that. To have come so far in transforming AT&T only to get stopped short by temporary balance sheet problems was just, well, short-sighted. Other board members agreed. The $110 billion cable strategy had been predicated on the grand idea that AT&T could sell customers a bundle of voice, data, and video services, all linked by the gold-plated brand name. Nobody ever said a word about breaking up AT&T and selling services à la carte. AT&T could have done *that* without ever spending a dollar, let alone $110 billion, to assemble one of the largest collections of cable TV assets on the planet. Keeping all the assets under one roof was critical to the larger plan, which offered huge cost benefits over time.

Noski's response?

Prove it.

He had arrived at AT&T long after the cable strategy had been adopted, so he had no way to vouch for the veracity of its underlying business assumptions. So show me the financial analysis that makes the case for the one-stop-shopping theory, he badgered, ever so diplomatically. Then convince me why it still makes sense in the current business environment. Noski's pessimism was influenced, no doubt, by his personal belief that there was no way to keep AT&T together and also deal with the crushing debt load. Some directors were taken aback that Noski would be so willing, even anxious, to tear asunder what Armstrong and the board had spent more than two years piecing together. But that was, indeed, precisely what Noski was talking about—a full-fledged breakup.

Noski made no apologies. The way he looked at it, his job as CFO wasn't to salvage AT&T's cable dreams. It was to come up with a new financial plan that the credit-rating agencies would buy, Wall Street would believe, and the board would accept. That was the only way to stop AT&T from defaulting on billions upon billions of dollars in short-term commercial paper.

Armstrong wasn't convinced. The company was bloodied and bowed, no question. But AT&T wasn't a flat-liner just yet. Okay, so the MediaOne financing didn't work out and the markets had tanked along with the stock price. It happens. Not often, if you're lucky. But it happens. Instead of hitting the panic button, why not just figure out a way to ride out the storm? Get creative: Sell assets, put a lid on capital expenditures, slow-roll telephony, or do what you must. But don't forfeit the game, for God's sake.

Dan Somers thought a breakup was a terrible idea. Sure, it would clean up the balance sheet in a hurry, but at what cost? If AT&T ceased to exist, did it really matter that it had a clean bill of health from the ratings agencies? That was like performing a heart transplant on a dead person. Utterly useless. Others privately agreed. But nobody, including Somers, bothered to press the point publicly. By then it seemed clear to the old guard that the outcome was inevitable, and nobody wanted to wind up on the wrong side of a losing argument. In short, it was classic AT&T.

The board continued to debate the breakup question through the summer of 2000 and into the fall. From there it was a very short walk to the next painful subject: what to do about the AT&T dividend.

The dividend was sacred around AT&T. It was also a proud reminder of AT&T's legacy, fortitude, and strength. To the coolly detached eye of Chuck Noski, however, it was just another bill that AT&T couldn't afford to pay. The dividend was only costing AT&T about $3 billion a year, chump change by most big-company standards. But that was $3 billion that AT&T didn't have to spare.

When Noski first proposed slashing the dividend, it didn't go over so well. Walter Elisha, the retired chairman of Springs Industries and an AT&T director since 1987, was almost wide-eyed with disbelief. "Over the past century," Elisha responded incredulously, "we've had 470-plus quarters of stable or increasing dividends through two world wars and the Great Depression. And now you want us to eliminate or significantly reduce the cash dividend to AT&T's shareholders, the classic widows and orphans stock?"

Noski didn't even try to sugarcoat the news.

"Yes."

Elisha's reaction was understandable. Since its debut in 1881, the AT&T dividend had never been cut, not by even a penny. During the Great Depression, AT&T had slashed costs to the bone just to scrape by. Thousands of workers were fired or laid off. But the dividend? Untouched.

None of that mattered. AT&T was out of options, and out of time. Noski dryly pointed out that if the board was that adamant, AT&T could take out a loan to cover the $3 billion cost of the annual payout. Nobody laughed, mostly because the directors weren't so sure he was kidding. He was. The dividend, after all, was supposed to be a tangible reminder of how well the business was performing. Only the business wasn't performing. It was dying. And the MediaOne deal had only made a bad situation worse. More to the point, taking out a loan to fund the dividend would have been totally antithetical to the mission at hand—cleaning up the balance sheet. Still, the gallows humor spoke volumes about AT&T's misery.

BY THE FALL everybody was in agreement that the time had come to decide AT&T's fate. And what a bitter Hobson's choice it was: AT&T could hew to its cable strategy and risk financial peril. Or it could break up the company and pray that the rupture unlocked AT&T's value in the marketplace. One path was strewn with possible glory; the other, while safer, at least for the short term, would signal a bitter defeat.

The final vote was taken in late October. There wasn't a lot of emotion. No pounding on tables. No heartfelt speeches about pulling one out for the Gipper. Just quiet regret over what might have been, accompanied by the sorrowful realization that it was the end of AT&T, as the world had always known it.

To be sure, Armstrong could have dug in his heels and tried to convince the board to stand by his one wire, one company vision. But this wasn't about vision. Or the cable strategy. It wasn't even about Armstrong. This was simply about survival. By then there had been too many bad management decisions, too many lost opportunities, too many tough breaks. AT&T's financial health, which had been tested beyond all reason by an ill-fated cable deal that never should have been attempted in the first place, was so broken that there was no way to fix it. At least that's what Noski believed, and his dispassionate reasoning carried a lot of weight with the AT&T board. Too much, perhaps.

Armstrong was devastated. He'd never imagined in his wildest dreams that he'd be presiding over the breakup of one of America's grandest, and most enduring, corporate icons. The enormity of that weighed on him. It ate at him. Constantly. By then he'd spent a lot of sleepless nights just lying awake staring at his ceiling—and pondering. He mostly thought about AT&T's future. Being human, he also thought about his own future. If AT&T got broken up, he'd always be known as the guy who killed Ma Bell. Could he live with that?

The weight of the decision wasn't lost on the board. This was the same board, after all, that had cheered Armstrong and cheered his bold cable strategy. A few directors were openly embarrassed. "We're going to look like a bunch of doofuses," George Fisher lamented out loud to nobody in particular. Nobody disagreed.

AT&T'S DECISION TO break up the company was announced on Wednesday, October 25, 2000.

In its release, AT&T said that it planned to create a family for four new companies: AT&T Wireless, AT&T Broadband, AT&T Business Services, and AT&T Consumer Services. AT&T said each of the units would become a publicly held company, trading as common stock or as a tracking stock of AT&T. All four companies would continue to support each other's services in the marketplace thanks to a series of intercompany agreements that were being executed. In short, the one-wire, one-company idea wasn't dead. It was just being reconstituted.

Armstrong tried his best to sound upbeat. "This is a pivotal event in the transformation of AT&T we began three years ago," he said in a prepared statement. The four new companies, he cheerily noted, would be "even better equipped" to deliver high-quality broadband services. The AT&T chief reiterated that the new companies would sell services under the same famous brand name, AT&T. In short, his fabled cable strategy hadn't failed. And even more important, perhaps, neither had he.

As part of the same release, AT&T lowered fourth-quarter financial guidance, marking the second reduction in just six months. The company also noted, almost as an aside, that it was reviewing its dividend policy.

Investors roared. AT&T's shares plunged by $3.50 a share in heavy trading on the New York Stock Exchange, closing at $23.38. The bloodletting pushed AT&T shares down 54 percent for the year, wiping out a staggering $105 billion in stockholder wealth. About half of AT&T's $90 billion market value, excluding debt, was tied up in Wireless. That meant the rest of the business, including the famed cable assets for which AT&T had just paid $110 billion, was now worth a grand total of just $45 billion.

Ken McGee, an analyst with Gartner Group, summed up the feelings of many that day. "It's hard to escape the feeling that a corporate funeral took place today," he told *The Wall Street Journal.* "It's really the end of an icon, and no matter how they try to put a positive spin on it, it's the death of a corporate giant."

Armstrong was stunned. All the months of polite boardroom discussion about the "restructuring"—nobody ever said "breakup"—had helped to lull him into a new reality, and it was a rose-colored reality shaped by hope. It didn't take long for reality to smack him in the face. During a packed investors' briefing that morning, one person asked him to elaborate on the reasons for AT&T's strategic "reversal." Armstrong, whose nerves were already frayed, lost it.

His eyes narrowing in anger, Armstrong boomed that the decision to break up AT&T was not a "reversal or repudiation" of his strategy. Moreover, the AT&T chief scolded, he found such a characterization to be "not only wrong, but offensive." "Structure is not strategy," Armstrong insisted loudly trying his best to shake the room into embracing his reality. "Structure must *serve* strategy, not the other way around."

Needless to say, nobody asked any more questions about AT&T's "reversal" after that. But his comment, which had been hurled with so much force and emotion that it caught a lot of people off-guard, sent a shudder through the room. Was Armstrong really *that* out of touch? Some investors couldn't help but wonder.

AT&T's public relations executives, who'd been standing off to the side listening to the whole exchange, were shocked. For some, it was like watching a car crash in slow motion—every awful second of his white-hot response seemed to hang in the air for an eternity. Adele Ambrose, a senior communications executive, was practically apoplectic. "He's dead!" she wailed to one of her colleagues. "He can't be saying that—the strategy *has* changed!"

Armstrong's comment drew jeers on Wall Street. It also became an instant classic. In historical terms, it was right up there with Alexander Haig's famous directive—"I'm in charge"—and President Clinton's notorious half-confession that he smoked but "never inhaled" marijuana.

Why'd Armstrong say it?

Because that's what he believed. Unable to accept the fact that his beloved cable strategy had failed to save AT&T, he simply concocted a new reality with a much happier ending. In Armstrong's rose-colored world, the $110 cable strategy lived on in perpetuity, and so did the American dream known as AT&T.

THE OTHER SHOE dropped in December. Right before Christmas, AT&T announced that it was slashing its famed dividend by 83 percent to just 3.75 cents a quarter. AT&T noted that the move would save the company a cool $3 billion a year in payouts. Trying to put a positive face on things, the company also pointed out that, at 15 cents a share annually, AT&T's dividends would be more in line with its industry peers.

In absolute terms, it was a truthful statement. But it was also pure spin. AT&T was slashing its dividend for one reason and one reason only: It needed the cash to help pay down debt. That was the same reason it had spun out Wireless. And the same reason it planned to spin out Broadband: All to pay down debt. In short, Armstrong's grand cable strategy, which had been hatched with the goal of turning AT&T into a media powerhouse, one that could last into the next century and beyond, was now being handed over to the debt markets. It was a fast way

to feed the debt beast, which had swelled to preposterous proportions—
more than $65 billion—on the back of the hydra-headed MediaOne
deal.

There was more bad news. In addition to slashing the dividend to almost nothing, AT&T warned that its fourth-quarter revenue would be
lower than expected, marking its third such reduction for the year.
Broadband, meantime, still wasn't living up to its promises. The profits
weren't there and its new phone-over-cable business was costing a lot
more to roll out than everybody had expected. But AT&T needn't have
worried. Comcast, as it turned out, was already working on a plan to fix
that.

15

THE END

THE FIREWORKS BETWEEN Comcast and AT&T began, appropriately enough, on the weekend of July 4th.

It was a Sunday. Early that morning Steve Burke, Comcast's cable chief, went out to buy a newspaper near his home in Bay Head, New Jersey. As he was leaving the store with his paper tucked under his arm, he passed by Robert Allen, AT&T's former chairman and CEO, who happened to be walking in the door at the exact same moment. It was the first in a series of odd omens that would leave their indelible mark on the day.

Three-quarters of the way across the country, the current chairman and CEO, Mike Armstrong, was preparing to return to New York. He was in exceptionally good spirits. Armstrong and his wife had just spent the weekend visiting with their three daughters and, collectively, their 10 children—five boys and five girls—at his mountain retreat in Telluride, Colorado. A doting grandfather, Armstrong loved spending time with his brood. And he especially loved spending time with his brood at his mountain retreat in Telluride, his home-away-from-home for more than 20 years. His upbeat mood would be short-lived.

A BEAUTY CONTEST was set to convene in Manhattan the very next day. The "contestants," in this case, were the big investment banking firms—J. P. Morgan, Merrill Lynch, Goldman Sachs, and others. AT&T

was planning an initial public offering of Broadband later in the year, with an eye on issuing a separate tracking stock for its cable assets. The banking fees stood to be enormous, so all the big Wall Street firms wanted to participate. Chuck Noski was overseeing the selection process, and he had a string of interviews scheduled to begin at 9 a.m. sharp.

AT&T had high hopes for the tracker. Owing to mounting concerns over long distance, AT&T's stock price was taking a beating. Shares were trading for around $18, representing a 40 percent drop in less than a year. Armstrong was incredibly frustrated. He'd just shelled out $110 billion to assemble one of the finest collections of cable TV assets in America. Yet he was getting no credit for that from the market. By setting up a separate cable tracker, Armstrong hoped to jolt investors and "unlock" the value of those underlying assets.

It was a familiar argument. Back in 1998, when John Malone first sold TCI to AT&T, he'd strongly urged Armstrong to proceed with a cable tracker right away. In addition to giving AT&T a separate currency for future cable deals, Malone figured the tracker would be a good way to put some distance—emotional as well as financial—between AT&T's cable and long-distance assets. As far as Malone was concerned, it was just common sense: cable was poised for fast growth, and long distance was headed to the graveyard. Why wrap that millstone around TCI's neck?

Armstrong initially agreed, but changed his mind about six months later. Thanks to Wall Street's warm embrace of the cable strategy in 1998, AT&T's stock price had almost doubled, and to all appearances it would head north from there. (And, indeed, it would continue to gain ground for several weeks, peaking at $95 on February 3, 1999.) Given the strength of the stock price, Armstrong concluded that a second currency—the tracker—just wasn't necessary.

Malone thought Armstrong was making a terrible mistake. To be sure, Wall Street was high on the cable strategy right then. But how long was that going to last? If investors turned and the stock price crashed—and given the rapid decline of long distance, that was a definite possibility—AT&T would quickly lose its financial flexibility. That's why Malone had proposed the cable tracker in the first place—so AT&T could have a separate deal currency that wasn't dependent on the vagaries of the long-distance business.

Malone held his tongue. When the AT&T chief delivered the bad news—that he was killing the tracker—in the first few days of 1999, the cable titan basically said okay, it's your call.

It might seem incongruous that Malone, a man known for his steely-eyed resolve at the negotiating table, would have chosen to remain mute, especially considering his misgivings. But consider the circumstances: The TCI deal had just been announced, and AT&T's stock price was soaring. About the last thing he wanted to do was to rattle investors by pointing out all the warts. Bowing to human nature, perhaps, Malone also wanted to demonstrate to his new partners at AT&T that he was a team player. That's why he later agreed, at Armstrong's personal request, to show up at an analysts' meeting to voice his support for dumping the tracker.

It was quite a show. Bedeviled by his private reservations, Malone wound up parsing his words like crazy, telling the standing-room-only audience that he thought it was perfectly okay for AT&T to not issue a tracker "at this time." Then he quickly segued over to the grander promise of the AT&T-TCI merger. Nobody seemed to notice his scrimmage-line punt. That was a shame, too, because if anybody had bothered to ask him to explain, Malone, no doubt, would have given everybody an earful.

WALL STREET'S ENTHUSIASM didn't last.

By the summer of 2000, AT&T's stock price had lost more than 60 percent of its value. The problem was no mystery: long distance. Just as Malone had feared, the business was collapsing, taking AT&T's stock price with it.

The outlook was bleak. Escalating price wars were eating a big hole in revenues, forcing all the big carriers to do more with less. AT&T was trying to make it up in volume, but it couldn't rake in new business accounts fast enough to offset its jaw-dropping losses on the consumer side of the house. Adding to AT&T's headaches, WorldCom seemed to be defying gravity. Under Bernie Ebbers, the carrier was racking up double-digit gains in revenues and profits. Chided by Wall Street to keep up, AT&T slashed costs and reworked its retail pricing structure so that it would be more competitive—over and over again.

None of it did much good. Federal investigators would later accuse WorldCom of using accounting trickery—$11 billion worth—to prop up its books. But it would take a while for that dead body to float to the surface. In the meantime, investors were pummeling AT&T's stock price into a fast retreat. By June of 2000 the stock was trading for just $35. That was 20 percent less than the $45 it had commanded two and a half years earlier when Armstrong first walked in the door. And that $45 had been for an AT&T with zero cable TV assets.

Malone was fixated on the stock price. Thanks to the nosedive, he'd *personally* lost more than $1 billion. And his paper losses were continuing to pile up. He was still a wealthy man. Most of Malone's net worth—about $2 billion at the time—was tied up in Liberty Media, which traded as a separate tracking stock of AT&T. Still, like any investor, he wasn't too happy at seeing his personal portfolio get creamed like that.

To get AT&T back on track, Malone became convinced that emergency action was needed. But what?

The answer came to him at the Allen and Co. media conference that summer. The media confab, held in the bucolic setting of Sun Valley, Idaho, is considered the ultimate summer camp for CEOs. Everybody who is anybody is there—Bill Gates of Microsoft is a regular. So is Sumner Redstone of Viacom, Howard Stringer of Sony, and Michael Eisner of Disney. Malone was another regular. A loner by nature, Malone didn't attend many industry events. But he liked the Allen conference, mostly because he never knew who he was going to run into.

On the first day of the conference he bumped into two old friends: Brian and Ralph Roberts of Comcast. For Malone, seeing the Robertses was always a treat. He'd known Ralph for more than 30 years, and they talked and laughed easily like the old friends they were. Malone also had a soft spot for Brian. Malone had watched Brian grow up, and he admired the man—and the cable executive—that he'd become.

The conversation quickly turned to AT&T Broadband. Everybody agreed: The company was stumbling badly under Armstrong's management, and the financial deterioration was painful to watch. As for AT&T's anemic stock price, that was just stupid. At $35 a share, AT&T was getting hardly any credit for its $110 billion worth of cable properties. As far as the stock price was concerned, in fact, they didn't exist.

It was a short walk to the end of the pier from there.

"Somebody really should buy Broadband," Malone finally told the startled pair. "And I think it should be Comcast."

It was a spontaneous, heartfelt sentiment. But the invitation, as it turned out, was also unnecessary. By then the Robertses had been tracking Broadband's performance for months. And what they saw gave them a lot of hope.

Under the wobbly leadership of Dan Somers, Broadband's operating margins, considered a key benchmark of cable health, had sunk into the high 20s. Comcast and the other big operators were agog. Most big companies, including Comcast, had rock-solid margins of 40 percent or better. Even TCI, as challenged as it was, had managed to get its margins up to 42 percent just before it was handed over to AT&T. And that was with cable systems that, in some cases, were strung together with the network equivalent of chicken wire and glue.

Somers had a raft of explanations. Because TCI's systems were in such sorry shape, he insisted, AT&T was being forced to spend heavily for upgrades. But if you backed out those expenditures, AT&T's basic cable TV business was actually performing quite well. To support his argument, Somers pointed to his RGUs—short for revenue generating units—which are considered a yardstick of future earnings potential. (One RGU equals one "service," be it a phone, high-speed data, or cable application.) Broadband's RGUs were soaring in comparison to other operators. He also suggested that AT&T's operational challenges were unique, owing to its back-to-back purchases of TCI and MediaOne. The upshot: All things considered, Broadband was actually doing quite well.

Cable executives were unimpressed. To be sure, AT&T was spending heavily to upgrade its cable systems. But so was every other cable operator in America, and nobody else was having such prolific problems. And, yes, Broadband did have big integration challenges. But that was a problem of AT&T's own making. Nobody had forced AT&T to double down on cable in two massive, back-to-back deals. Like that old saw goes: If you can't take the heat, stay out of the kitchen.

As for those RGU figures, nice try. As cable veterans were well aware, all RGUs aren't created equal. And AT&T's growth spurt, unfortunately, was heavily weighted toward the least profitable RGU of them all—

traditional "circuit-switched" phone service. The returns on circuit phone were incremental in comparison to high-margin services like Internet access and cable TV. That's why Broadband's margins were plunging even though its RGUs were going through the roof. To be sure, circuit-switched phone had the potential to become a big moneymaker over time. The only question was whether AT&T would have a viable cable TV business left by the time that happened.

COMCAST'S OFFICIAL COURTSHIP of AT&T began in January 2001. Not that AT&T recognized it as such.

Salomon Smith Barney was holding its annual media conference in Palm Springs that month. The event was being hosted by Jack Grubman, who was the premier telecom analyst at the time. He made sure that it was packed with A-listers, including Bernie Ebbers of World-Com, Gary Winnick of Global Crossing, and Bert Roberts of MCI. Also on the list: Brian Roberts of Comcast, and Mike Armstrong and Chuck Noski of AT&T.

Brian Roberts put in a call to Armstrong's office. Since they were both going to be at the conference anyway, Roberts suggested they get together to talk. They'd attempted to get together shortly after AT&T's big restructuring plan had been announced. Armstrong canceled at the last minute after *The New York Post* ran a story saying the two companies were meeting to discuss a possible merger. By January the buzz had died down, so Armstrong agreed to take the meeting. At Armstrong's request, Noski agreed to accompany him.

Neither Armstrong nor Noski expected the meeting to yield much. AT&T, after all, was in the middle of a major restructuring. An IPO for Broadband was also in the works. In addition, AT&T Wireless was set to be spun off to shareholders later in the year. The spin-off date wasn't firm. But there was wide expectation that it would happen by the summer.

Because their expectations were so low, perhaps, they didn't bother to tell the AT&T board about the meeting. Nor did they do much prep work. From their point of view it probably seemed reasonable. Nothing was going to happen, so why rattle the board?

All in all, it was a smug, even arrogant, view. Even worse, it failed to take into account the tough dealmaking profile of the Robertses, who had a long history of launching surprise attacks on unwary targets.

Consider the MediaOne deal. Brian and his father plotted the $60 billion merger while AT&T was in the middle of large debt financing. Because AT&T was in a quiet period, it was difficult for the company to respond right away. When AT&T emerged from its quiet period a few weeks later, it came out swinging. The telecom giant eventually succeeded in wrestling MediaOne away from Comcast, but it had to pay a sky-high price to do it. Leo Hindery, who was working behind the scenes with Dan Somers to topple Comcast's deal, would later admit in his own business memoir (co-written by this author) that the Robertses had completely blindsided him.

Barry Diller, regarded as one of the wiliest deal makers around, also got bushwhacked. In 1994 Diller announced plans to roll up shopping giant QVC into CBS in a reverse merger, with Diller as the CEO of the combined company. Diller, who'd longed to run his own network for years, was ecstatic.

Enter Ralph Roberts. He'd been a ground-floor investor in QVC, and he was none too happy at the prospect of being cut out of the power structure like that. (Federal rules prevented anybody from owning cable and broadcast TV networks in the same market, so Comcast was out.) Comcast only had a 16 percent stake in QVC, so he didn't have enough juice to block the deal. Even so, Roberts wasn't happy about the direction of things and he let Diller know as much.

The QVC chief wasn't very sympathetic. "If you're that upset about it," Diller joked, "you can always make a counteroffer."

The idea stuck.

When Roberts got back to Philadelphia, he immediately rounded up his advisors. Could Comcast make a counteroffer at that late stage in the game? Absolutely, his lawyers replied. Upon hearing that, he uttered two words: "Do it."

A few weeks later Comcast lobbed in a $1.4 billion counteroffer for the part of QVC that it didn't already own, sabotaging Diller's deal. The surprise attack startled CBS. The Tiffany Network had no interest in getting involved in a bidding war, and it quickly pulled out of the deal.

Diller was furious. But there was also nothing he could do. It would mark one of the few times in Diller's storied business career that he would get outfoxed on a deal. And by a grandfatherly type in a bow tie, no less.

Comcast struck again in 1997. The target this time was TCI.

The circumstances were unfortunate: Bob Magness, TCI's beloved founder, had just died, and there was a family dispute about his will. The disputed inheritance included a large block of controlling TCI stock. Malone had already cut a deal to buy back the block, ensuring that the company stayed in friendly hands. But TCI's share price had hitched up in the months since the deal had been struck, and Magness's two sons wanted more money. Malone and his lawyers refused, arguing that the price TCI was offering represented fair market value.

Sensing a rare opportunity, Brian Roberts teamed up with Microsoft to make an offer for the stock. Under the terms of their anonymous bid, Comcast and Microsoft would have owned the block 50–50. The offer was delivered through Steve Rattner, an investment banker in New York who had long ties to Comcast. As instructed, Rattner refused to tell TCI whom he was representing. The blind offer put everybody at TCI into a panic. Malone was most panicked of all, however, because whoever controlled that big block of stock effectively controlled TCI. Malone finally chipped in a big counteroffer, securing the coveted Magness shares—as well as TCI's future.

The episode caused quite a sensation in the cable TV industry. Roberts later claimed he'd been invited by a third party to bid for the stock. The insinuation was that Magness's sons had used Comcast as leverage to get Malone to increase his bid. That said, few people would have dared to attempt a stunt like that, invited or not. Messing with Malone was like messing with the Godfather. Not done.

But those sorts of messy details only obscure the real point of all these stories, which is this: Ralph and Brian Roberts weren't the sort of people you ever wanted to ignore, or dismiss lightly. Ralph might have looked like everybody's favorite grandfather. But he had ice water in his veins and a hit man's sense of timing when it came to looking out for Comcast's business interests. And his ever-faithful son, Brian, was the acorn that didn't fall far from the tree.

THE PALM SPRINGS meeting got off to a friendly enough start.

The trio—Brian Roberts, Mike Armstrong, and Chuck Noski—agreed to meet at Armstrong's hotel suite. It was a breakfast meeting. After exchanging some pleasantries over coffee and rolls, Roberts got down to business.

At the first break in the conversation he pulled out some charts that had been put together by his investment bankers. The charts showed what Comcast and Broadband might look like if they were combined. On paper, at least, the merged company looked impressive—it would have 22 million subscribers and a commanding position in 8 out of the top 10 markets in the country.

Roberts didn't mince words.

So, have you ever thought about doing a merger with Comcast?

The question, which had been delivered with a purposeful mix of wide-eyed wonder and polite detachment, landed with a dull thud.

"It's not a bad idea," the AT&T chief shot back, a broad smile washing across his face. "But it is a bad time."

Noski, always sensitive to keeping his boss out of harm's way, jumped in and cut off the conversation. He quickly explained what Roberts already knew: AT&T was in the middle of a "quiet period," so it was unable to discuss any new business opportunities. (During quiet periods, companies are allowed to engage in merger talks but they must update their public securities filings to say as much. Since most companies don't want to tip their hand in this manner, they usually wait until the quiet period is over.) The quiet period owed to an $8 billion stock swap that was under way. Shares of AT&T were being swapped for shares of AT&T Wireless, which was set to start trading as an independent company later in the year.

Roberts nodded, indicating that he understood. Privately, however, he was already running the angles in his head.

Noski, he quickly concluded, was stalling. Comcast's attorneys had already warned him that Noski might try to back him off by playing the quiet-period card. Even so, Comcast's attorneys didn't think AT&T *needed* to be in a quiet period—Noski just didn't want to talk. Quiet periods, after all, are self-imposed. Some events, like an IPO or a debt financing, clearly qualify. Others don't, leaving it up to the company to make a judgment call as to when to impose a quiet period, and for how long.

To Roberts's way of thinking, putting AT&T into an open-ended quiet period because of a simple stock swap was absurd. But it was also effective, particularly if Noski didn't want to run the risk of disrupting AT&T's carefully crafted restructuring plan.

Roberts didn't tip his hand. Instead, he did what he always did anytime he was confronted with intractable opposition from a deal target: He smiled, said okay, and silently plotted his next move.

By the time the meeting wrapped up about an hour later, all three men were feeling optimistic, but for wildly different reasons. Armstrong and Noski, for their part, seemed to feel that they'd handled Roberts pretty well. So well, in fact, that they didn't even think the meeting rated a discussion with the AT&T board. The way they looked at it, there was really nothing to report: Roberts had broached the idea of a merger, and Noski had shut it down. End of story.

And Roberts? Just two words described his emotions that day: Mission accomplished. He'd gone into the meeting with exactly one goal in mind: to let AT&T know that Comcast had serious intentions about buying Broadband. So to his mind, AT&T was officially on notice.

ROBERTS DIDN'T let up.

He kept calling AT&T. His message was always the same: Let's talk merger.

Citing the quiet period, Noski and Armstrong took turns trying to back him off. Roberts's persistence made it clear he didn't buy AT&T's explanation. Exasperated, Armstrong and Noski finally had AT&T's top outside lawyer, Dick Katcher of Wachtell Lipton, talk with Comcast's lead outside-deal lawyer, Dennis Hersch of Davis Polk. It didn't do any good. Hersch was convinced that AT&T was using the quiet period as a shield to avoid talking, Katcher was just as insistent that AT&T couldn't engage in merger talks, not unless it wanted to disclose that fact publicly, that is.

There was nothing to prevent Armstrong and Noski from talking to the AT&T board. (Quiet periods have no impact on internal board discussions.) But that didn't happen, either. Instead, they just talked to each other—for five long months. AT&T finally submitted its exchange offer prospectus to the Securities and Exchange Commission on April 19, 2001. About a month later, AT&T emerged from its marathon quiet period. By then it was the end of May.

Almost immediately, Roberts was on the phone to Armstrong's office. "Let's talk," Roberts implored. "How about dinner?"

At Armstrong's request, Noski agreed to take the meeting.

The dinner took place on June 6. The two men agreed to rendezvous at the St. Regis Hotel in midtown Manhattan. To ensure absolute privacy, arrangements were made for them to dine in a little-used ballroom off the main floor. It was an odd setting. Because the room was so large, their voices tended to echo off into the dark. But it served the purpose, and for several hours they ate, drank good red wine, and talked about the futures of their respective companies.

It was understood by both sides that what they were talking about was a full-blown merger, not just a joint venture or a lesser business arrangement. Valuation was not discussed, but they did talk about who the CEO of the combined company might be. Noski made it clear that Armstrong had a lot of interest in following the cable business once it was spun off, so he was clearly a candidate. They also talked about how such a deal might be structured.

By the time they shook hands to say good night, each had reached a few conclusions about the other. Noski's takeaway was the following: Roberts was proud of his company, and proud of the fact that his family controlled Comcast. Noski admired the Robertses' business acumen. But he also thought Comcast's corporate governance was going to be a huge problem for the AT&T board. The Roberts family—the shares were actually under Brian's name alone—owned just 2 percent of Comcast's equity, but exercised 87 percent voting control. AT&T had a long history of offering its investors one vote for every share they owned.

For his part, Roberts liked Noski right off the bat. It was also clear to him that Noski was a total pro who knew his business well. And Noski seemed to have few emotional ties to AT&T. After two years he was still commuting to Basking Ridge from his home in Los Angeles. The way Roberts looked at it, that sort of emotional detachment couldn't hurt, especially considering the volatile state of Noski's boss.

Armstrong was Roberts's biggest worry, by far. Armstrong considered his legacy to be inextricably intertwined with AT&T's cable strategy. The AT&T chief was also convinced that his cable strategy could live on once the company was broken up. The glue? Inter-company contracts. By having all of the units—Consumer Services, representing long distance; Broadband; and Wireless—sign long-term service agreements with each other, Armstrong believed the piece-parts could function as one. Sort of a loose federation, like the British Commonwealth, only with the AT&T logo instead of the Union Jack as the national flag.

The source of Armstrong's optimism? Who knows? During Armstrong's fast and furious run, AT&T's senior executives had *never* managed to work together collegially. Quite the contrary, they'd largely comported themselves like junkyard dogs fighting over the last bone. And the notion that they would magically mesh once AT&T was broken up into pieces was fanciful at best. As one of Armstrong's own top lieutenants put it: "The idea was crap. And crap is crap, no matter how well you spin it."

Noski, always respectful of Armstrong's views, left the impression he didn't necessarily buy the we-are-one strategy either. But he also made it clear that Armstrong wanted to go out on a high note. Roberts got the message: To get a merger done with AT&T, he'd have to find a way to accommodate Armstrong's bruised ego, which was tethered to his failed cable strategy. And he'd have to do it in a way that was respectful of Armstrong, but also true to Comcast's larger business goals. That was going to be quite a trick.

ROBERTS AND NOSKI agreed to meet for a second dinner a few weeks later. This time they met in Philadelphia. The date was June 17. It was Father's Day. A Sunday. Noski, who'd spent the weekend at his home in Los Angeles, was flying back east that day. Roberts picked him up at the airport in his BMW, and they tooled off to the Four Seasons for dinner. To ensure complete privacy, they dined in one of the hotel's suites.

Roberts was polite but unrelenting: Comcast wanted to buy AT&T Broadband. By combining the companies, Roberts thought he could ramp up the productivity of Broadband significantly, translating into a win-win for both companies. Roberts pointed out that AT&T was spinning off Broadband, anyway, so why not just sell it to Comcast? That way, AT&T shareholders wouldn't have to go through all the uncertainty associated with an IPO. Instead, they'd have the security of knowing that Broadband was going to a company with a proven track record of delivering results to its shareholders.

Noski was just as resolute. Comcast's corporate governance was a big problem. To gain the approval of the AT&T board, Roberts had to be willing to roll back his voting stake significantly. Another big issue was Armstrong's cable strategy—he expected it to live on once Broadband was spun off. There was also the matter of Armstrong himself. The AT&T chief wanted a prominent role in the combined company. How prominent? Noski said the AT&T chief would probably like to be the CEO. Nothing was said about the chairman's title, per se. But since the two titles were bookends, the presumption was that it would go to Armstrong, as well. Roberts could become the chief operating officer, or COO, reporting to Armstrong.

Noski, who'd been conferring with Armstrong every step of the way, also thought it might make sense to put the combined company in New York City. The Big Apple, after all, was the center of the media world. In addition, Noski suggested that a name change was in order. How about AT&T Comcast? Armstrong, he explained, felt the AT&T name connoted a worldly view that might be more appropriate if the two companies combined. There was also the cable strategy to consider. Once AT&T was carved up into pieces, the gold-plated name would be the only thing linking them. Armstrong considered the linkage to be critical.

By the time the two men pushed back from the table to say good night several hours later, each felt he'd managed to make some headway with the other. In reality, however, their respective positions were only hardening.

Privately, Roberts thought Noski was living in fantasyland. As far as he was concerned, Comcast's corporate governance was a benefit, not a liability. Since going public in 1972, Comcast had delivered double the returns of the S&P 500 on an annual, compounded basis. A mere $7,000 invested in Comcast in 1972 was worth, as of 2001, $3.9 million.

And AT&T? Under Armstrong's hit-and-miss leadership, the company's stock price had lost almost 60 percent of its value in two years—and that was on the heels of two massive, back-to-back cable deals. As for the suggestion that Comcast needed to embrace AT&T's cable strategy—come again? Like nearly everybody else in the cable television industry, Comcast considered Armstrong's $110 billion phone-over-cable strategy to be a bust. Indeed, one of the main reasons AT&T was breaking up was because the strategy had done a big belly flop.

As for the idea of relocating to New York City—get real. Broadband was based in Denver; Comcast was based in Philadelphia. Why put the combined company in Manhattan? Just because it was convenient for Armstrong? Not a chance. Ditto for the idea of letting Armstrong run the show. The AT&T chief had already had his shot at running Broadband. Now it was time for him to move out of the way so that people who actually knew something about the cable TV business could step in. And forget about changing the name of the combined company to AT&T Comcast—no way. That would only cause confusion in the marketplace.

Noski also had a few takeaways. For starters it was clear that Comcast wasn't going away. Roberts had been pushing the idea of a merger, at that point, for almost six months. And his verbiage, if anything, was only getting more aggressive. It was also clear that Roberts wanted to maintain voting control. That was a huge red flag. So long as Comcast refused to budge on that point, there was really nothing to talk about.

Flying back to New Jersey that night, Noski rolled the conversation over in his head. He had a good framework for a deal, no question. By then he'd talked through the social issues, deal structure, and corporate governance. But he also thought it was time to brief the board, which, remarkably, still had no clue about Comcast's interest. Part of his motivation, no doubt, was defensive. Roberts had given no indication that he planned to make a hostile run on Broadband. But Noski probably didn't want to take any chances either.

WHY SO SLOW to engage the AT&T board? AT&T would later cite the quiet period as its biggest hindrance. But even then, it was a hollow argument. Quiet periods don't preclude companies from talking to their own boards. It's also questionable as to whether AT&T even needed to be in a quiet period, much less for an open-ended one that dragged on for five long months. Most companies try to minimize their quiet periods for precisely the reason that AT&T's experience illustrates: If opportunities crop up, things can get messy real fast. AT&T's argument that it had merely been following the advice of its outside legal counsel also doesn't hold water. In the real world, corporate lawyers tend to be awfully good at finding ways to accommodate the wants and needs of their clients.

A better guess is that AT&T—Noski and Armstrong, that is—just didn't want to engage. A big IPO for Broadband was in the works, and AT&T Wireless was set to start trading as a separate company. Human nature being what it is, Noski and Armstrong probably just didn't want the hassle of having to reset the strategic clock and start all over again.

Institutional bias, in all likelihood, was also a factor. If the aggressor had been, say, Lou Gerstner of IBM or Michael Eisner of Disney, it's a good bet that the board would have been alerted much earlier. But this wasn't a marquee name like Gerstner or Eisner—it was Brian Roberts of Comcast, the polite son of the patrician founder of a nice-sized cable operation based in Philadelphia. That's not to say that Noski and Armstrong weren't respectful of what Roberts had to say. But it does seem clear, at least in hindsight, that they didn't consider Comcast to be much of a threat.

It's impossible to say how the extra six months might have affected the outcome. The delay gave Dan Somers an extra six months to run Broadband. It also caused AT&T to push its auction into the black hole of time around 9/11. That horrific event would roil the financial markets for months, rattling investors and lopping billions off the market values of Comcast and all the other would-be bidders. If the auction process had wrapped up earlier, maybe Comcast would have agreed to a "collar" to guarantee its stock price. This was, after all, the most important deal of Comcast's life. If the talks had been friendly, not hostile, maybe Comcast would have been willing to bend on other terms, as well. We'll never know.

One thing is for certain, however. The delay gave Comcast ample time to plan its ambush. By the time Noski and Armstrong finally decided to brief the AT&T board, Brian Roberts and Larry Smith, Comcast's lead deal maker, had been meeting with a team of Wall Street advisors for almost three months. During these brainstorming sessions, which often lasted three hours or more, every scrap of intelligence—from financial filings to the movements of AT&T's senior executives, including, most notably, Noski and Armstrong—was collated and analyzed, all with the aim of figuring out the best way to take out Broadband.

And AT&T? As of June 17, 2001, it still had no clue that it was deep into a game of cat and mouse with Comcast. And AT&T, unfortunately, wasn't the cat.

WITH THE FATHER'S DAY discussion still fresh in his mind, Noski went to see Armstrong the very next morning. It was Monday, June 18.

After talking it over, the two men agreed that it was time to tell the board about Comcast's advances. There was a regularly scheduled board meeting on Wednesday. That was just two days away. But there was a problem that needed to be worked out first: John Malone.

It was no secret that the cable titan was unhappy with AT&T's performance. The stock price, in particular. Malone thought tracking stocks might help, and had been pushing the idea for awhile. He started to take his campaign public in the summer of 2000. That's when it all hit the fan.

In a move that shocked Armstrong and the other directors, Malone laid out his prescription for fixing AT&T in detail to *The Wall Street Journal.* (The article was written by the author of this book.) In the story, Malone repeated what he'd been saying in board meetings for months: AT&T should set up a tracking stock for its cable TV assets. He also thought AT&T should merge its struggling long-distance unit with Network Services to create one huge "network" division, then sell shares to the public in the form of a second tracker.

"You can't sell apples, peaches, and bananas together," Malone told *The Journal*, his frustration practically jumping off the page. "And right now AT&T is fruit salad."

Armstrong went nuts. By then his star had begun to fade on Wall Street, and he was being pilloried in the press on a regular basis. About the last thing he needed was to have a high-profile board member like John Malone spouting off to the world. To be fair, most CEOs have an almost manic obsession with maintaining the illusion that their boards are in 100 percent agreement with them 100 percent of the time. Directors inherently understand this, which is why Malone's comments caused such a stir. Malone, for his part, seemed taken aback that people would make such a fuss. After all, it wasn't like he'd said anything that the AT&T directors hadn't heard before.

The timing of its commentary struck some directors as odd. By then, there'd been a spate of negative stories in the press about AT&T, and many of them included quotes from anonymous sources. Nobody said anything directly to Malone. But privately some board members began to suspect that he was the source of some of those stories. Suspicions skyrocketed after verbatim quotes from board sessions made their way into the papers. That rattled everybody. Especially Armstrong.

Malone could feel the chill in the air. He even joked about it on occasion, referring to himself as the "turd in the punch bowl" at AT&T. He basically chalked it up to residual agitation over the *Journal* story. It never occurred to him that some of his fellow directors might actually think he was a snitch.

It was right around this time that Armstrong made a fateful decision: When it came time for him and Noski to talk about Comcast at the board meeting, he would ask Malone to leave the room. Marilyn Wasser, AT&T's corporate lawyer, felt strongly that Malone was conflicted because of his stead with Liberty Media. As the chairman of Liberty, she pointed out, Malone had stakes in dozens of media properties whose interests potentially collided with those of Comcast. To be sure, Armstrong could have kept Malone in the meeting, especially if he thought the positives outweighed any potential negatives. But since the AT&T chief had growing doubts of his own, he decided to take the path of least resistance and give Malone the boot.

It was a really bad call.

With more than $600 million in AT&T stock in his *personal* portfolio, it was hardly in Malone's interest to dribble out bad news that might tank the stock even more. The cable titan was miserable about AT&T's performance—he made no bones about that. And he was speaking up regularly about possible remedies—no question. But that was a far cry from sneaking around AT&T's back and leaking confidential board business to the press.

As for Wasser's contention that Malone was "conflicted"—take a number and get in line. Amos Hostetter, the other cable billionaire on the board, was the chairman of Pilot House Associates. The Boston-based firm had plenty of investments in media, including some cable TV networks. Hostetter was also a big investor in, and advisor to, Quadrangle Group, a media investment house in New York. The kicker? Quadrangle was managed by Roberts's longtime friend and banker, Steve Rattner, who was *advising* Comcast about the AT&T merger. (Many years later AT&T would insist that it never knew about Hostetter's relationship with Quadrangle, which is another issue entirely.)

Yet, nobody said a peep about Hostetter. Just Malone. The difference was trust. Armstrong and the other directors inherently trusted Hostetter. But not Malone.

The sad irony of this twisted tale was that Malone knew about the Comcast talks all along. Malone, after all, was one of the most plugged in guys in America. He had friends and business associates at every major and minor cable operator in America, including, most notably, Comcast. No deal of any import ever went down in the cable TV business without him hearing about it first. It was part of the unspoken code of the cable club, and Malone was a charter member.

So why didn't Malone speak up? Because the guy can keep a secret, that's why. Malone figured Armstrong would clue him in when he was ready to talk. The only thing he hadn't anticipated was getting iced out by the AT&T board. Indeed, on the day Armstrong excused Malone so he could talk about Comcast in private with the other directors, Malone just naturally assumed it was because he wanted to talk about Comcast in private with the other directors. So while Noski and Armstrong prattled on about Comcast, the one guy who was arguably best equipped to give advice on that very subject was cooling his heels outside in the hall.

Inside the boardroom, things were heating up. AT&T's directors immediately understood the importance of Comcast's interest. And they treated it accordingly. By the time the meeting concluded, the board had given Noski two very specific messages to deliver to Brian Roberts. First, if Comcast was serious about doing a deal with AT&T, it had to be willing to skinny down its voting control significantly. And second, the board wanted Comcast to sign a "standstill" agreement promising that it wouldn't make a hostile run at AT&T or its piece-parts. In short, the board was ready to engage in friendly talks, providing its ground rules were honored.

Noski caught up to Roberts on the phone two days later. It was Friday, June 22. "Gee, you really ruined my weekend," Roberts told Noski, friendly as ever. "Let me think about this and I'll get back to you."

THE LEAKS CONTINUED.

Since Malone was out of the picture, it seemed pretty clear that he wasn't the snitch. That was the good news. The bad news was that AT&T clearly had a leak at the highest levels of the company, and Armstrong had no idea who it was.

Just to make sure AT&T didn't have a corporate spy, security was finally called in to sweep the boardroom for listening devices. The room was clean—no bugs were found. Frustrated, Armstrong called up Jim Cicconi, AT&T's general counsel, and floated an idea: How about making people take lie detector tests? Cicconi was appalled, and shot down the idea immediately. What would AT&T do if a director took the test and failed, Cicconi asked: Fire him? And what if a director refused to take the test? AT&T couldn't exactly order its blue-chip board into action, much less over a hare-brained scheme like that. Armstrong dropped the idea on the spot. But the mere fact that he had even proposed it spoke volumes about his growing paranoia.

———

THE FIREWORKS BEGAN at 4 P.M. sharp on Sunday, July 8.

Comcast's hostile tender offer for AT&T Broadband was faxed to Armstrong's home. The letter was simultaneously released to the newswires, ensuring that Comcast's offer got maximum coverage on Monday morning. Comcast's all-stock offer valued Broadband's cable assets at $58 billion. (The offer included about $13 billion in assumed debt.) That was about half what AT&T had originally paid for them.

Armstrong had just walked in the door from his long holiday weekend in Telluride. When he picked up the fax and read it, his jaw just about hit the floor. He had no idea that Comcast was about to make a run on Broadband. Quite the contrary, he thought the two companies had made a lot of progress toward reaching a friendly deal. After all, Noski and Brian Roberts had spent hours talking through the issues on Father's Day. That had been followed up by a formal invitation from the AT&T board, delivered just three weeks earlier, to engage in friendly merger talks. Brian had told Noski he'd think it over and get back to him. And now *this*.

Ralph Roberts was on the phone within moments.

"Just wanted to make sure you got the fax," he told Armstrong, polite as always. The comment hung in the air like billowing, black smoke from a July Fourth cookout gone bad.

Armstrong was boiling, and he made no attempt to hide his displeasure. His voice rising with anger, Armstrong bellowed that he didn't like Comcast's hardball tactics. And he especially didn't like the public nature of the offer. Comcast's decision to fax the offering letter to the world offended him. Deeply. So did the late Sunday afternoon timing. And on July Fourth weekend, no less.

Within minutes the reality of the moment sunk in. And it hit Armstrong hard, like an anvil lodged right between his eyes. The fate of Broadband, which represented the future of his beloved cable strategy, was suddenly up for grabs. Not only that, but he'd just been bushwhacked in plain daylight by a company less than half AT&T's size. Humiliation didn't even come close to describing it.

"Can't we talk about this privately?" the AT&T chief finally asked almost pleadingly.

Roberts was taken aback by the request. Comcast's offer was plastered all over the newswires. Half the world knew that AT&T was in play. Roberts gently explained the situation: Because of Comcast's hostile tender offer, a private discussion was no longer possible. Roberts didn't mention the Father's Day meeting with Noski. If anything, Noski's overreaching—on corporate governance, the social issues, the relocation to New York, the name change—had only helped to convince him that AT&T wasn't taking Comcast very seriously. The board's insistence that Comcast needed to sign a standstill agreement also didn't sit well. Ditto for AT&T's idea that "vote had to follow value." It was a nice ditty. But coming from a company whose stock price was down almost 60 percent in just two years, it was almost laughable. That was the real reason Brian had never bothered to call Noski back—there was nothing to discuss. AT&T had made itself abundantly clear. Now Comcast was doing the same.

In the letter attached to Comcast's public tender offer, the Robertses pointedly noted that the only reason they were launching a hostile was because the two sides had been unable to reach agreement despite "months" of discussions. AT&T was silent on this point, and no wonder. AT&T's directors had only been told about Comcast's interest three weeks earlier. And they'd yet to have even a single discussion with Comcast or its representatives.

The Robertses were unapologetic. By then they'd been signaling their intentions clearly and openly for more than six months. Given the aggressiveness of Comcast's advances, they'd just naturally assumed that Noski and Armstrong had kept the AT&T board informed all along. It never occurred to them that Armstrong and Noski were only talking to each other.

Back in Philadelphia, Comcast was being flooded with congratulatory calls. One of the first calls to Ralph Roberts came from his old friend and business partner, John Malone. His jubilant opener: "What took you so long?"

Monday, as expected, was a three-ring media circus. And Comcast was commanding center ring. AT&T's "beauty contest," which had been in the works for months, proceeded as planned. But it went ahead without some major players, including J. P. Morgan, Morgan Stanley, and Merrill Lynch. All three firms were advising Comcast, so they had to beg off. Noski kept on his game face, but the absence of three of the biggest names on Wall Street was noticeable.

Popular wisdom would later hold that Comcast had timed its offer to bust up AT&T's beauty contest. But in fact the exact opposite was true. Because J. P. Morgan and the others had agreed to advise Comcast, they could not, as a matter of law or ethics, show up to talk about Broadband's IPO. But the firms just couldn't drop out without a word of explanation either. J. P. Morgan, after all, was AT&T's longtime banker. If Merrill and the others begged off at the last minute, the Robertses were afraid that Noski would connect the dots.

Even as Noski was trying to hold the tatters of his beauty contest together, Comcast was around the corner at the St. Regis holding court with more than 200 investors and analysts. Comcast wielded the spotlight like a club. Speaking to the standing-room-only crowd, Brian Roberts and Steve Burke, Comcast's cable chief, were blunt and to the point: The overall strategic direction of Broadband was wrong. Not only that, but they believed that AT&T was losing up to $500 million annually on Armstrong's failed phone-over-cable plan.

The pair beat on Broadband's operating margins like a drum. Thanks to heavy spending on phone, they pointed out, Broadband's margins had dropped to anemic levels—just 18 percent. Comcast, by comparison, was reporting rock-solid margins in the low 40s. Even the old TCI had a 40 percent operating margin when it was handed over to AT&T in 1998. Their insinuation was clear: AT&T was driving Broadband into the ground. Even more troubling, Broadband's basic cable TV business, which was supposed to be throwing off enough cash to fund the larger cable strategy, was starting to actually lose customers. Among the big operators, that was unheard-of. So were 18 percent operating margins, for that matter.

Roberts was careful not to dump on phone service as a potential moneymaker for the cable industry over time. But he thought AT&T's idea of using upgraded cable lines to sell "circuit-switched" services like the Bells was misguided. Roberts said Comcast would eventually offer Internet telephony, also known as "VoIP," short for Voice over Internet Protocol. But that was still a few years out.

Roberts and Burke didn't single out Armstrong by name. But then again, they didn't have to. Comcast was basically calling his $110 billion push into cable an abject failure. Somers was also on the hot seat. In the face of Comcast's withering dissection of Broadband's financial performance, his RGU defense, which had been the centerpiece of his pitch to Wall Street for more than a year, looked weak. So did Armstrong, who had defended him every step of the way.

Comcast held its breath waiting for AT&T's response. One of Roberts's biggest fears was that AT&T would jerk out Somers and replace him with a more credible executive. Wall Street might feel obliged to give AT&T the benefit of the doubt, ending Comcast's momentum. "If they did that," one Comcast executive would later recall, "we knew we were dead."

But Roberts didn't think Armstrong would be willing to go that far, if only because it would have been a tacit admission that he'd made a mistake. Given Armstrong's propensity to take every sling and arrow personally, Roberts was betting that the AT&T chief, once stung, would revert to form and dig in his heels. He also thought investors would see things his way. Comcast had just put a good deal on the table, and he was confident that investors would see that, even if AT&T didn't.

Roberts bet right.

Unaccustomed to being called out so directly, AT&T came back swinging. At Armstrong's insistence, Connie Weaver, AT&T's investor relations director, set up an investors' call to rebut Comcast's claims. She put Somers on the call—under the circumstances, she really didn't have a choice—playing right into Comcast's hands. When Comcast's deal team heard the news, high-fives went up all around the company's Philadelphia headquarters. The fact that AT&T was trotting out Somers so publicly, and so early, suggested that it intended to back him all the way. That, of course, was *exactly* the response that Comcast had been hoping for.

Somers was in a tough spot. He needed to respond forcefully to Comcast's accusations. But he couldn't come across as too defensive.

Somers did his best. He pointed out that Broadband's RGUs were taking off like a shot in comparison to other operators, including Comcast. But investors had heard that song-and-dance routine before. Thanks to Comcast's full frontal attack, which had been delivered with deadly force in broad daylight with the whole world watching, the only thing investors wanted to hear about, it seemed, was the operating margins. And for Somers, unfortunately, that's where his story skidded to a halt.

Wall Street listened closely—and promptly drove up AT&T shares by almost $2, or 12 percent, to close at $18.70. Comcast's shares dropped by almost $3, or 7 percent, to close at $38.95. The seesaw action suggested investors thought Comcast would prevail. AT&T was stunned. So was Comcast.

Indeed, for all its public bravado, Roberts and his deal team really didn't think they'd be successful. Comcast was less than half AT&T's size. So it had no leverage to force a deal. It couldn't wage a proxy fight either. Comcast was only trying to buy a *division* of AT&T, not the whole thing. If management turned thumbs down, Comcast basically had nowhere to go. Even Comcast's own advisors, which included such heavyweights as Paul Taubman, the co-head of mergers and acquisitions at Morgan Stanley; Dennis Hersch, a top deal lawyer with Davis Polk; Steve Rattner of Quadrangle; Rob Kindler of J. P. Morgan; and legendary investment banker Felix Rohatyn, weren't so sure the gambit—known on Wall Street as a subsidiary bear hug—would work. Most of them, in fact, were sure that it wouldn't.

Roberts knew the odds were against him. Just before he faxed over Comcast's offer to Armstrong, Roberts passed out pieces of paper to all 15 members of his deal team. Then he asked everybody to write down his or her most optimistic guesstimate of Comcast's odds of success. The highest estimate in the room was 40 percent. Most people thought Comcast had a 25 percent chance, at best. Since financial advisors tend to be overly optimistic by nature, the low scores said a lot.

Roberts refused to blink. If Comcast failed, he figured his pride would take a scuffing. He could live with that. As the heir-apparent-in-training at Comcast for most of his career, he'd learned early on to put his pride in his back pocket, especially when the stakes got high enough. But what he couldn't live with was the knowledge that he'd had a chance—not necessarily a *good* chance, but a chance—to pick off the top cable TV prize in America, and passed. As far as Roberts was concerned, having a 40 percent chance, or even a 25 percent chance, was better than no chance, which was exactly what he was looking at if he sat pat on the sidelines. His father, as usual, backed him up every step of the way. So did Julian Brodsky, Comcast's other legendary co-founder.

THE OTHER SHOE dropped less than 24 hours later.

On Tuesday, July 10, Malone abruptly resigned from the AT&T board. AT&T tried to downplay his resignation, noting that the cable titan had been scheduled to step off the board four weeks later, anyway, coincident with the spin-off of Liberty Media. (The spin-off was part of the larger "Grand Slam" restructuring plan.) But even AT&T's own statement left no doubt as to why the cable titan was leaving. In his prepared comment, Armstrong said that he understood Malone's decision to resign early, "in view of the fact that he is not participating in current discussions concerning Comcast." Translation: AT&T had frozen out Malone, and now Malone was returning the favor.

Armstrong closed by thanking Malone for his service, adding, "John Malone is a unique figure in American business history, and we have been fortunate to have the benefit of his insight and vision."

What the AT&T chief failed to point out, however, was that he had never really bothered to take advantage of Malone's insight or vision. And any attempts by Malone to promote his ideas, inside or outside the boardroom, only seemed to earn him derision. Contrast that with the board's handling of another director, Kathryn Eickoff, who sometimes fell asleep in meetings. People snickered, to be sure. But nobody ever complained. What to make of that? Catnapping through board business is okay, but campaigning aggressively for bold solutions to tough business problems is not? Go figure.

Malone kept his poker face on. Taking his cue from Wasser, perhaps, the cable titan steadfastly insisted the only reason he was stepping down early was because of his relationship with Liberty and its potential conflicts with Comcast. Behind the scenes, however, Malone was furious. And not just about Comcast either. To be sure, the fact that he'd gotten frozen out of a discussion to which he probably could have added a lot of value and insight was perplexing. And maybe a little hurtful. But the thing that really gnawed at him was the tremendous opportunity that had been lost forever. When he'd sold TCI to AT&T in 1998, he had every expectation that Armstrong would carry through on his grand plan for transforming AT&T into a New Age media Goliath that could outlast the Bells, regulators, and the fickle nature of Wall Street. What he got, instead, was a front-row seat to a financial disaster of historical proportions. The miscalculation had cost him plenty. More than $1 billion, and counting. Malone didn't lay awake at night thinking about the money. But he couldn't stop thinking about the wasted opportunity.

Malone partly blamed himself. For him, it all went back to the cable tracker in 1998. Malone couldn't help but wonder how things might have changed, for AT&T as well as himself, if he'd only dug in his heels and insisted that AT&T proceed with the cable tracker, as originally planned. It was a "what if" that would haunt him for years.

It's impossible to say how a cable tracker might have changed life for AT&T. So much depends on the variables, like management, market conditions, and execution. But it is tantalizing to think about that possibility. With a tracker, AT&T would have had a ready deal currency to use for MediaOne. So there would have been no need to turn to the commercial paper markets. Debt, which would eventually break the back of AT&T's balance sheet, would have been a lot easier to manage. With a separate tracking stock at its disposal, Broadband could have issued as many new shares as it needed to cover its obligations, and carried on.

Malone's decision to stand down on the tracker would eventually become one of the two biggest regrets of his life. His other major regret was selling TCI to AT&T. If he'd known that Armstrong was going to mangle the cable opportunity so badly, he would later say, he never would have sold.

THE LEAKS CONTINUED.

In September that same year, *Business Week* published a story saying that AT&T was talking to BellSouth about a possible merger. The story even had the code name of the super-secret project: Brazil. Armstrong went nuts. He was incensed that somebody would dare to leak such confidential information to the press, and he was determined to find out who was talking. Under marching orders to find and plug the leak immediately, AT&T's general counsel, Jim Cicconi, brought in an outside security firm to do some snooping around. Working off company cell phone records, investigators quickly focused on an attorney who worked in Marilyn Wasser's office. The attorney was subsequently confronted by investigators and resigned from AT&T a short time later.

Some people insisted the leaks slowed down after that. But they never completely stopped. As for all the negative stories in the press about AT&T, they were about to get a whole lot worse.

THANKS TO COMCAST'S relentless attacks on Broadband's financial performance, it was suddenly open season on Dan Somers.

By then Somers had missed a string of internal financial targets, leading to growing dissatisfaction with his performance. But the directors didn't want to pull him out of the job right then for fear that it would look like AT&T was caving. Since the board was in the unenviable position of having to defend Somers, the directors thought it might be prudent to get a better feel for what, and whom, they were defending. AT&T had yet to respond to Comcast's offer, and the board wanted to make sure it was on firm ground before it crafted a formal response.

With that goal in mind, the board decided to make a road trip to Denver. The board had two objectives: First, to gain a better understanding of Broadband's unique operational challenges, and second, to gain a better understanding of how Somers was dealing with those issues. In short, the board wanted to make sure that its strident defense of the most derided executive in cable was, indeed, warranted.

For two solid days, the entire AT&T board sat through a series of presentations by Broadband's senior managers. Then it was Somers's turn to talk. That's when the air fizzled out of the balloon.

With his usual bravado, Somers proudly waxed on about the many accomplishments of his team in Denver. Among other things, he noted, Broadband had managed to upgrade dozens of TCI systems, often under crushing deadlines. Not only that, but Somers and his team had rolled out AT&T-branded local phone service in key markets across the United States. Broadband was also making remarkable progress in meshing the crazy quilt of billing and customer service support functions that it had inherited as a result of the TCI and MediaOne mergers. As for those operating margins—not to worry. Broadband's RGUs were soaring. Other cable operators should do as well, he chided. To hear Somers talk, in fact, Broadband was red hot, and hitting on all cylinders.

Silence fell over the room like a wet blanket. A few people studied Somers's face, as if looking for any trace of recognition or acknowledgment that Broadband was, at that very moment, in the middle of the fight of its life. Somers's reputation was also being shredded. Comcast had basically accused him of being inept, and trotted out scorching evidence to back up its claims. And what to make of those 18 percent margins? They were an embarrassment, and Comcast was using them to beat AT&T over the head at every turn. Yet, to hear Somers talk, it was business as usual.

Trying to toss him a life preserver so that he could haul himself back to shore, one director—nobody seems to remember who—finally asked Somers to reflect on his experiences at Broadband. If you had it to do all over again, the director asked, coaxing him along, what would you do differently, given what you know now?

As softball questions go, they don't get much better than that. AT&T's board was composed of a blue-chip roster of top CEOs like George Fisher of Kodak, Ken Derr of Chevron, Ralph Larsen of Johnson & Johnson, and Sandy Weill of Citigroup. These were people who understood, on a really gut level, how incredibly difficult it is to manage large, complex businesses on a day-to-day basis. Nobody expected miracles. But they did expect candor. In posing the question "What would you do differently?" the director was merely asking Somers to show his humanity, as well as his humility. All he had to do was follow the bouncing ball and go for the layup.

Somers blew it.

Jutting out his jaw like a prizefighter going for the knockout punch, Somers immediately launched into an impassioned defense of his record. As the stunned directors looked on, Somers bragged that there was absolutely nothing he'd do differently given the opportunity to go back in time and do it all over again. And for one simple reason: He'd done it all right the first time. And anybody who suggested otherwise, he loudly instructed, just didn't understand the situation very well. Somers had no regrets. No doubts. Not a shred of equivocation about the correctness of his business decisions. Somers was rock solid, self-assured, and openly proud of his many accomplishments.

He lost the board's confidence on the spot. The directors had come out to Denver looking for some affirmation that their continued support was deserved. And maybe even appreciated a little. What they got, instead, was incontrovertible proof that Comcast was right: Dan Somers was the wrong man for the wrong job at the wrong time. And the more Somers talked, the farther he sank into the black hole that had once been his promising career at AT&T.

AT&T put out a press release that night. The telecom giant said it was turning down Comcast's offer. AT&T also said that it had decided to delay its Broadband IPO so that it could consider other "strategic alternatives." Comcast was ecstatic. In just 10 short days it had managed to turn a 25 percent shot at success—40 percent at the outside—into a credible threat. Not only that, but it had forced AT&T, which had insisted all along that Broadband wasn't for sale, to push off its IPO and seriously consider a sale of the company. It wasn't quite a grand slam out of the park. But it was close enough.

AT&T DID ITS BEST to gin up a bidding war. It wasn't very successful. But thanks to Chuck Noski, it did manage to put on a hell of a show.

By the summer of 2001, AT&T had managed to draw interest from the three biggest cable TV operators in America: AOL Time Warner, based in New York; Cox Communications, based in Atlanta; and, of course, Comcast.

AOL Time Warner's entry into the fray created a lot of heat. The company, after all, was the largest entertainment house in the world, with annual revenues of more than $35 billion. It was also the No. 2 cable operator, with more than 13 million subscribers. The CEO, Jerry Levin, was also a longtime believer in the power of cable TV lines to change the world, making him a kindred spirit, of sorts, with Armstrong.

Levin hoped to combine Broadband with Time Warner Cable, and then spin it out as an independent company. Armstrong would have been the CEO, at least for a while. Armstrong loved the idea. (He liked it so much, in fact, that after a while he was openly campaigning for Time Warner to win. Noski, who was running the auction, finally had to tell his boss, gently but firmly, to cut it out.)

But Time Warner's bid was doomed from the start. The company was still struggling to realize the promised synergies of its $147 billion merger with AOL, which had largely been derided as a failure. There was also growing strain between Levin and Steve Case, AOL Time Warner's then-chairman, about the future direction of the company. Case had no interest in seeing Time Warner spend any more money chasing Levin's pipe dreams. Levin, in turn, was growing tired of listening to Case's blue-sky blather about the future of the Internet.

Just two weeks before final bids were due, Levin abruptly announced plans to retire. Absent an internal champion like Levin, the company's interest in Broadband began to wane. Dick Parsons, who was Levin's longtime No. 2, did his best to keep the Broadband project on track. But even Parsons, as influential as he was, could only convince the AOL Time Warner board to go so far. Levin tried to move things forward. But in his weakened political state he was simply unable to jam the deal through. (Ironically, the Broadband deal is probably the transaction that Levin should have done in the first place—not AOL. Had he done that, Levin, in all likelihood, would have gone out looking like a hero.) Time Warner still submitted a final bid. But according to many people, it was a water-weak effort. The mere fact that it would allow a relative pip-squeak like Comcast to outbid it by such a commanding margin—more than $2 billion—is testament to that.

Even if Levin had managed to pull a rabbit out of his hat, it's doubtful the deal would have passed muster with the Justice Department, at least not without a lot of onerous conditions. AT&T Broadband and Time Warner Cable represented the No. 1 and No. 2 cable operators in the country—never a good combination in the eyes of regulators.

Cox, at least on paper, was the perfect marriage partner. It shared AT&T's belief in the power of cable to provide Bell-quality phone service. But it was also the smallest of the three bidders, with annual revenues of just $4 billion. It also had the fewest customers—just 4 million. The company's handling of Armstrong, while not a deal-breaker, probably didn't help.

Unlike Time Warner and Comcast, Cox made it clear early on that Armstrong wouldn't have a prominent role—or really *any* role—in the combined company. Part of Cox's reticence owed to Paul Rizzo, who sat on the board of the parent company, Cox Enterprises. Rizzo had been IBM's vice chairman during Armstrong's reign, and he remembered the experience well. Rizzo liked Armstrong personally. But he had little confidence in Armstrong's business acumen, and he shared his views liberally with Cox's senior management.

Jim Kennedy, Cox's chairman, personally delivered the news. In a face-to-face meeting with Armstrong, Kennedy, joined by Jim Robbins, Cox's CEO, told the AT&T chief that Cox would be pleased to have him on the board of the combined company. But an operating role was not in the cards. Noski, for his part, always insisted that Armstrong's role was a nonissue. That said, Noski went out of his way to make sure that all the bidders knew that Armstrong wanted, and expected, a prominent position. While Kennedy's candor is admirable, the wisdom of the move is debatable. In the end, however, it wasn't Cox's size or manners that cost it the race. It was its lackluster bid.

That left Comcast.

With its strong balance sheet, impressive management team, and strong track record of delivering shareholder value, Comcast was always the one to beat. Unlike Time Warner, it didn't have any regulatory complications hanging over it. And unlike Cox, it had enough size and heft to give satisfaction to the AT&T board that it wasn't swapping one set of problems for another.

Comcast was confident. But it was never so cocky as to take its win for granted, as evidenced by its willingness to step up with sweetened terms, over and over again. Noski, to his credit, managed to squeeze Brian Roberts for an extra $1 billion in the closing hours of the auction. Roberts gave his final offer while he was riding up the escalator at New York's Pennsylvania Station. He'd just come in on the train from

Philadelphia, and he was desperate to get the deal sealed. Roberts was utterly exasperated. By then he'd been on the edge of his seat for days, and Noski was still banging him for more money.

"Will this do it?" Roberts wailed, his voice trailing off into the din of Penn Station. Noski indicated that it would—or at least that's how Roberts read his response.

By the time Roberts got to the top of the escalator, his stomach was a nest of butterflies. He spent the rest of the day holed up at the St. Regis with his deal team waiting for Noski's call. By 5 P.M., the tension in the room was off the charts. Trying to lighten things up, Larry Smith went into the bathroom and put in a call to Brian—just to watch him dive for the phone. Everybody in the room got a good laugh at that. Especially Brian.

Back in New York at the law offices of Wachtell Lipton, the AT&T board was still deadlocked over what to do. Three directors were still refusing to approve a deal with Comcast. The ringleader, Amos Hostetter, was threatening to vote against the transaction. Kathryn Eickoff and Shirley Jackson were threatening to follow his lead.

Armstrong and Noski were desperate for a unanimous decision. Being forced to sell Broadband was bad enough. But having to do that and also admit that three AT&T directors, including the sole cable TV executive who was left on the board, were dead set against it would have been beyond humiliating.

Some people thought Hostetter was just being stubborn because the deal involved Roberts. Brian, in particular, seemed to grate on his nerves. Some people said Hostetter's prickliness owed, at least in part, to Comcast's ill-fated merger with MediaOne in 1999. (Hostetter, you might recall, was instrumental in convincing AT&T to break up that deal.) Others thought he just didn't like Brian because he was younger, richer, and more influential in a cable TV industry that Hostetter still dearly loved. It's also possible that Hostetter just didn't like the deal. After all, he'd bought into the idea of the grand cable strategy, just like everybody else. But regardless of the reason, he was digging in his heels hard.

After a lot of haggling, Hostetter finally agreed to go along, provided the Robertses agreed to some last-minute givebacks aimed at strengthening AT&T's shareholders' rights. Eickoff and Jackson, who'd been following Hostetter's lead all day, quickly backed him up. Noski was so steamed his face was flushed. But he got on the phone with Armstrong to deliver the last-minute demand to Brian Roberts, who was still holed up at the St. Regis.

After a flurry of calls, the issue was quickly resolved. Around 6:30 that night Noski and Armstrong got on the phone together to deliver the good news: Comcast was the hands-down winner. Roberts and his deal team sped over to Wachtell to sign the final paperwork. As soon as the Comcast team walked in the door, cheers went up all across the floor. One hour and a dozen signatures later, the cable deal of the century was done.

In the end, Comcast agreed to buy Broadband for $72 billion—$47 billion in stock, plus the assumption of another $25 billion in debt. That was a whopping 24 percent more than Comcast's original offer of $58 billion—$44.5 billion in stock and $13.5 billion in debt—just six months earlier. In exchange for agreeing to take on the extra debt, Comcast got a little something extra: Time Warner Entertainment. The venture, known as TWE (pronounced "twee") included most of Time Warner's cable TV systems, as well as HBO, Warner Bros., and Road Runner, which was Time Warner's high-speed Internet access service. Comcast's opening offer in July did not include AT&T's 25.5 percent stake in TWE, which had an estimated value of $7 billion to $9 billion.

In keeping with Armstrong's wishes, he got a prominent role in the new company. Comcast agreed to give Armstrong the title of chairman, leaving Brian Roberts as the CEO. Comcast also embraced AT&T's phone strategy, suggesting it would continue rolling out AT&T-branded phone service in key markets across the country. In another nod to Armstrong, Comcast agreed to change the combined company's name to AT&T Comcast. The headquarters stayed in Philadelphia. But Comcast did agree to set up an executive office in New York. The Robertses also agreed to roll back their voting control to just 33 percent, leaving AT&T's investors with a respectable 66 percent voting interest.

In raw numbers, Comcast's final winning offer was $2 billion higher than what Time Warner had offered, and about $4.5 billion more than what Cox had offered. In hindsight, you have to give Noski a lot of credit for being able to squeeze that much extra value out of Comcast. Anytime an auctioneer can get the winning bidder to pay $2 billion more than the next guy, it ain't too bad. But almost any way you look at it, it was still a fabulous deal for Comcast. At $72 billion, Comcast was only paying about 75 cents on the dollar for assets that had cost AT&T, in round numbers, around $110 billion to assemble.

Ralph Roberts, who was 82 at the time, would later call the deal a "breathtaking moment" in Comcast's long history. "It's one of those things that happens once in a lifetime."

IN CLASSIC, BLOODLESS STYLE, Comcast asserted itself quickly. The day before the deal closed, the AT&T Comcast name was summarily dumped. Armstrong's successor, Dave Dorman, wasn't wild about the idea of having another "AT&T" in the marketplace. Neither was Comcast. The AT&T board agreed. Dorman left it to his able general counsel to put in the proper fixes. Cicconi tried to keep the change under wraps until the last possible moment, mostly because he knew Armstrong would pitch a fit. Which he did.

The night before the deal closed, the AT&T board held a dinner at the Four Seasons in New York. The purpose of the dinner was two-fold: to celebrate the closing of the deal, and to honor Armstrong, who was leaving AT&T the next day to join Comcast. It was also a big night for Dorman, who was set to succeed him. Unlike most board dinners, this one included wives.

There was a lot of uncertainty in the air. Nobody knew what the future might hold for AT&T, or even if it had a future. By then the tracking stock for Consumer Services, which had been part of the original restructuring plan, had been scrapped. The tracker got dumped after the senior staff, including Dorman, questioned the wisdom of going forward. By then, MCI had issued a tracking stock for its long-distance business, and it was tanking. The market's reaction didn't bode well for AT&T. After a lot of debate, the Consumer tracker was quietly tabled. AT&T's long-distance revenues, meantime, were evaporating like rain on hot pavement. None of this got brought up at the Four Seasons, however. This was, after all, Armstrong's night to shine.

About halfway into the dinner, Dorman read a congratulatory letter from President George Bush. (Cicconi, a former White House deputy with long ties to the Bush Administration, had secured the letter.) After that, a few directors got up to toast the AT&T chief, heaping praise on him for his loyalty, courage, and diligence. Armstrong was openly moved by the show of support. Collecting himself, the AT&T chief rose to give his farewell speech. With all eyes turned his way, Armstrong launched into a passionate defense of his leadership, booming that he had "always tried to give my all to the IBM company."

IBM. There it was again. The word radiated like a red neon sign in a fog. All around the table, people winced. Nobody said a word, but a few did exchange side glances. Armstrong quickly corrected himself, and carried on. But the cat was out of the bag. After five hard years at the helm of the most legendary telecommunications company on Earth, its CEO was still, in the final analysis, a Big Blue kind of guy. As if there was ever any doubt about that.

AT&T'S FAMED CABLE strategy went out the window. For Comcast, it was just a matter of dollars and cents. (Some might say dollars and sense.) By then Broadband's operating margins were still shockingly low, and it was losing thousands of basic cable TV subscribers with each passing quarter. In the year between the deal's announcement and the close, more than 500,000 basic cable TV subscribers would bolt, putting the onus on Steve Burke, Comcast's cable chief, to pump up the margins quickly. By then AT&T had shown Somers the door and brought in an experienced cable veteran, Bill Schleyer, formerly of Continental Cablevision (Armstrong had a hard time letting Somers go. To prepare, he practiced his speech ahead of time, with an executive from human resources in the role of Somers). But to some extent that was like closing the barn door after the horse is gone. It was too late.

Armstrong's management role evaporated in no time flat. He kept the chairman's title, at least for a while. But there was no question as to who was calling the shots—Brian and Ralph Roberts. Armstrong earnestly showed up for his first board meeting with a laundry list of things he hoped to accomplish as chairman. David Cohen, Comcast's executive vice president, took Armstrong aside afterward to gently explain how things worked in Philadelphia. Armstrong didn't show up with any more laundry lists after that.

True to his word—and in keeping with the merger agreement—Brian Roberts rolled back his voting control to just a third. But he got the right to pick five out of the 12 directors. AT&T also got the right to pick five directors; the remaining two were selected jointly. Though Comcast's voting control was reduced, it will never get watered down, no matter how many new shares of the company get issued in the years ahead.

Comcast got the right to staff the combined company. Out of the top dozen or so executives, all but two were from the Comcast side of the house. Armstrong initially objected, arguing that it would send the wrong message to Wall Street. His preference was to divvy up the top jobs equally. Burke flatly refused, arguing that it would send a far worse signal if Comcast appointed executives who were plainly unqualified for their jobs.

Burke won, setting the tone for the new Comcast, which, at its heart, was really just the old Comcast, only a whole lot bigger. Armstrong, always good at dealing with life's curveballs, took it all in stride. In reality, however, he really had no choice. After all, the Armstrong Era was over.

EPILOGUE:
THE NEXT 100 YEARS

IN THE WEE HOURS of January 31, 2005, AT&T announced that it was selling itself to SBC Communications for $16 billion. The sale is expected to take about a year to close. At that point, the fabled company, including the iconic brand name, will become the sole property of the Texas-based Bell.

The weight of the moment wasn't lost on Ed Whitacre, SBC's chairman and CEO. Whitacre is a big man with a big reputation for being one tough, tough son-of-a-gun at the negotiating table. But talking to reporters on a conference call that day, the SBC chief was practically misty-eyed. "We are preserving an American icon," Whitacre declared, his Texas twang warming a bit at the mere mention of the AT&T name. Then he extended a warm greeting to the beleaguered employees, stockholders, and customers of the world's most famous phone company: "Welcome home, and welcome to the future."

People who were in the room with Whitacre that day said his voice actually cracked a bit as those closing words left his lips. A 41-year veteran of the telephone business, Whitacre understood better than most, I suspect, the magnitude of what had just happened. To be sure, the SBC deal was, after a fashion, saving AT&T from the disgrace of withering away to nothing before the public's eyes. But the deal also marked the end of AT&T's long life as a proud, independent company.

Dave Dorman, AT&T's chairman and CEO, was just as moved. Like most telecom executives, he'd spent his whole life working for, or working in the shadow of, AT&T. To go down in history as the guy who sold the business, thus marking its official end, wasn't something he took lightly.

The night before his board was to assemble in New York to take the final vote, Dorman had the official portraits of Alexander Graham Bell and Theodore Vail, AT&T's storied general manager in the early 1900s, moved into the boardroom. Later, when asked why he moved the paintings, Dorman would say that he had simply been heeding his gut. "This is an historic company, one of the most enduring and widely used by mankind," he said, referring to the ubiquitous Bell telephone. "I just wanted them there."

AT&T and SBC held a special meeting with financial analysts in New York two days later. The meeting, which attracted more than 100 analysts, was held at the Plaza Hotel. Afterwards, Dorman and Whitacre, accompanied by their respective top executives, went over to AT&T's offices at the GM Building, located across the street. There Dorman presented Whitacre with a very special gift: the oil portrait of Theodore Vail, the same one that had hung in the boardroom two nights earlier.

When he presented the painting, Dorman said he thought Whitacre showed the same sort of courage and vision that had been demonstrated by Vail more than 100 years earlier. It was no small compliment. Thanks to Vail's fortitude and unwavering vision of the future, AT&T became the most famous—and successful—communications company of all time. To all appearances, Whitacre is well on his way to duplicating that feat with SBC. He inherited the smallest Bell right after divestiture—Southwestern Bell—and has used dealmaking and pure moxie to turn it into the biggest. Once the AT&T deal closes, SBC will become the largest communications carrier in America.

So what's ahead for AT&T? Thanks to SBC, which is a sturdy amalgam of three of the seven original Baby Bells, AT&T finally gets a new lease on life. At least that's what AT&T's backers are hoping. "This is not the end of AT&T," Dorman said right after the deal was announced. "It's another beginning." He has a valid point. Tethered to SBC, AT&T will have a chance to flourish, grow, and contribute—to telecom, to our society, and, indeed, to the world at large. For its $16 billion, SBC will also pick up AT&T Labs. There's no telling if the labs will ever invent anything that even comes close to having as much impact on mankind as the Bell telephone. But in the new digital world we live in, the opportunities for innovation are virtually boundless. So you never know.

The famous AT&T name also seems destined to live on. Enigmatic as ever, Whitacre has so far declined to say whether he'll adopt the legendary brand as his corporate moniker. But in an interview with this writer, he made it abundantly clear that he's leaning in that direction. Asked if he'd consider adopting the AT&T name, Whitacre's enthusiasm was almost palpable. "Absolutely," he said, not missing a beat. "It's a great name, and an icon in American business." Likewise, the SBC chief has indicated that he is seriously considering holding onto AT&T's famous "T" trading symbol, which has been a fixture on the New York Stock Exchange for decades. So even if AT&T is going away, technically, it would appear that some of the more visible parts will live on.

Some people are already accusing Dorman of selling the family jewels too cheaply, and too quickly. This writer begs to disagree. Mike Armstrong's mismanagement, coupled with his unfortunate decision to lop off the future of the company by selling off the wireless and cable TV assets, left AT&T stranded and destitute. By the time Dorman became CEO in the fall of 2002, many people had written off AT&T for dead. A lot of people forget that. Dorman never did. Faced with the certainty of a slow slide to extinction, Dorman did exactly what he needed to do: he made the tough calls, and played his hand well.

So it ends for AT&T. It was a hell of a run—more than 130 years in all. During that time, AT&T was an eyewitness to history. It also made history, and in the process left its indelible mark on our country, and on our legacy as a nation. It remains to be seen how the new super-sized SBC will fare. As AT&T's experience has so aptly demonstrated, no company, no matter how big or sturdy or seemingly impervious, is infallible. It is a lesson worth remembering as AT&T, secure in the arms of her former offspring, begins her next century.

Appendix A

SO HOW DID
INVESTORS FARE?

I ASKED MIKE BALHOFF, the former head of Telecom Equity Research at Legg Mason Wood Walker in Baltimore, to answer this very question. My goal was rather simple: I wanted to know how AT&T investors made out, on a straight-up financial basis, during the Armstrong era. Mike, who has been following telecom for more than 16 years, graciously agreed. I left it up to him to figure out the best—and fairest—way to crunch the numbers.

Within a few days, Mike, who is now the managing partner of Balhoff & Rowe in Baltimore, came back with a one-page summary. His analysis, in its entirety, follows:

Investors in AT&T shares have been sorely disappointed over the past decade. The shares had already declined by 17.3 percent from the end of June 1994 to the day before Armstrong was named CEO of the company.* However, the damage had only begun and the subsequent collapse proved far more sobering.

AT&T's (New York Stock Exchange symbol: "T") stock price closed at $45.19 on Friday, October 17, 1997. That was one day before Armstrong was officially named chairman and CEO of the company. When he resigned five years and one month later, on November 18, 2002, the shares had imploded, closing at $13.51.

Various adjustments are required to calculate the precise price

---

*The share price was calculated from the end of June 1994, with adjustments for the 1996 spin-offs of Lucent Technologies and NCR; each AT&T shareholder received 0.324084 shares of Lucent for each AT&T share, and 0.0625 shares of NCR for each AT&T share.

288

change, since, in the interim, there was a 3-for-2 split in AT&T shares and then investors received about one-third of a share in AT&T Wireless.* Making the appropriate recalculations, an AT&T shareholder would discover that he or she had lost 53.6 percent during that five-year period. In the same time frame, the S&P 500 declined 4.6 percent, even as the market was digesting the severe contraction that began in early 2000.

Viewed in annual terms, AT&T shares lost value at a compounded annual rate of approximately 14 percent in that half-decade. The S&P 500, by comparison, declined at an annual rate of approximately 0.9 percent over the same period.

Another and harsher view of the collapse comes into focus when you consider the high price of AT&T's stock price during the cable-acquisition period.

Right after Armstrong joined the company, there was a lot of enthusiasm around his strategic vision, and AT&T's stock price reflected as much. AT&T's stock price peaked on February 3, 1999, with shares closing at $95, up 110.2 percent from their closing price on the day before Armstrong was named CEO. The S&P, by comparison, was up by a far more modest 34.7 percent. Calculated from that peak, AT&T's collapse was even more stunning—77.9 percent. The S&P, during the same period, fell by more palatable but still painful 29.2 percent.

In the two years since Armstrong resigned, AT&T shares have continued to slip badly as the company has grown weaker. Avoiding further complexities in analyzing the individual pieces into which AT&T shares were divided on November 18, 2003, as well as the 5-for-1 reverse stock split, it is disturbing to note that the shares of AT&T's core long-distance operations deteriorated an-

---

*A 3-for-2 stock split occurred on April 15, 1999, when AT&T shareowners received one additional share of stock for every 2 shares owned on the record date of March 31, 1999. In lieu of any fractional shares, cash was received unless the shareowner participated in the company's Dividend Reinvestment and Stock Purchase Plan on the record date. Also, AT&T shareowners of record on June 22, 2001, received a distribution of 0.3218 shares of common stock of AT&T Wireless Services, Inc. (AWE) on July 9, 2001, for every AT&T share owned. Shareowners entitled to a fractional share of AWE received a cash payment instead.

other 46.2 percent between November 19, 2002 and the end of the second quarter of 2004, when the stock price ended at $14.21.* Granted, this is a somewhat simpler analysis. But the dramatic implosion is impossible to ignore.

Since the time we prepared this analysis in mid-December, a lot has happened. On January 31, 2005, AT&T agreed to be purchased by SBC Communications in exchange for SBC shares and a special dividend.** AT&T shares have appreciated to reflect the combination. But they are still 21 percent lower than what they were trading for when Michael Armstrong left the company.*** The further erosion is primarily a reflection of a long-distance industry that has contracted sharply over the last several years, with no end in sight. The removal of certain regulatory systems——most notably "UNE-P" (a federal rule that for a time required the Bells to lease their "last mile" connections to the home to AT&T and other rivals)—has also been a factor in the stock's decline.

The reader should be cautioned that it is a mistake to simply add the recent decline to the previous collapse, since AT&T was significantly altered in the November 2002 restructuring. But the import is clear—that longtime holders of AT&T have participated in a titanic collapse over the last decade.

Michael J. Balhoff, CFA Balhoff & Rowe, LLC
Baltimore, Maryland
February 12, 2005

---

*It is not correct to add the 46.2 percent decline after Armstrong left office to the decline in value we calculated earlier, since there were other investments assigned to the shareholder in AT&T Broadband and Comcast, and we did not make further adjustments for AWE shares.

** On January 31, 2005, the merger terms announced by SBC and AT&T implied $19.71 per share, or approximately $16 billion, for AT&T shareholders, who are scheduled at closing to receive 0.77942 shares of SBC common stock for each common share of AT&T, plus a special tax-free dividend of $1.30 per AT&T share.

***AT&T closed at $19.37 on February 11, 2005, 20.6% lower than $24.41 where the shares were the day after the November 2002 restructuring. We excluded the performance of Comcast's stock in the earlier analysis, since the question we were asked concerned management of AT&T during the Armstrong Era. However, to provide a complete picture, we note that Comcast-Broadband shares rose by 20.2% until February 11, 2005. Making the necessary adjustments, the two securities—Comcast and AT&T—generated a total return of 5.3% percent through that date.

Appendix B

HOW THIS BOOK
WAS PUT TOGETHER

A BOOK LIKE THIS doesn't come together without a lot of participation by a lot of thoughtful, informed people, and *End of the Line* is no different.

Over the course of my research, I conducted interviews with more than 100 people, some of them repeatedly. The makeup of this group was as diverse as AT&T; it included current and former executives, current and former employees, regulators, historians, and many others. The only common link was their shared interest in the company, either by dint of their jobs, personal experiences, or some other connection, directly or indirectly, to the complex world of AT&T.

The input of my interviewees was invaluable in helping me compile *End of the Line*. But the conclusions, criticisms, and commendations contained herein are solely my own. (The only exception is the stock analysis on pages 288–290, which was done by an independent telecom analyst, Mike Balhoff.) To that end, I do not expect everybody to agree with all, or even any, of my opinions. That includes some of the people who are portrayed in this book.

There are no footnotes in this book. This is by design. As a reader of business narratives, I have never liked to see pages of text littered with tiny numbers or symbols referencing footnotes. (I personally think it tends to slow down the flow of a story.) But I would like to acknowledge that I did make use of a wide range of public documents, including magazines, newspapers, broadcast transcripts, and the like. For the chapter on AT&T's history, I referred to a couple of books, most notably *Deal of the Century: The Breakup of AT&T,* written by Steve Coll, and *Telephone: The First Hundred Years,* by John Brooks. I highly recommend them both. Coll's book, published in 1986, focuses on the dramatic string of events that led up to the 1984 breakup of Ma Bell. Brooks's book, published in 1976, is a straightforward historical account that starts at the very beginning—the invention of the telephone by Alexander Graham Bell. I also referred to *Cable Cowboy,* written by Mark Robichaux. The book, which is also a wonderful read, tracks John Malone's rise to power in the cable TV business.

INDEX

About the Author

LESLIE CAULEY is a telecom writer for *USA Today*. She has been a business journalist for more than twenty years, spending nine years as a staff writer and editor for *The Wall Street Journal*. She has been nominated for the Pulitzer Prize three times for her journalism. She lives in New York City.

Printed in the United States
By Bookmasters